Managing Business Ethics

A Reader on Business Ethics for Managers and
Students

Edited by John Drummond and Bill Bain

BUTTERWORTH
HEINEMANN

To Carole: for overcoming the trials and tribulations, never mind the slings and arrows of outrageous fortune. But most of all for being there when needed. Also to Australia's finest exports – Alison, Kate and Diana.

To Glynis: for all sorts of really good reasons including (but certainly not limited to) supporting me during the last four years of my education.

Butterworth-Heinemann Ltd
Linacre House, Jordan Hill, Oxford OX2 8DP

ℛ A member of the Reed Elsevier group

OXFORD LONDON BOSTON
MUNICH NEW DELHI SINGAPORE SYDNEY
TOKYO TORONTO WELLINGTON

First published 1994

British Library Cataloguing in Publication Data
A catalogue record for this book is available from the British Library

ISBN 0 7506 0663 0

Composition by Genesis Typesetting, Rochester, Kent
Printed and bound in Great Britain by Clays Ltd, St Ives plc

Contents

Preface

When I was asked to put together a book consisting of the most useful business ethics material for managers and students of management, it seemed, at first, a daunting task.

First, I am not an academic with a background in teaching. Second, I am not a theologian with a concern about the flaws of business life. Third, I have not had time to pursue an interest in any of these areas because I have been involved in business over the last three decades, since starting work as a fifteen-year-old.

During that time I have worked in multinational companies, in high-tech corporations, in financial services; and in a variety of capacities, ranging from apprentice to director. My work has seen me operate as a purchaser of expensive materials and a supplier of high-quality services.

In addition, I have operated as a consultant inside companies and as an external consultant. So I have seen companies from all sides now, and I have studied business people and their actions throughout this period. Some of those I have studied have performed well under difficult circumstances, some have performed badly under very favourable conditions. A few have been stinkers, and fewer still have been saints.

In all cases, it seems to me, they would have profited from a deeper understanding of business ethics. But all, saints and sinners and the vast majority in between, would have challenged me to show them ways to apply this ethical understanding to the resolution of the commercial difficulties they faced.

My experience of running Integrity Works, a consultancy which helps organizations and business people deal with ethical problems, has underscored this need to combine theory with practice.

So, perhaps the publishers made a wise choice after all in asking me to compile this material. Business is not easy and it never has been, except for a charmed few. In today's rapidly changing environment, coupled with tough economic conditions, business life is arguably more demanding than ever.

The professionalism of modern managers is being tested in ways that few could have anticipated. There are greater demands on today's executive to understand general issues and strategies, but at the same time to be able to respond quickly to rapidly changing local conditions. In other words, more managers are now required to think globally and act locally.

For this to have any meaning, executives need to comprehend the contributions that philosophers, researchers and others can make to helping them solve business problems. Too often, however, it seems it is difficult for these worlds to interact in ways that would be meaningful and useful to both. Therefore one goal of this book is to encourage the view that executives should be philosophical and philosophers need to be practical. Read on.

John Drummond

For further information about Business Ethics, please contact:

Integrity Works
47 Marloes Road
LONDON
W8 6LA

Tel: 071 938 2025
Fax: 071 938 2241

Acknowledgements

Grateful acknowledgement is made to the following for permission to reprint previously published material:

Nash, Laura L. 'Why business ethics now?' *Good Intentions Aside* (Boston, MA: Harvard Business School Press, 1990). Reprinted by permission of Harvard Business School Press. Copyright 1990 by the President and Fellows of Harvard College.

Carr, Albert Z. 'Is business bluffing ethical?' *Harvard Business Review*, **46**, January/February 1968; 162–169. Reprinted by permission of *Harvard Business Review*. Copyright 1967 by the President and Fellows of Harvard College; all rights reserved.

Hoffman, W. Michael. 'What is necessary for corporate moral excellence?' *Journal of Business Ethics*, 5, 1986; 233–242. Copyright 1986 by D. Reidel Publishing Company. Reprinted by permission of Kluwer Academic Publishers.

Stead, W. Edward, Worrell, Dan L. and Stead, Jean Garner, 'An integrative model for understanding and managing ethical behaviour in business organizations'. *Journal of Business Ethics*, **9**, 1990; 233–242. Copyright 1990 Kluwer Academic Publishers. Printed in the Netherlands. Reprinted by permission of Kluwer Academic Publishers.

Pastin, Mark. 'Ethics as an integrating force in management'. *New Jersey Bell Journal*, **8**, No. 2. Summer 1985; 1–15. Reprinted by permission of *New Jersey Bell*.

Bird, Frederick B. and Waters, James A. 'The moral muteness of managers'. *California Management Review*, **32**, Fall 1989; 74–88. Copyright 1989 by The

Regents of the University of California. Reprinted from the *California Management Review*. By permission of The Regents.

James, Gene G. 'Whistleblowing: its moral justification', 1990. Original essay used by permission of the author.

Mahoney, Jack. 'The ethics of advertising and sponsorship'. Lecture 2 in a series 'Ethical choices in business', Gresham College, 19 March 1991. Original lecture used by permission of the author.

Donaldson, Thomas. 'Multinational decision-making: reconciling international norms'. *Journal of Business Ethics*, 4, 1985; 357–366. Copyright 1985 by Thomas Donaldson. Reprinted by permission of Kluwer Academic Publishers.

Hoffman, W. Michael. 'Business and environmental ethics'. *Business Ethics Quarterly* 1, 1991; Original essay used by permission of author.

Lynch, James J. 'The future shape of ethical banking'. *Ethical Banking*. London: MacMillan Academic and Professional, 1991, 11–28. Copyright James J. Lynch 1991. Reprinted by permission of MacMillan Press Ltd.

Jack, Andrew. 'Accountancy and ethics' (1993). Original essay used by permission of author.

McDonald, Gael M. and Zepp, Raymond A. 'Business ethics: practical proposals'. *Journal of Management Development*, 8, no. 1. 1989. 55–66. Reprinted by permission of MCB University Press.

The articles using American spelling have been changed to UK spelling. When the context allowed, some American terms were changed to ones more familiar to European readers. For example, in Nash's first paragraph, 'congressman' was changed to 'politician'.

Contributors

Bird, Frederick B. and Waters, James A.
Frederick B. Bird, PhD, Professor, Religion, Concordia University, Montreal, Canada.

James A. Waters, late Associate Dean, Wallace E. Carroll School of Management, Boston College, Massachusetts

Carr, Albert Z.
Albert Z. Carr was Assistant to the Chairman of the War Production Board during World War II and later served on the White House staff and as a special consultant to President Truman.

Donaldson, Thomas
Thomas Donaldson is the John F. Connelly Professor of Business Ethics, Georgetown University, School of Business Administration, Washington, DC.

Hoffman, W. Michael
W. Michael Hoffman, PhD, Director, Center for Business Ethics, Bentley College, Waltham, Massachusetts.

Jack, Andrew
Andrew Jack, Journalist with the *Financial Times*, London.

James, Gene G.
Gene G. James, Department of Philosophy, Memphis State University, Memphis, Tennessee.

Lynch, James J.
James J. Lynch is founder of Service Excellence Associates, Kent.

Mahoney, Jack
Jack Mahoney, Dixon's Professor of Business Ethics at the London Business School.

McDonald, Gael M. and Zepp, Raymond A.
Gael M. McDonald and Raymond A. Zepp, University of East Asia, Macau.

Nash, Laura L.
Laura Nash, principal of Nash Associates and adjunct associate professor at the Boston University Graduate School of Management, Massachusetts.

Pastin, Mark
Dr Mark Pastin, Director of the Center for Ethics and Professor of Management at Arizona State University.

Stead, W. Edward, Worrell, Dan L. and Stead, Jean Garner
Edward Stead, PhD, Professor of Management, East Tennessee State University.

Dan Worrell, PhD, Professor of Management, Appalachian State University, North Carolina.

Jean Garner Stead, PhD, Associate Professor of Management, East Tennessee State University.

Introduction

This reader aims to provide managers and students with a solid introduction to business ethics issues. It consists of classical and contemporary material from leading figures in the field worldwide.

While it is certain that the future will see more work from European authors, and the establishment of the journal *Business Ethics – A European Review* is a very significant step in this direction, none the less the bulk of the seminal work in the subject stems from the USA. However every effort has been made to include contributions from experts closer to home. Some of the contributors are academics and some are business people, but all have important statements to make about the ethics of business.

Never has the subject of business ethics excited more interest. In June 1992, the Cadbury Committee on Corporate Governance in the UK advised that all companies should have a code of ethics which should be communicated externally and internally. All well and good, but some business observers might argue that top management ought to have – as a very minimum – a clear sense of their company's ethos. But how far does this extend in practice?

Clearly it must be difficult for managers and executives to cope with ethical issues if they are morally mute – that is, if they are incapable or reluctant even to talk about ethical problems.

In our book *Good Business – A Guide to Corporate Responsibility and Business Ethics* [1], it is suggested that this muteness about ethics in the business community has led to the low regard that the general public has for senior executives.

To what degree are business schools responsible for this moral muteness? Some would argue that ethical processes should be developed before the start of business life. Recent evidence that senior school students in the UK do not even understand what the word 'ethical' means suggests that action is called for [2].

The reader contains arguments from those who believe that companies have a responsibility for ethics training. In these days of financial stringency, companies accepting this viewpoint may then have to decide what other forms of training must be sacrificed to make possible the inclusion of ethics. There is then a question of who should be trained. Top management or all managers? Specialist staff or all staff?

There can be little doubt that the drive for increased profitability through devolved and decentralized decision-making is bringing its own pressures. As management layers are removed, a company's ethos can be jeopardized. There are fewer experienced managers around, perhaps, for staff to consult; and junior executives eager to demonstrate their worth to the organization may be tempted to sacrifice integrity for short-term advantage.

In many cases the erring executive may not suffer the immediate consequences of an unethical decision, because the problem so created very often surfaces first in another part of the decentralized organization.

Breaches of ethics can make even the most responsible and respectable company look foolish or disingenuous. Worse still, some unethical decisions can also appear to be illegal, thereby confronting the company with legal action; and such action may have very serious implications in terms of cost and reputation. Loss of reputation can be extremely serious because a growing proportion of European consumers now base purchasing decisions on their empathy with the values of supplier companies.

It is our contention that the European debate on business ethics is presently at the same stage that the quality debate was at 10 years ago. Then, most companies regarded quality as a useful concept, but had difficulty in recognizing the practical and important benefits to be secured in giving quality considerations a high priority. The companies who placed themselves in the vanguard of the move to become quality suppliers obtained a significant competitive advantage. By contrast, those who tarried found themselves having to make up ground quickly; and not all were successful.

This is not to say that the introduction and implementation of quality processes in some companies have been uneventful. Mistakes have been made, but none of these invalidates the quality principle.

Equally important, geopolitical changes are casting a greater spotlight on the market system. One result is that pressure groups are seeking to become involved in areas of corporate activity which were perceived in the past to be the exclusive province of management.

Rapid technological change is also a growing issue for corporate executives. Markets once dominated by suppliers whose advantage lay in the possession of innovative technology are being rapidly penetrated by smaller-scale competitors, whose lower overheads and easy access to advanced engineering make possible more attractive offerings.

Some business observers have argued that to decentralize and devolve company operations without a set of clearly understood and enforced corporate values is to court disaster. In a rapidly changing business environment it is suggested that effective performance and maximum profitability can best be secured by empowering individuals through moving decision-making authority to the lowest possible level, while at the same time insisting that the company's ethics are not negotiable.

What this means in practice is that unethical behaviour is not rewarded, regardless of how well the individual performs in other respects. This is far and away the most powerful message that company executives can send about their commitment to ethical standards.

How many companies place the integrity of their business dealings above all else? Indeed, is it advisable that they should? More fundamentally, what is ethics? Is there such a thing as business ethics? If such exists, how does a busy manager deal with it? Does an ethics code make an organization ethical? What else might be required?

This reader contains contributions which aim to answer all of these questions, and many others of crucial importance to business as it heads for the twenty-first century.

The organization of this book

The material has been compiled in such a way that the reader can study whatever aspect of business ethics makes a contribution to his or her greater understanding, simply by referring to the appropriate section.

The chapter arrangement begins with questions that feature in every discussion on business ethics; then moves through a number of considerations which apply to specific forms of business operations; and concludes with practical recommendations.

In the opening chapter, Laura L. Nash introduces the study of business ethics and explains why it is a vital area for concern. This is followed by a contribution by Albert Z. Carr in which it is argued that business people need not follow the ethical rules of society but instead the rules of the business game. This is analogous to poker players following the specific rules of that game.

In Chapter 3, W. Michael Hoffman first addresses the question of whether a company as an entity can be held morally responsible for its actions or whether only people can be treated in such a manner. Hoffman then discusses what is necessary for corporate moral excellence.

The following two chapters approach the topic of business ethics by looking at its impact on the company as a whole. W. Edward Stead, Dan L. Worrell and Jean Garner Stead have contributed 'An integrative model for understanding and managing ethical behaviour in business organizations' and Mark Pastin writes on 'Ethics as an integrating force in management'.

In Chapter 6, Frederick B. Bird and James A. Waters discuss the reluctance of managers to describe their actions in moral terms even when they are acting for moral reasons. The negative effects of this and ways to rectify the situation are reviewed.

The topic of whistleblowing is presented by Gene G. James as he discusses its moral justifications and factors to consider when contemplating blowing the whistle.

Chapter 8 deals with the ethics of advertising and sponsorship. Jack Mahoney discusses the information and the pressures that advertising brings and relates sponsorship with advertising.

In Chapter 9, Thomas Donaldson looks at what a business person should do when working overseas and confronted with different norms. His practical algorithm is an essential study for those doing business abroad.

Michael Hoffman looks at the timely topic of business and environmental ethics. He highlights the dangers of justifying environmental protection solely on the grounds that it is good for business and he introduces the biocentric view of environmental ethics.

In Chapter 11, James J. Lynch writes about the future shape of ethical banking. Topics include the trends in European, Japanese and Islamic banking along with trends in alternative banking.

As a financial journalist, Andrew Jack of the *Financial Times*, London, brings his experience to bear on the moral issues affecting a key business group in the chapter 'Accountancy and ethics'.

Throughout the reader, the aim has been to provide material that gives a solid description of the theoretical concepts, while keeping a clear focus on their practical application. In the final chapter, Gael M. McDonald and Raymond A. Zepp concentrate on practical proposals for implementing business ethics initiatives.

The study of business ethics

The study of business ethics has its roots in moral philosophy and as a result many approach the topic by first reviewing the relevant philosophical theories. While this may very well lead to a thorough understanding, it has one significant drawback. *Business people and philosophers do not tend to speak the same language.* Beginning a study on business ethics with an in-depth review of Kant's categorical imperatives may be enough to turn some people off.

What we have provided is a combination of practical advice written by business practitioners along with important academic articles that have specific points to drive home.

For those readers who want to deepen their knowledge of ethics by reviewing the moral philosophies, many references are available. One excellent introduction to the topic is by Donaldson and Werhane [3]. One can also turn to Goodpaster's 'Ethical frameworks for management' [4].

Additional reading

A sample of annotated references is provided at the end of each chapter to assist those who want to investigate further the topic covered. These references and those cited by the contributors are confirmation of both the depth and breadth of the work being done in the field of business ethics.

Discussion questions

Discussion questions are provided at the end of each chapter. These can be used to stimulate discussions in the office or in the classroom. Some may argue that each of these questions can be answered in several sentences. We maintain, however, that each can lead to an in-depth debate.

Another way to stimulate group discussion is to turn to the prepared cases. Unfortunately, European cases have been slow to appear on the scene. Two excellent collections of American cases (which have many parallels to Europe) are *Case Studies in Business Ethics* [3] and *Policies and Persons: A Casebook in Business Ethics* [4].

References

1 Carmichael, S. and Drummond, J. *Good Business – A Guide to Corporate Responsibility and Business Ethics*, London: Century Business Books, 1989.
2 *Sunday Times*, 16 August, 1992.
3 Donaldson, T. and Werhane, P.H. Introduction to ethical reasoning. In: Donaldson, T. and Gini, A.R. (eds) *Case Studies in Business Ethics*, 2nd edn, Englewood Cliffs, NJ: Prentice-Hall, 1990.
4 Goodpaster, K.E. Ethical frameworks for management. Harvard Business School case 9–384–105 1983. Reprinted in: Matthews, J.B., Goodpaster, K.E., Nash, L.L. (eds) *Policies and Persons: A Casebook in Business Ethics*, New York: McGraw-Hill, 1985.

Chapter 1

Why business ethics now?

In 'Why business ethics now?' Laura Nash gives an excellent introduction to the subject. She tackles the important reasons for the growing interest in this field and provides in addition a definition of the term 'business ethics'. She notes that: 'business ethics is not a separate moral standard, but the study of how the business context poses its own unique problems for the moral person who acts as an agent for this system'.

The reader may wish to compare this definition with that provided in our book *Good Business* (p. 89) [1]: 'A person's ethics are the basic ground rules by which he or she acts. We often give complex explanations of our actions, but in fact we act for simple reasons. These ground rules are a framework for defining which actions are personally permissible, and which are not'.

Most of the companies noted in Nash's contribution operate worldwide, and their contention that high personal standards of conduct are a major asset, as economically valuable as good will, should be considered alongside the views of Albert Carr in the next chapter.

British readers, in particular, will recognize the business excesses described in this chapter, and might like to reflect on the fact that US regulations, particularly in financial services, are often regarded as being more exacting than those applying elsewhere.

It is a moot question as to how many business people are comfortable with the description of the free market ethos as 'managed greed'. The collapse of the communist system in most parts of the world has added piquancy to this point.

Many executives will find the discussion on the three basic areas of business ethics – choices about the law; choices about the economic and social issues beyond the law's domain; and choices about the pre-eminence of one's own self-interest – of fundamental interest. These bear upon precisely the choices that managers need to make in everyday business life.

Choices about the law, for example, relates to the debate about Sunday opening in England and Wales, and the dilemma confronting executives of those companies whose decision to open may be in breach of local laws.

Economic and social issues beyond the law's domain has a pertinence in the way redundancies are handled and, for example, about what happens to those who lose out after merger and acquisition processes are finalized.

Furthermore, the increasing diversity of the workplace requires greater ethical awareness. Companies that pride themselves on their record for fairness in employee relations are having to explain how this priority squares with targets for women managers. Both objectives are laudable but questions remain, particularly in the minds of many white, middle-aged, male employees, about how these possibly conflicting goals are being met.

Choices about the pre-eminence of one's own self-interest are also an increasing concern for many executives. The debate about corporate governance has thrown the role of the company in society into sharper relief. An increasing number of managers at all levels are experiencing difficulties about how to prioritize the interests of different stakeholder groups. In particular it can sometimes be very challenging to decide how an executive's self-interest can be reconciled with the interests of a major stakeholder.

The contention in this chapter that the erosion of trust is a key factor in organizational life today is borne out by our own research which indicates that corporate loyalty could become a rarity. In the majority of cases the most viable defence against the erosion of trust is a sound ethics process, in our experience.

In the face of these changes Laura Nash makes a plea for 'a covenantal business ethic' whereby corporate self-interest would be subordinated to other motivations, such as value creation and service to others. This view, as she notes, is very much in line with the thinking of Tom Peters and Rosabeth Moss Kanter, although their recommendations spring primarily from the perspective of organizational change.

Reference

1 Carmichael, S. and Drummond J. *Good Business*, London: Century Business Books, 1989.

Why business ethics now?
Laura L. Nash

Reader, suppose you are a businessman. Now suppose you are of ruthless and greedy character. But I repeat myself.

The activity of moneymaking has always stood in somewhat uneasy alliance with people's private sense of morality. Jokes about business ethics – the above epigraph is a paraphrase of Mark Twain's description of a [politician] – have regularly appeared in the popular press over the past two centuries. Many an executive today voices a similar cynicism about the relevance of moral inquiry to managerial practice. For many reasons, from the eternal fact of greed to the very different ways in which we tend to think about managing and morality, ethics and business have often seemed if not downright contradictory, at least several worlds apart. Even those wedded to the notion that integrity in business might be an obtainable ideal have nevertheless tended to leave the exploration of ethical dilemmas to each manager's private conscience.

In the past ten years American business has blasted through the Chinese wall that traditionally separates the discussion of management problems and personal morality. Whereas the voicing of ethical standards was formerly a concern of a few exceptional leaders, today the topic of business ethics is acknowledged to pervade every area of the corporation just as it is a recurrent issue in the media. Corporate codes of conduct are now the norm rather than the exception [1]. Corporate leaders have become more vocal about their own commitment to ethical standards. Respected business groups such as the Business Roundtable . . . and The Conference Board are sponsoring major ethics programmes. In the consulting world, business ethics seminars and conferences comprise a new cottage industry. And many a respected corporation has embarked on an organized attempt to encourage ethical conduct among its employees.

The reasons for the newly elevated place of ethics in business thinking are many. Managers have seen the high costs that corporate scandals have exacted: heavy fines, disruption of the normal routine, low employee morale, increased turnover, difficulty in recruiting, internal fraud and loss of public confidence in the reputation of the company. A body of literature has even developed, at this point tentative, outlining the economic costs of a damaged reputation. Business leaders at such outstanding companies as Johnson & Johnson, IBM, Goldman Sachs, Hewlett-Packard, Ford, 3M . . . and many others are emphasizing that high personal standards of conduct are a major asset, as economically valuable as that equally elusive intangible called good will.

Although many managers are committed to high ethical standards, many others are unconvinced that ethics can be reconciled with economics, or they regard morality as being exclusively a matter of personal character. In a recent MBA business policy class the students were asked to critique an impressive corporate credo that combined practical business functions with ethical ideals. One student asserted that the document was flawed because it tried to combine two very different things. It violated his sense of order. 'After all', he said, 'ethics doesn't have any direct relation to market share or earnings. It should be in a separate document. You know, ethics are very personal, they're about yourself.' Most of the students nodded sagely. A few days later I heard a similar group agreeing with Albert Carr's classic article in which he contended that it was morally acceptable to lie in business as long as you played within the unwritten rules of the game [2].

The challenges of today's marketplace and the serious ethical lapses that are occurring in nearly every industry demand a more sophisticated approach to ethical dilemmas, one that is more than simply game-playing or indulging in personal feelings about oneself. The root of the word 'integrity' means 'to hold together'. Integrity in business today requires incredible integrative powers: the power to hold together a multitude of important and often conflicting values, and the power to bring personal morality and management concerns into the same dimension. No manager can afford, from an economic or moral standpoint, to keep his or her moral notions in a separate compartment, reserved for the narrowest and most obvious cases.

Facing up to fallibility

The idea that ethical conduct in business is a fairly straightforward notion is at first glance persuasive. One could argue that most if not all of the values that comprise ethical business conduct – honesty, fairness, respect for others, service, promise-keeping, prudence and trustworthiness – are a familiar part of most managers' upbringing. However, it is an unfortunate fact that these common-sense values have frequently suffered meltdown in the marketplace. The headline-gathering corporate scandal and the petty whisperings of office gossip are evidence that business managers – like the rest of humankind – are not always capable of making good ethics an actual fact of business conduct.

When you couple the undeniable pervasiveness of human fallibility with the age-old temptations of money and power, the need for a deliberate exploration of the moral challenges of management becomes clear. Throw in the organizational factors of delegating the execution of one's decisions and having to defer to higher authorities, and the realities of moral fallibility slam home with all the force of a year-end earnings loss.

Unless one is the sole owner of a company that produces no products and hires no employees and creates no waste, merely being raised right will not provide sufficient ammunition against the ever-present opportunities to abandon one's basic moral standards. Every manager regularly faces decisions that are problematic from a moral standpoint and over which he or she does not have total control: decisions where people will inevitably get hurt; where trade-offs must be made between equally desirable values and constituencies; where the commitments of the organization and a manager's performance goals are at odds with the individual needs of certain employees or customers. On these occasions it may or may not be legitimate to compromise professional standards, but clearly the inevitable compromise of moral values which accompanies such decisions should be seen as truly problematic. The gap between a well-thought-out policy at the top level and the messy, hurtful people-problems surrounding its execution is great. A good leader cannot assume that by merely plugging in a decent person the moral lights will shine like beacons for every activity in the company.

Achieving and sustaining business integrity is harder and less automatic than that. What is more, every manager has a responsibility not only to *be* above reproach, but for it to be *perceived* that he or she is above reproach, and expects the same standards from others who execute company policy. Otherwise, the well-intentioned and personally upright manager becomes an unintentional contributor to a 'look-the-other-way' climate which invites ethical abuses. Thus, from the standpoint of managing the large organization, a manager is not an autonomous moral entity. Rather, he or she must be a moral leader, responsible for the behaviour of other people and the institution itself, as well as his or her own character.

Addressing this responsibility requires at a minimum an explicit investigation and stand on the ethical aspects of corporate activity, from strategy to compensation.

Defining business ethics

But what, exactly, is to be investigated? Surely most executives already believe that they support honesty, fairness and apple pie? What else needs saying? As a first step, then, in understanding the nature of ethical decision-making in business – as well as the reasons for moral failure – it is important to agree on some general term for the inquiry.

What is business ethics? *Business ethics is the study of how personal moral norms apply to the activities and goals of commercial enterprise. It is not a separate moral standard, but the study of how the business context poses its own unique problems for the moral person who acts as an agent of this system.*

Aristotle defined virtue as a matter of habit or the trained faculty of choice (*Nichomachean Ethics* II.6). Business ethics reflects the habits and choices managers make concerning their own activities and those of the rest of the organization. These activities and choices are informed by one's personal moral value system, but that system often suffers a transformation of priorities or sensitivities when it operates in an institutional context of severe economic constraints and pressures, as well as the potential for acquiring power.

Although there are many different moral aspects of business, business ethics generally falls into three basic areas of managerial decision-making:

1 *Choices about the law* – what it should be and whether or not to obey it.
2 *Choices about the economic and social issues that are beyond the law's domain* – usually called the 'grey areas' or 'people values'. These concern the tangible and intangible ways one treats others, and include not only the moral notions of honesty, promise-keeping and fairness, but also the avoidance of injury and the voluntary reparation for harm done.
3 *Choices about the pre-eminence of one's own self-interest* – the degree to which one's own well-being comes before the interests of the company or of other people inside and outside the company. Included are decisions concerning rights of ownership and how much money is to be retained or distributed elsewhere.

The ways in which such choices are framed, analysed and either maintained or abandoned form the basis of the business ethics inquiry. The validation of *business ethics*, however unpopular the term, is simply a way of acknowledging that, indeed, there are choices to be made concerning the means and ends of business which have an essentially moral ingredient.

Shifting concerns

Often the discussion of these choices grows out of a major collapse of moral standards in a specific business activity. The issues that receive widespread attention are in those areas where the normal rules have broken down. Thus the topical issues of business ethics shift over time. In the 1950s, two major concerns were price-fixing and dehumanization in the work force (e.g. Arthur Miller's *Death of a Salesman* and Sloan Wilson's *The Man in the Gray Flannel Suit*). In the 1960s, the Vietnam War aroused general moral indignation over the political and military aggressiveness of the military–industrial complex and its multinational conglomerates. Perhaps in reaction to the demonstrated destructiveness of business overseas, managers were also faced with new constraints on environmental and social destructiveness. A series of social conscience reforms – from pollution control to Equal Employment Opportunities standards – were instituted inside the corporation and in the legislative arena.

In the 1970s, corporate internationalism and new-found markets in Asia and the Middle East shifted the nation's corporate conscience to issues of bribery here and abroad. Watergate raised an outcry against political contributions activity, and led to a major revamping of reporting requirements and internal auditing procedures. Corporate codes of conduct were a tangible response. Meanwhile, a rapidly rising consumer movement was forcing attention on the deceptive and/or injurious practices in development, advertising, packaging and labelling of goods.

Consumer issues and cultural differences abroad continued to dominate business ethics in the first half of the 1980s. But in the last half of the decade, the central issues of collective moral concern took new shape. Whereas during the past two decades most business ethics issues centred on problems of *institutional* responsibility and *institutional* mechanisms for encouraging conformity to high standards, the focus is now on the *moral capacity of individuals*. Insider-trading, hostile takeovers and the break-up of well-known and dependable corporate entities such as the major retail chains have shifted public attention back to the age-old problems of individual greed and dishonesty. The egregious behaviour of extremely wealthy individuals in both the insider-trading and [Savings and Loan] débâcles has ruptured the thin membrane of impersonality that formerly surrounded most discussions of business ethics.

A manager's personal values and strength of character have become urgent issues for the corporation. In a survey by Korn/Ferry International and Columbia University Graduate School of Business, over 1500 executives from twenty countries rated personal ethics as the number one characteristic needed by the ideal chief executive officer in the year 2000 [3]. As Delbert 'Bud' Staley, former chairman of NYNEX, remarked, personal integrity is a business leadership essential: 'We have to depend on every one of our employees for the good reputation of this firm'. So, too, Johnson & Johnson's Jim Burke has asserted that most individuals in his company welcome the emphasis on high ethical standards which their credo represents. 'After all', he said, 'everybody wants to believe in something'.

Even the best people have ethical problems

Despite the widespread agreement today on the need for ethical *people* in business, it is still hard for individuals to feel that they personally face ethical problems. This point was made succinctly when NYNEX's current chairman, William Ferguson, remarked that he never viewed 'Gab-lines' as his own ethical problem, because he was so clear on his own moral stand: he was personally against pornography. And yet First Amendment issues and legal obligations of the carrier demanded that the company provide service for these activities. In retrospect, says Ferguson, he had a moral obligation to address the issue more aggressively. The service was re-examined and NYNEX made a breakthrough in selective blocking technology, which allowed consumers to exercise choice in this matter.

Familiar ethical quandaries

Such circumstances arise daily. The rules of the marketplace and pluralism of our society present opportunities and needs for action which do not on the surface seem to give rise to personal moral doubt, but which do, on closer examination, represent important moral problems for the individual. Ethics is everywhere. A quick survey of most managers would be likely to include participation in, if not direct initiation of, at least twenty of the thirty following situations. All are important from a managerial standpoint, and all contain moral issues of honesty, fairness, respect for others or fulfilment of promises. I have compiled the list simply from the comments of executives with whom I have worked. The reader may wish to check how many he or she has personally encountered in the past two years.

1 Greed.
2 Cover-ups and misrepresentations in reporting and control procedures.
3 Misleading product or service claims.
4 Reneging or cheating on negotiated terms.
5 Establishing policy that is likely to cause others to lie to get the job done.
6 Overconfidence in one's own judgement to the risk of the corporate entity.
7 Disloyalty to the company as soon as times get rough.
8 Poor quality.
9 Humiliating people at work or by stereotypes in advertising.
10 Lockstep obedience to authority, however unethical and unfair it may be.
11 Self-aggrandisement over corporate obligations (conflict of interest).
12 Favouritism.
13 Price-fixing.
14 Sacrificing the innocent and helpless in order to get things done.
15 Suppression of basic rights: freedom of speech, choice and personal relationships.
16 Failing to speak up when unethical practices occur.

17 Neglect of one's family, or neglect of one's personal needs.
18 Making a product decision that perpetrates a questionable safety issue.
19 Not putting back what you take out of the environment, employees and/or corporate assets.
20 Knowingly exaggerating the advantages of a plan in order to get needed support.
21 Failing to address probable areas of bigotry, sexism or racism.
22 Courting the business hierarchy versus doing the job well.
23 Climbing the corporate ladder by stepping on others.
24 Promoting the destructive go-getter who outruns his or her mistakes.
25 Failing to cooperate with other areas of the company – the enemy mentality.
26 Lying by omission to employees for the sake of the business.
27 Making an alliance with a questionable partner, albeit for a good cause.
28 Not taking responsibility for injurious practices – intentional or not.
29 Abusing or just going along with corporate perks that waste money and time.
30 Corrupting the public political process through legal means.

What is most interesting to me about this list is its length. Moreover, these are not hothouse problems that occur once in a career – they are familiar dilemmas. A company has at least twenty on the table every day. A manager has at least twenty on his or her desk every year. What I find equally impressive is their elusive nature. These are the kinds of situations that seem obviously wrong from a distance, but are so embedded in other concerns and environmental circumstances that the demarcations between right and wrong are blurred. Even price-fixing has been regarded by many otherwise high-minded executives as not really significant from a moral standpoint [4].

With the possible exception of price-fixing, each example poses a choice to step over the moral line or not. An ethical resolution to these situations requires discretional judgement about degree, overall goals, immediate logistical problems, other trade-offs, chances of success, and so on. There is no canned programme or magical mirror to help you determine what is right and wrong.

Such dilemmas are at the core of every manager's job, and their resolution rests partly on the foundation of values he or she brings to the task, but also on many conditions beyond a manager's direct control. Being raised right presumably provides the foundation for moral conduct. But how many managers with good backgrounds nevertheless end up as players in a commercial effort that puts other people's lives at risk [5]? How many succumb to an 'everybody-for-him-or-herself' culture because those who were greedy and dishonest seem to get all the rewards? How many employees, disgruntled over a superior's conduct, feel no qualms when they choose to lie to a customer rather than solve the customer's problem?

Or say you are confronted with a potentially flawed product that would not physically injure a customer but certainly would cost him or her time and money. You have to determine whether to delay its introduction, and for how long, while you run time-consuming tests and make adjustments. Meanwhile the company has set your division a hard-and-fast sales target for the quarter, you are in a declining market with unethical competitors and have a smaller staff, and the investment community is breathing down your boss's neck. How does being raised right provide an automatic solution, even at the theoretical level, to the many ethical choices that must be made about one's obligation to customer, shareholder, boss and organization?

Good business leadership and ultimately the fate of capitalism depend on the deliberate maintenance of a complex web of ethical values in the face of these many conflicting pressures. No moral artifice such as the law or corporate policy can mechanically solve the difficult trade-offs and painful decisions a responsible manager continually faces.

The moral calculus with which a manager would evaluate the current currency of his or her corporate activities must include more than what was learned at parental knees. It is cavalier to imply that maintaining ethical standards is easy as long as you're strong enough. Everyone faces hard issues whose solutions are not always obvious. The reconciliation of profit motives and ethical imperatives is an uncertain and highly tricky matter.

What is more, theoretical frameworks for reconciliation, though important, are obviously not enough. There is an old proverb: The road to hell is paved with good intentions. Many analysts of business ethics have noted that most instances of business wrong-doing are committed by people who never deliberately set out to commit unethical acts [6]. The potential for fallibility is not confined to the business person, but it also does not escape him or her. One is reminded of Hannah Arendt and Primo Levi's sobering conclusions that the truly frightening thing about the Holocaust was that it was carried out not by the fiendishly evil or maladapted, but by ordinary people who, under other circumstances, would appear to fit our common definitions of goodness. Wrote Levi in a moving analysis of the average Nazi in the SS [7]:

> They were made of the same cloth as we, they were average human beings, averagely intelligent, averagely wicked: save the exceptions, they were not monsters, they had our faces, but they had been reared badly. They were, for the greater part, diligent followers and functionaries . . . many indifferent, or fearful of punishment, or desirous of a good career, or too obedient.

History and developmental psychology have indicated that members of almost any group, though individually well-intended, can sink to immoral depths they would never dare test as individuals.

Today's manager needs to be armed with an awareness of what habits of thought and action are most likely to subvert moral common sense and the intellectual tools for breaking through these ethical snags.

A system at risk

The need for a second look at one's own approach to business ethics is particularly urgent in the 1990s. In the past, attention to the ethics of business centred largely on money matters. Corporate standards were primarily a matter of procedural rules about the pursuit of self-interest and welfare state instructions about the responsible distribution of the assets accrued. In a simplistic perversion of the Hebrew commandments, these standards consisted of a promise and a curse: Do this and you will prosper; fail to do so and you will be cursed. 'This', to put it in free market terms, was the pursuit of self-interest within the bounds of law and custom.

This contract for conduct has informed the basic motivational and allocation mechanisms in the corporation for at least the past forty years. Its assumption that personal goodness will follow fairly easily has rested on four important conditions:

1 Sustained economic growth.
2 An expectation of lifetime employment.
3 A homogeneous work force.
4 A national educational system that stresses literacy, [mathematics] ability and basic Judeo-Christian values.

Immediate and dependable cash rewards, people whose norms were similar, an effective educational background and the prospect of working with much the same group throughout one's career were sufficient to stimulate teamwork and productivity. People were relatively competent by the time they finished their higher-education goals, and they were willing to cooperate and be self-sacrificing and work hard because it paid to do so. They stayed more or less within the bounds of acceptable behaviour because: the players were all reasonably like-minded; the pie was big and growing; and the legislative arena was relatively benign. George Gilder's description of the humane nature of the free market would generally have been said to be accurate, if somewhat exaggerated.

Granted there were downsides to this ethos – smothering conformity, humiliating obedience to a hierarchical social system, and more recently the decline of market responsiveness – but in general, business could rely on informal cultural mechanisms and formal controls to motivate success within acceptable bounds of conduct and still use profit as the driving concept. A manager could informally voice a question about the right way of doing business and likely be understood by others without seeming to invade someone else's privacy or putting the business at unacceptable risk.

It was also possible for a manager to have direct oversight of other people's behaviour. Robert Baldwin, former chairman of Morgan Stanley, recounted how in his early days at the company all the traders sat in a circle with Mr

Morgan occupying a prominent position on a platform at one end. 'You can believe me', said Baldwin, 'this was a powerful incentive to conduct yourself ethically'.

Even as late as the early 1980s, the established reaction to scandal – whether it was environmental pollution, consumer injury or overseas bribery – was to increase the control mechanisms within the company, pass laws or set company restrictions, and leave it at that. The essential motivational patterns and approaches to problem-solving remained firmly rooted in a 'my profit/my company's profit-first' orientation.

As one astute manager expressed it in 1989, 'Essentially you motivate for greed and set up a strong system of controls to ensure that if someone steps over the boundaries, they'll get caught and be penalized'.

Although this formula for ethics and success may still hold strong currency in some managers' thinking about business morality, the environment that supported it has been steadily eroding since 1970. In the 1990s, it is all but gone. Economic recession in many industries and a multipolar array of strong competitors have undermined the promise of universal and immediate cash rewards among like-minded people. Downsizing, mergers and extreme work force mobility have destroyed any remaining illusions about lifetime employment. Homogeneity and coincident value systems are all but gone. The work force is now international, multiracial, dual sexual, and on its way to being even more so. The legislative arena is redefining (with customary difficulty) every standard of corporate behaviour from import quotas to drug testing. The schools have abandoned values education for so long that even a free-market president speaks of a values crisis in this country and calls for a kinder, gentler nation. As for hard work and sacrifice, US personal savings rates dropped from over 10% of income to under 2% between 1973 and 1987.

In short, the familiar free-market ethos of managed greed has become unmanageable. The already fragile bonds between people in the marketplace are fast disappearing as the cash rewards fail to materialize, and traditional methods of leadership such as personal contact and communication with the top become all but obsolete as the corporation becomes larger and geographically more scattered.

The situation is further exacerbated by massive disruptions of company traditions through ownership change and the increasing impersonalization of work as technology progresses into everyone's barnyard. Excessive wage gaps between the top and the bottom distance people still further and breed resentment. A resentful worker is one more likely to rip off a company or at least fail to go the extra mile for its customers. Moreover, without massive investment in re-education, many workers could not effectively respond to entrepreneurial opportunities even if they wished to do so.

These environmental changes have meant bad news for many companies' performance records as teamwork, cooperation and self-sacrifice fail to inform managerial attitudes and behaviour. The accompanying decline in trust levels makes it increasingly difficult to motivate intracompany cooperation and responsiveness to customers, or to count on employee loyalty in situations where the rewards must be down the road, and not guaranteed at that. Meanwhile, consumers are able to survey a wider and wider arena of alternatives to choose from.

The impact of these changes is not just economic. They also spell danger for the moral capacity of business and the people in it. Technology and financial complexity have created many more opportunities to cheat and many more corners to hide in. New environmental concerns and a more educated consumer pose additional quandaries about products, markets, manufacturing and financing. When growth is relatively constant and lifetime membership in the corporate family assured, it is easier for a person to invest time, money and reputation to solve such problems. But today's survival environment stimulates a me-first business ethic which seems to justify exploitation and cheating because the lifeboats are filled. Game-playing and indifference to others are inevitable results. The trust factor is eroded at every level of corporate activity. The spontaneity, enthusiasm and personal risk-taking that characterize many start-up, high-growth businesses are being lost in the economic and social turmoil that embroils most large corporations today.

In such an environment the old models of motivating for self-interest and passively leaving other values to chance or outside regulation simply fail to be effective moral or market motivators. In the 1980s, we saw the emergence of a materialistic, get-rich-quick, lean-and-mean ethos which is creating a self-destructive confidence gap in individual corporations and the marketplace. It has also set up many executives for a certain identity crisis as their material achievements either diminish in the face of economic downturn or fail to nourish their spiritual needs.

Those who voice confidence in the private sector's ability to carry on as usual in the face of such changes should not forget that until quite recently the securities industry, resting on a bedrock of self-regulation and after-the-fact regulatory oversight, was frequently cited as the model for encouraging high ethical standards in business. As the moral fabric of this industry unravelled in the late 1980s, all the environmental factors mentioned above battered the companies at which wrong-doing occurred: dramatically abrupt changes in ownership and leadership patterns, a more diverse work force with more individualistically centred values, heightened complexity of transaction procedures providing more places to hide, a globalized and faster-paced playing field, and legislative rules that did not keep up with changing practices and increased volume.

Moving beyond compliance concerns

The quiet tragedy is that so many securities companies, by failing to address the devaluation of personal standards, which would be the inevitable fallout of such conditions, ended up victimizing not only the public but themselves as well. As one executive in the industry put it, the system worked in the sense that some people eventually got caught, but what do you do next? For many whose business approach was formed by this system, the only operating questions on the table are, will we be staying within the procedural rules, and will we make money? In such questions one finds no deep foundation of values to help reverse the recent overemphasis on greed.

Theologian Paul Tillich has described the truth of a faith as its ability to express adequately an ultimate concern. He defines adequacy of expression as something that 'creates reply, action, and communication' [8].

Laissez-faire ethics, i.e. relying on everyone's home-rearing or creating a lot of sticks to punish after the fact, is no longer able to create the kind of communal reply, communication and action that is adequate for expressing the ultimate concerns about profit and morality, namely whether there is real value creation and how the standard way of doing business affects people in the system and those who are objects of its activity.

The chief issue for business ethics and the manager intent on sustaining high corporate standards of behaviour is not the detection of all the business people who are unethical. Compliance oversight is needed, but it is not the whole answer to ensuring ethical business conduct. The task at hand for every corporate leader is to concentrate not just on what should *not* be done, but also on what the ethical manager *should* be thinking from moral and economic standpoints. Here is where the real moral leadership will occur in corporations.

Enlightened self-interest?

To begin the journey, it must be recognized that standard managerial approaches to problem-solving and motivation are failing to keep basic moral standards and the overarching goals of a capitalistic society alive in today's changed competitive and social environments. Traditional self-interest models of problem-solving and motivating do not adequately stimulate either the moral or performance outcomes for which they were developed. They no longer provoke truly enlightened self-interest, with its implication of suspended self-interest for long-term self-enhancement. Rather, they are being perverted into a justification for what I call the survival ethic, i.e. everyone for him- or herself for the sake of the company's survival. As increasingly dire depictions of American industry's demise are accompanied by calls for breaking the rules, the survival ethic becomes more and more persuasive and equally unmanageable. The obvious outcome is a no-holds-barred approach to business which renders impotent our hoped-for constraints on predatory behaviour. It also introduces into the system a hidden and lethal 'exploitation virus' that causes well-intended team-building and joint venture efforts to self-destruct.

New kinds of competitive alliances, new arrangements of the work force, and old problems of unresponsiveness call for a more socially oriented approach to management which can stimulate the ethical values that build rather than impede cooperation, hard work, personal empowerment and value creation as a first goal. If business and society are to thrive, we need a stronger moral ballast for business than thoughts of self-advancement.

It is time to strike a new bargain for capitalism, one that recognizes that voluntary exchange, individual and social health, and the cooperation of large groups of people are based on more than the management of personal self-interest. To the degree that they fail to go beyond the appeal to self-interest, current goal-setting and other motivational frameworks for problem-solving are setting companies up for moral and financial failure.

A new foundation of assumptions is needed that elicits the normal array of ethical values *despite* the current economic and social upheavals. Without these values, which would include honesty, trust, value creation, fairness and self-sacrifice, potentially destructive ethical dilemmas such as the thirty mentioned above can become the unremarkable norm. Should that occur, current corporate efforts towards innovation, responsiveness and teamwork will be futile. A company's reputation – for that matter the integrity of our economic system – ultimately rests not on self-aggrandisement but on the cultivation of genuinely self-respecting employees who have the welfare of others firmly seated in their value system. The legitimacy of capitalism depends on managers who have the necessary understanding and skill to maintain these other-oriented standards as the pressure to abandon them increases.

The ethics issue of the 1990s will surely be the search for a set of management assumptions that can stimulate personal integrity and responsiveness to others in the marketplace within the changing competitive context of most industries. To be successful, this inquiry cannot remain isolated from other business issues today. One must understand the moral underpinning of a success theory, if excellence is ever to be obtained and sustained.

Some business leaders and long-standing corporate traditions have already found the kind of business philosophy needed to respond to the ethical complexities of commercial endeavour. Increasingly, they are shedding the traditional anonymity of the chief executive officer's role in favour of a more explicit assertion of ethical standards. This new style of leadership, exemplified by such people as Wal-Mart's David Glass, Johnson & Johnson's James Burke, and Xerox's David Kearns, *has underscored the importance of individual integrity and the relevance of private moral values to the achievement of excellent performance* [9]. Likewise, Tom Peters echoes the thinking of a number of his admired executives when, in *Thriving on Chaos*, he cites 'integrity' as the capstone of his forty-five-point list of competitive attributes. These people not only have a theoretical commitment to ethical conduct; they have already successfully applied familiar ethical values like honesty, trustworthiness, loyalty, fairness, self-knowledge and beneficent results to the realm of moneymaking and managing. John Casey's *Ethics in the Financial Marketplace* [10] and Max DePree's *Leadership is an Art* [11] are two outstanding examples of this leadership philosophy. My purpose here will be to build on the tenor of such works and to explore systematically the major themes of the excellence literature in terms of the *moral* premisses on which outstanding performance is based and motivated.

The covenantal ethic

The most noteworthy feature of a Johnson & Johnson credo, or Max DePree's management approach, is the way in which self-interest is reoriented. It is not that these business leaders ignore profit motives – far from it. But they subordinate self-interest to other motivations, the most prominent of which are value creation and service to others. Their experience, the way they define goals, and how they describe the way they resolve problems provide the basis for what I will call a Covenantal Business Ethic. This label is a deliberate echo of the social contracts that early New England communities established for the mutual well-being of their members. The Covenantal Ethic provides a coherent blending of profit motive and the other-oriented values that help create trust and cooperation between people. It has three essential aspects:

1 It sees value creation in its many forms as the primary objective.
2 It sees profit and other social returns as a result of other goals rather than the overriding objective.
3 It approaches business problems more in terms of relationships than tangible products.

Building upon this framework, a Covenantal Ethic stresses service to others and deliberately draws on some of the non-rational impulses, such as caring, which secure people's commitment to organizations and tasks even when doing so is not obviously to their immediate advantage. As such, this ethic differs from traditional approaches not just in focus but in the vehicles by which moral conduct is made an active part of management. Emotional phenomena have for the most part been absent from the vocabulary and theoretical frameworks that business people have applied to moral problems. Morality has been a question of legal obligation, a weighing of rights, a cost–benefit calculation of consequences. A Covenantal Ethic does not preclude these kinds of thinking, but it also draws on the workings of the heart. It is a radical departure from the eat-or-be-eaten, sweat-or-be-beaten theories of motivating hard work and innovation one hears so often in executive seminars and analyses of, for example, why we've fallen behind, say, Japan.

Not only does a Covenantal Ethic promise a more communal morality in business thinking, it also holds the prospect of increasing a manager's sense of self-worth. Covenantal thinking's foundation is the belief that *all* individuals are worthy of respect and service, rather than being of worth only in terms of what they might cost or gain you. Simply stated, it is an assertion of humanism, in that it holds every life to be of value, even in the economic context of serving a corporate entity. Thus a Covenantal Ethic, or for that matter any other business ethic, is a statement about the relative significance of individuals and the society to which they are committed. I see these significances not just in terms of productivity, though that is important, but also in terms of vitality. A Covenantal Ethic places the energy and intrinsic worth of individuals above the mechanics of an organizational system and its preordained financial strategy. As such, it is an ethic that directly complements recent arguments such as Tom Peters' [12] or Rosabeth Moss Kanter's [13] about the need for increased individualism and autonomy in today's competitive environment.

Though I agree with their theses, to my mind this need is not a new one precipitated by the need for new organization structures in the face of changing competition. In the 1950s and 1960s, it was argued that the corporation needed to pay more attention to individualism because of the very success of its hierarchical bureaucracy. Now it is argued that the corporation needed to pay attention to individualism because of its failures. It seems more likely that individualism is quite simply an ever-present human need, independent of economic fortune. The society that is vital and moral must have individuals who are vital and moral. This is especially true for business.

It is important to note at the outset of this inquiry that the Covenantal Ethic suggested here is not a theoretical wish-list about . . . corporate leadership, but a reality in many of the country's most successful organizations. Covenantal thinking has a proven economic and moral track record, as Herman Miller Company's legendary annualized earnings growth and product quality demonstrate, or J.C. Penney's continued and successful responsiveness to customers illustrates.

[My contention is] that it is possible for a manager to carry his or her moral concerns beyond the realm of good intentions into actual application in the achievement of economic success. The approach I suggest here conforms to what one would call 'good business sense'. It tries to enhance the way managers think about the concept by systematically analysing the moral and humanistic dimension of good business judgement. This perspective is crucial if capitalism's moral objectives of social good and individual well-being are not to become obsolete. I firmly believe that there is a deep reservoir of decency in American management, but that too frequently the way in which managers set goals and measure success fails to tap that resource adequately. The number one American business challenge in the 1990s is to transform a manager's allegedly good intentions into a profound and enacted covenant with customers, employees and the general public. None of these groups are limited to American shores. The global nature of this covenant only adds to its urgency, for how well it is fulfilled could either destroy or secure the tenuous foothold that democratic capitalism has in so many nations today.

References and notes

1 Berenbeim, Ronald E., *Corporate Ethics*, The Conference Board Research Report no. 900, New York: 1988.
2 Carr, Albert Z., 'Is Business Bluffing Ethical?' *Harvard Business Review*, **46**, January–February 1968; 143–153.
3 Korn/Ferry International and Columbia University Graduate School of Business. *21st Century Report: Reinventing the CEO* Los Angeles: 1989, p. 41.
4 Relatively low penalties for the act indicate that the judicial system concurs. For a discussion of attitudes towards price-fixing, see Clinard, Marshall and Yeager, Peter C. *Illegal Corporate Behaviour*, Washington, DC: National Institute of Law Enforcement and Criminal Justice, 1979.
5 For example, over 100 000 deaths per year are attributed to occupationally related diseases, the majority of which are caused by wilful violations of health and safety laws by corporations. See Kramer, Ronald, C. 'Corporate Crime: An Organisational Perspective'. In: *White Collar and Economic Crime*, Wickman, Peter and Dailey, Timothy (eds) Lexington, MA: Lexington Books, 1982, p. 76.
6 For example, Gerald E. Ottoson states: 'Most of the unethical acts I have seen committed in business were performed essentially by honest people'. See Ottoson, Gerald E. 'Winning the War against Corporate Crime'. *Ethikos* 2.4: January–February 1989, 3.
7 Levi, Primo *The Drowned and the Saved*, New York: Summit Books, 1986.
8 Tillich, Paul *Dynamics of Faith*, New York: Harper Torchbooks, 1965, p. 96.
9 For a study of 'values-driven' leadership, which describes some of this new explicitness, see Badaracco, Joseph L. Jr and Ellsworth, Richard R. *Leadership and the Quest for Integrity*, Boston, MA: Harvard Business School Press, 1989.
10 Casey, John L., *Ethics in the Financial Marketplace*, New York: Scudder, Stevens & Clark, 1988.
11 DePree, Max *Leadership is an Art*, Garden City, NY: Doubleday, 1989.
12 Peters, Tom, *Thriving on Chaos*, New York: Harper & Row, 1987.
13 Kanter, Rosabeth, Moss *The Change Masters: Innovation and Entrepreneurship in the American Corporation*, New York: Simon & Schuster, 1983; and, more recently, *When Giants Learn to Dance*, New York: Simon & Schuster, 1989.

Additional reading

This contribution by Nash is from her book *Good Intentions Aside* (Boston, MA: Harvard Business School Press, 1990) where she expands on the covenantal ethic introduced here. Hard-hitting chapters include 'The seductive power of ego incentives' and 'Wearing two hats: when private conscience and corporate viewpoint conflict'.

One opinion that runs counter to Nash's is Albert Carr's 'Is business bluffing ethical?', which is reprinted in the next chapter of this book.

Questions for discussion

- Compare Nash's definition of business ethics with that of Carmichael and Drummond printed in the introduction to this chapter.
- What insight do you obtain from each definition?
- Relate each definition to examples from your working experience.

Chapter 2

Is business bluffing ethical?

Albert Carr explores the case for a special kind of ethics for business people by employing a form of game theory, because in his view business is a game.

Anyone with a modicum of business experience will be able to relate to the material covered in this chapter. Much of it will ring a bell with experienced managers, because it is based upon practical, real-life business experience.

Carr's concern is that in order to be successful it is necessary not that business people abandon *all* personal morals at the office door – just some of them – and this is possible provided the bluffs employed are 'ethically justified'.

Further, he contends that 'no one should think any worse of the game of business because its standards of right and wrong differ from the prevailing traditions of morality in our society'. Therefore, business people must be guided by a different set of ethical standards, as poker players follow the rules of poker.

Some would argue that the rules of poker are well-defined, despite not being codified in law, whereas those of business are much less so; and some might also take issue with the view that the law provides sufficient definition of the rules of business.

Carr's view, which is common in a number of business circles, is that it is sufficient that a company obeys the law, and that provided it does so then it has the legal right to shape its strategy without reference to anything but its profits.

Readers might ask if a company also has a moral right to take this view, or if they agree that strategy can be devised independently of ethics, provided legal criteria are satisfied. Or is it the case that 'the major tests of every move in business, as in all games of strategy, are legality and profit'? The point is also made that business people 'do not make the laws': however, it might also be argued that everyone in a company contributes to the making of laws through the democratic process of electing law-makers. Furthermore, as Carr himself notes, large companies do think it prudent to advance their corporate interest through lobbying legislators.

Carr discusses the issue of spying on competitors and this is of course not confined to the US. For example, the Bath School of Management claims that 2500 UK companies are involved in such activities, and an estimated 100 000 bugs are sold every year in the UK.

His use of the example of cigarette manufacturers may prove to be especially prescient in the light of recent US legal judgements, which perhaps make legal action more likely.

Many managers will be familiar with the description in this chapter of the difficulties experienced by executives in explaining business decisions to those not familiar with business operations, such as family members. It is interesting to note, in this regard, that in the best designed codes of ethics, staff are encouraged to apply certain tests to guide their decision-taking. One of the tests most commonly suggested is to ask the question: How would I feel if my friends or family knew of this decision?

Is business bluffing ethical?
Albert Z. Carr

The ethics of business are not those of society, but rather those of the poker game.

A respected businessman with whom I discussed the theme of this article remarked with some heat, 'You mean to say you're going to encourage men to bluff? Why, bluffing is nothing more than a form of lying! You're advising them to lie!'

I agreed that the basis of private morality is a respect for truth and that the closer a businessman comes to the truth, the more he deserves respect. At the same time, I suggested that most bluffing in business might be regarded simply as game strategy – much like bluffing in poker, which does not reflect on the morality of the bluffer.

I quoted Henry Taylor, the British statesman who pointed out that 'falsehood ceases to be falsehood when it is understood on all sides that the truth is not expected to be spoken' – an exact description of bluffing in poker, diplomacy and business. I cited the analogy of the criminal court, where the criminal is not expected to tell the truth when he pleads not guilty. Everyone from the judge down takes it for granted that the job of the defendant's [lawyer] is to get his client off, not to reveal the truth; and this is considered ethical practice. I mentioned Representative Omar Burleson, . . . who was quoted as saying, in regard to the ethics of Congress, 'Ethics is a barrel of worms' [1] – a pungent summing-up of the problem of deciding who is ethical in politics.

I reminded my friend that millions of businessmen feel constrained every day to say *yes* to their bosses when they secretly believe *no* and that this is generally accepted as permissible strategy when the alternative might be the loss of a job. The essential point, I said, is that the ethics of business is game ethics, different from the ethics of religion.

He remained unconvinced. Referring to the company of which he is president, he declared:

> Maybe that's good enough for some businessmen, but I can tell you that we pride ourselves on our ethics. In 30 years not one customer has ever questioned my word or asked to check our figures. We're loyal to our customers and fair to our suppliers. I regard my handshake on a deal as a contract. I've never entered into price-fixing schemes with my competitors. I've never allowed my salesmen to spread injurious rumours about other companies. Our union contract is the best in our industry. And, if I do say so myself, our ethical standards are of the highest!

He really was saying, without realizing it, that he was living up to the ethical standards of the business game – which are a far cry from those of private life. Like a gentlemanly poker player, he did not play in cahoots with others at the table, try to smear their reputations, or hold back chips he owed them.

But this same fine man, at that very time, was allowing one of his products to be advertised in a way that made it sound a great deal better than it actually was. Another item in his product line was notorious among dealers for its built-in obsolescence. He was holding back from the market a much-improved product because he did not want it to interfere with sales of the inferior item it would have replaced. He had joined with certain of his competitors in hiring a lobbyist to push a . . . legislature, by methods that he preferred not to know too much about, into amending a bill then being enacted.

In his view these things had nothing to do with ethics; they were merely normal business practice. He himself undoubtedly avoided outright false-hoods – never lied in so many words. But the entire organization that he ruled was deeply involved in numerous strategies of deception.

Pressure to deceive

Most executives from time to time are almost compelled, in the interests of their companies or themselves, to practise some form of deception when negotiating with customers, dealers, labour unions, government officials, or even other departments of their companies. By conscious misstatements, concealment of pertinent facts, or exaggeration – in short, by bluffing – they seek to persuade others to agree with them. I think it is fair to say that if the individual executive refuses to bluff from time to time – if he feels obligated to tell the truth, the whole truth, and nothing but the truth – he is ignoring opportunities permitted under the rules and is at a heavy disadvantage in his business dealings.

But here and there a businessman is unable to reconcile himself to the bluff in which he plays a part. His conscience, perhaps spurred by religious idealism, troubles him. He feels guilty; he may develop an ulcer or a nervous tic. Before any executive can make profitable use of the strategy of the bluff, he needs to make sure that in bluffing he will not lose self-respect or become emotionally disturbed. If he is to reconcile personal integrity and high standards of honesty with the practical requirements of business, he must feel that his bluffs are ethically justified. The justification rests on the fact that business, as practised by individuals as well as by corporations, has the impersonal character of a game – a game that demands both special strategy and an understanding of its special ethics.

The game is played at all levels of corporate life, from the highest to the lowest. At the very instant that a man decides to enter business, he may be forced into a game situation, as is shown by . . . a magazine space salesman who, owing to a merger, suddenly found himself out of a job. This man was 58 and, in spite of a good record, his chance of getting a job elsewhere in a business where youth is favoured in hiring practice was not good. He was a vigorous, healthy man, and only a considerable amount of grey in his hair suggested his age. Before beginning his job search he touched up his hair with a black dye to confine the grey to his temples. He knew that the truth about his age might well come out in time, but he calculated that he could deal with that situation when it arose. He and his wife decided that he could easily pass for 45, and he so stated his age on his résumé.

This was a lie; yet within the accepted rules of the business game, no moral culpability attaches to it.

The poker analogy

We can learn a good deal about the nature of business by comparing it with poker. While both have a large element of chance, in the long run the winner is the man who plays with steady skill. In both games ultimate victory requires intimate knowledge of the rules, insight into the psychology of the other players, a bold front, a considerable amount of self-discipline, and the ability to respond swiftly and effectively to opportunities provided by chance.

No one expects poker to be played on the ethical principles preached in churches. In poker it is right and proper to bluff a friend out of the rewards of being dealt a good hand. A player feels no more than a slight twinge of sympathy, if that, when – with nothing better than a single ace in his hand – he strips a heavy loser, who holds a pair, of the rest of his chips. It was up to the other fellow to protect himself. In the words of an excellent poker player, former President Harry Truman, 'If you can't stand the heat, stay out of the kitchen'. If one shows mercy to a loser in poker, it is a personal gesture, divorced from the rules of the game.

Poker has its special ethics, and here I am not referring to rules against cheating. The man who keeps an ace up his sleeve or who marks the cards is more than unethical; he is a crook, and can be punished as such – kicked out of the game or, in the Old West, shot.

In contrast to the cheat, the unethical poker player is one who, while abiding by the letter of the rules, finds ways to put the other players at an unfair disadvantage. Perhaps he unnerves them with loud talk. Or he tries to get them drunk. Or he plays in cahoots with someone else at the table. Ethical poker players frown on such tactics.

Poker's own brand of ethics is different from the ethical ideals of civilized human relationships. The game calls for distrust of the other fellow. It ignores the claim of friendship. Cunning deception and concealment of one's strength and intentions, not kindness and open-heartedness, are vital in poker. No one thinks any the worse of poker on that account. And no one should think any the worse of the game of business because its standards of right and wrong differ from the prevailing traditions of morality in our society.

Discard the golden rule

This view of business is especially worrisome to people without much business experience. A minister of my acquaintance once protested that business cannot possibly function in our society unless it is based on the Judeo-Christian system of ethics. He told me:

> I know some businessmen have supplied call girls to customers, but there are always a few rotten apples in every barrel. That doesn't mean the rest of the fruit isn't sound. Surely the vast majority of businessmen are ethical. I myself am acquainted with many who adhere to strict codes of ethics based fundamentally on religious teachings. They contribute to good causes. They participate in community activities. They cooperate with other companies to improve working conditions in their industries. Certainly they are not indifferent to ethics.

That most businessmen are not indifferent to ethics in their private lives, everyone will agree. My point is that in their office lives they cease to be private citizens; they become game-players who must be guided by a somewhat different set of ethical standards.

The point was forcefully made to me by . . . [an] executive who has given a good deal of thought to the question:

> So long as a businessman complies with the laws of the land and avoids telling malicious lies, he's ethical. If the law as written gives a man a wide-open chance to make a killing, he'd be a fool not to take advantage of it. If he doesn't, somebody else will. There's no obligation on him to stop and consider who is going to get hurt. If the law says he can do it, that's all the justification he needs. There's nothing unethical about that. It's just plain business sense.

This executive (call him Robbins) took the stand that even industrial espionage, which is frowned on by some businessmen, ought not to be considered unethical. He recalled a recent meeting . . . where an authority on marketing made a speech in which he deplored the employment of spies by business organizations. More and more companies, he pointed out, find it cheaper to penetrate the secrets of competitors with concealed cameras and microphones or by bribing employees than to set up costly research and design departments of their own. A whole branch of the electronics industry has grown up with this trend, he continued, providing equipment to make industrial espionage easier.

Disturbing? The marketing expert found it so. But when it came to a remedy, he could only appeal to 'respect for the golden rule'. Robbins thought this a confession of defeat, believing that the golden rule, for all its value as an ideal for society, is simply not feasible as a guide for business. A good part of the time the businessman is trying to do unto others as he hopes others will *not* do unto him [2]. Robbins continued:

Espionage of one kind or another has become so common in business that it's like taking a drink during Prohibition – it's not considered sinful. And we don't even have Prohibition where espionage is concerned; the law is very tolerant in this area. There's no more shame for a business that uses secret agents than there is for a nation. Bear in mind that there already is at least one large corporation – you can buy its stock over the counter – that makes millions by providing counterespionage service to industrial firms. Espionage in business is not an ethical problem; it's an established technique of business competition.

'We don't make the laws'

Wherever we turn in business, we can perceive the sharp distinction between its ethical standards and those of the churches. Newspapers abound with sensational stories growing out of this distinction . . . . Critics of business regard such behaviour as unethical, but the companies concerned know that they are merely playing the business game.

Among the most respected of our business institutions are the insurance companies. A group of insurance executives meeting recently in New England was startled when their guest speaker, social critic Daniel Patrick Moynihan, roundly berated them for 'unethical' practices. They had been guilty, Moynihan alleged, of using outdated actuarial tables to obtain unfairly high premiums. They habitually delayed the hearings of lawsuits against them in order to tire out the plaintiffs and win cheap settlements. In their employment policies they used ingenious devices to discriminate against certain minority groups [3].

It was difficult for the audience to deny the validity of these charges. But these men were business game-players . . . . If the laws governing their businesses change, or if public opinion becomes clamorous, they will make the necessary adjustments. But morally they have in their view done nothing wrong. As long as they comply with the letter of the law, they are within their rights to operate their businesses as they see fit.

The small business is in the same position as the great corporation in this respect. For example, in 1967 a key manufacturer was accused of providing master keys for automobiles to mail-order customers, although it was obvious that some of the purchasers might be automobile thieves. His defence was plain and straightforward. If there was nothing in the law to prevent him from selling his keys to anyone who ordered them, it was not up to him to inquire as to his customers' motives . . . . Until the law was changed, the key manufacturer could regard himself as being just as ethical as any other businessman by the rules of the business game [4].

Violations of the ethical ideals of society are common in business, but they are not necessarily violations of business principles. Each year the Federal Trade Commission orders hundreds of companies, many of them of the first magnitude, to 'cease and desist' from practices which, judged by ordinary standards, are of questionable morality but which are stoutly defended by the companies concerned.

In one case, a firm manufacturing a well-known mouthwash was accused of using a cheap form of alcohol possibly deleterious to health. The company's chief executive, after testifying in Washington, made this comment privately:

> We broke no law. We're in a highly competitive industry. If we're going to stay in business, we have to look for profit wherever the law permits. We don't make the laws. We obey them. Then why do we have to put up with this 'holier than thou' talk about ethics? It's sheer hypocrisy. We're not in business to promote ethics. Look at the cigarette companies, for God's sake! If the ethics aren't embodied in the laws by the men who made them, you can't expect businessmen to fill the lack. Why, a sudden submission to Christian ethics by businessmen would bring about the greatest economic upheaval in history!

It may be noted that the government failed to prove its case against him.

Cast illusions aside

Talk about ethics by businessmen is often a thin decorative coating over the hard realities of the game. Once I listened to a speech by a young executive who pointed to a new industry code as proof that his company and its competitors were deeply aware of their responsibilities to society. It was a code of ethics, he said. The industry was going to police itself, to dissuade constituent companies from wrong-doing. His eyes shone with conviction and enthusiasm.

The same day there was a meeting in a hotel room where the industry's top executives met with the 'czar' who was to administer the new code, a man of high repute. No one who was present could doubt their common attitude. In their eyes the code was designed primarily to forestall a move by the . . . government to impose stern restrictions on the industry. They felt that the code would hamper them a good deal less than new federal laws would. It was, in other words, conceived as a protection for the industry, not for the public.

The young executive accepted the surface explanation of the code; these leaders, all experienced game-players, did not deceive themselves for a moment about its purpose.

The illusion that business can afford to be guided by ethics as conceived in private life is often fostered by speeches and articles containing such phrases as, 'It pays to be ethical', or, 'Sound ethics is good business'. Actually this is not an ethical position at all; it is a self-serving calculation in disguise. The speaker is really saying that in the long run a company can make more money if it does not antagonize competitors, suppliers, employees and customers by squeezing them too hard. He is saying that oversharp policies reduce ultimate gains. That is true, but it has nothing to do with ethics. The underlying attitude is much like that in the familiar story of the shopkeeper who finds an extra [£20 note] in the cash register, debates with himself the ethical problem – should he tell his partner? – and finally decides to share the money because the gesture will give him an edge . . . the next time they quarrel.

I think it is fair to sum up the prevailing attitude of businessmen on ethics as follows: We live in what is probably the most competitive of the world's civilized societies. Our customs encourage a high degree of aggression in the individual's striving for success. Business is our main area of competition, and it has been ritualized into a game of strategy. The basic rules of the game have been set by the government, which attempts to detect and punish business frauds. But as long as a company does not transgress the rules of the game set by law, it has the legal right to shape its strategy without reference to anything but its profits. If it takes a long-term view of its profits, it will preserve amicable relations, so far as possible, with those with whom it deals. A wise businessman will not seek advantage to the point where he generates dangerous hostility among employees, competitors, customers, government, or the public at large. But decisions in this area are, in the final test, decisions of strategy, not of ethics.

The individual and the game

An individual within a company often finds it difficult to adjust to the requirements of the business game. He tries to preserve his private ethical standards in situations that call for game strategy. When he is obliged to carry out company policies that challenge his conception of himself as an ethical man, he suffers.

It disturbs him when he is ordered, for instance, to deny a rise to a man who deserves it, to fire an employee of long standing, to prepare advertising that he believes to be misleading, to conceal facts that he feels customers are entitled to know, to cheapen the quality of materials used in the manufacture of an established product, to sell as new a product that he knows to be rebuilt, to exaggerate the curative powers of a medicinal preparation, or to coerce dealers.

There are some fortunate executives who, by the nature of their work and circumstances, never have to face problems of this kind. But in one form or another the ethical dilemma is felt sooner or later by most businessmen. Possibly the dilemma is most painful not when the company forces the action on the executive but when he originates it himself – that is, when he has taken or is contemplating a step which is in his own interest but which runs counter to his early moral conditioning. To illustrate:

● The manager of an export department, eager to show rising sales, is pressed by a big customer to provide invoices which, while containing no overt falsehood that would violate a . . . law, are so worded that the customer may be able to evade certain taxes in his homeland.

- A company president finds that an ageing executive, within a few years of retirement and his pension, is not as productive as formerly. Should he be kept on?
- The produce manager of a supermarket debates with himself whether to get rid of a lot of half-rotten tomatoes by including one, with its good side exposed, in every [pack of tomatoes].
- An accountant discovers that he has taken an improper deduction on his company's tax return and fears the consequences if he calls the matter to the president's attention, though he himself has done nothing illegal. Perhaps if he says nothing, no one will notice the error.
- A chief executive officer is asked by his directors to comment on a rumour that he owns stock in another company with which he has placed large orders. He could deny it, for the stock is in the name of his son-in-law and he has earlier formally instructed his son-in-law to sell the holding.

Temptations of this kind constantly arise in business. If an executive allows himself to be torn between a decision based on business considerations and one based on his private ethical code, he exposes himself to a grave psychological strain.

This is not to say that sound business strategy necessarily runs counter to ethical ideals. They may frequently coincide; and when they do, everyone is gratified. But the major tests of every move in business, as in all games of strategy, are legality and profit. A man who intends to be a winner in the business game must have a game-player's attitude.

The business strategist's decisions must be as impersonal as those of a surgeon performing an operation – concentrating on objective and technique, and subordinating personal feelings. If the chief executive admits that his son-in-law owns the stock, it is because he stands to lose more if the fact comes out later than if he states it boldly and at once. If the supermarket manager orders the rotten tomatoes to be discarded, he does so to avoid an increase in consumer complaints and a loss of good will. The company president decides not to fire the elderly executive in the belief that the negative reaction of other employees would in the long run cost the company more than it would lose in keeping him and paying his pension.

All sensible businessmen prefer to be truthful, but they seldom feel inclined to tell the *whole* truth. In the business game truth-telling usually has to be kept within narrow limits if trouble is to be avoided. The point was neatly made a long time ago (in 1888) by one of John D. Rockefeller's associates, Paul Babcock, to Standard Oil Company executives who were about to testify before a government investigating committee: 'Parry every question with answers which, while perfectly truthful, are evasive of *bottom* facts' [5]. This was, is, and probably always will be regarded as wise and permissible business strategy.

For office use only

An executive's family life can easily be dislocated if he fails to make a sharp distinction between the ethical systems of the home and the office – or if his wife does not grasp that distinction. Many a businessman who has remarked to his wife, 'I had to let Jones go today' or 'I had to admit to the boss that Jim has been goofing off lately', has been met with an indignant protest. 'How could you do a thing like that? You know Jones is over 50 and will have a lot of trouble getting another job.' Or, 'You did that to him? With his wife ill and all the worry she's been having with the kids?'

If the executive insists that he had no choice because the profits of the company and his own security were involved, he may see a certain cool and ominous reappraisal in his wife's eyes. Many wives are not prepared to accept the fact that business operates with a special code of ethics. An illuminating illustration of this comes from a . . . sales executive who related a conversation he had with his wife at a time when a hotly contested political campaign was being waged in their [area]:

I made the mistake of telling her that I had lunch with Colby, who gives me about half my business. Colby mentioned that his company had a stake in the election. Then he said, 'By the way, I'm treasurer . . . for Lang. I'm collecting contributions. Can I count on you . . . ?'

Well, there I was. I was opposed to Lang, but I knew Colby. If he withdrew his business I could be in a bad spot. So I just smiled and wrote out a cheque then and there. He thanked me, and we started to talk about his next order. Maybe he thought I shared his political views. If so, I wasn't going to lose any sleep over it.

I should have had sense enough not to tell Mary about it. She hit the ceiling. She said she was disappointed in me. She said I hadn't acted like a man, that I should have stood up to Colby.

I said, 'Look, it was an either–or situation. I had to do it or risk losing the business'.

She came back at me with, 'I don't believe it. You could have been honest with him. You could have said that you didn't feel you ought to contribute to a campaign for a man you weren't going to vote for. I'm sure he would have understood'.

I said, 'Mary, you're a wonderful woman, but you're way off the track. Do you know what would have happened if I had said that? Colby would have smiled and said, "Oh, I didn't realize. Forget it." But in his eyes from that moment I would be an oddball, maybe a bit of a radical. He would have listened to me talk about his order and would have promised to give it consideration. After that I wouldn't hear from him for a week. Then I would telephone and learn from his secretary that he wasn't yet ready to place the order. And in about a month I would hear through the grapevine that he was giving his business to another company. A month after that I'd be out of a job'.

She was silent for a while. Then she said, 'Tom, something is wrong with business when a man is forced to choose between his family's security and his moral obligation to himself. It's easy for me to say you should have stood up to him – but if you had, you might have felt you were betraying me and the kids. I'm sorry that you did it, Tom, but I can't blame you. Something is wrong with business!'

This wife saw the problem in terms of moral obligation as conceived in private life; her husband saw it as a matter of game strategy. As a player in a weak position, he felt that he could not afford to indulge an ethical sentiment that might have cost him his seat at the table.

Playing to win

Some men might challenge the Colbys of business – might accept serious setbacks to their business careers rather than risk a feeling of moral cowardice. They merit our respect – but as private individuals, not businessmen. When the skilful player of the business game is compelled to submit to unfair pressure, he does not castigate himself for moral weakness. Instead, he strives to put himself into a strong position where he can defend himself against such pressures in the future without loss.

If a man plans to take a seat in the business game, he owes it to himself to master the principles by which the game is played, including its special ethical outlook. He can then hardly fail to recognize that an occasional bluff may well be justified in terms of the game's ethics and warranted in terms of economic necessity. Once he clears his mind on this point, he is in a good position to match his strategy against that of the other players. He can then determine objectively whether a bluff in a given situation has a good chance of succeeding and can decide when and how to bluff, without a feeling of ethical transgression.

To be a winner, a man must play to win. This does not mean that he must be ruthless, cruel, harsh or treacherous. On the contrary, the better his reputation for integrity, honesty and decency, the better his chances of victory will be in the long run. But from time to time every businessman, like every poker player, is offered a choice between certain loss or bluffing within the legal rules of the game. If he is not resigned to losing, if he wants to rise in his company and industry, then in such a crisis he will bluff – and bluff hard.

Every now and then one meets a successful businessman who has conveniently forgotten the small or large deceptions that he practised on his way to fortune. 'God gave me my money', old John D. Rockefeller once piously told a Sunday school class. It would be a rare tycoon in our time who would risk the horse laugh with which such a remark would be greeted.

In the last third of the twentieth century even children are aware that if a man has become prosperous in business, he has sometimes departed from the strict truth in order to overcome obstacles or has practised the more subtle deceptions of the half-truth or the misleading omission. Whatever the form of the bluff, it is an integral part of the game, and the executive who does not master its techniques is not likely to accumulate much money or power.

References and notes

1 *The New York Times*, 9 March, 1967.
2 Henderson, Bruce D. 'Brinkmanship in Business'. *Harvard Business Review*, 45, March-April 1967; 49.
3 *The New York Times*, 17 January, 1967.
4 Cited by Nader, Ralph in 'Business Crime'. *The New Republic*, 1 July, 1967; 7.
5 Babcock in a memorandum to Rockefeller (Rockefeller Archives).

Additional reading

Carr's article has generated much discussion since it was published a quarter-century ago. A sample of some of the first responses are in *Harvard Business Review*, 46, May–June 1968; 162–170.

Another contribution by Carr to the discussion of ethics is his article 'Can an Executive Afford a Conscience?' in *Harvard Business Review*, 48, July–August, 1970; 58–64.

See Jack Mahoney's contribution (Chapter 8) for a discussion on the bluffing used in the advertising trade.

Questions for discussion

- Identify several examples from your working experience where bluffing, exaggerating or withholding information occurs and is an accepted method of doing business.
- A competing view to Carr's is as follows:

  Treating business like a poker game results in an adversary relationship where one party wins at the expense of others. If business were to approach relationships with a spirit of cooperation (e.g. the way many large Japanese firms approach negotiations with their work force and their suppliers), not only would all parties win but each would be better off than if it took the bluffing route.

  Do some of your examples listed above, or any others, support this perspective? If this competing view is (at times) true, what is it that determines when bluffing is self-defeating?

Chapter 3

What is necessary for corporate moral excellence?

In his first of two contributions to this book, Michael Hoffman tackles a question that is key to the discussion of business ethics. Before he delves into the specifics of what is necessary for corporate moral excellence, however, he first discusses whether it is at all appropriate for us to attribute moral characteristics to a company.

It is often assumed that it makes perfectly good sense to say that companies are 'morally responsible' for their actions. But a moment's reflection might give pause for thought before so easily attributing moral responsibility to corporate groups. What does it mean, for example, to say the bank BCCI is 'morally responsible' for causing distress to so many people? Clearly it is not meant that everyone in BCCI should be blamed or punished.

Hoffman summarizes the various arguments surrounding the debate of corporate moral agency and this serves a springboard to his thoughts on how a morally excellent corporation can come about. He argues that the two necessary criteria are a moral corporate culture and the moral autonomy of the individual within the corporate culture.

Corporate culture and its relationship to ethics is one of the basic issues which frequently crops up in discussion with senior executives. Corporate culture is a popular concept – there appears to be an endless number of books spelling out its importance to corporate success. But if it is strong enough, it can strangle a company and destroy its vitality.

A common definition of organizational culture is 'the way things are done around here'. It is about *how* things are done rather than *why*. It is essentially conservative: it judges the future by the past. Because it is rooted in tradition it reflects what *has* worked rather than what *will* work.

A strong culture is predisposed not to change. The stronger the culture, the more resistant it is. But in order for a culture to exist, and to serve those who work and play in it, it must be able to learn and to profit from those lessons – in other words, to change.

The connection between ethics and culture is made when the organization is in crisis. To change a culture it is essential to talk about ethics. To change a culture without ethics is like trying to change a flat tyre without a jack. The only effective change mechanism is through ethics because only ethics asks *why* things are done.

By its very nature, a strong culture can subjugate the individual. As Hoffman points out, this is why some people admire companies with strong cultures but 'wouldn't want to work for one'. Hoffman looks at alternative ways to approach corporate culture and argues that it need not eliminate individual autonomy.

Much of what Hoffman affirms relates to the specifics addressed by other contributors to this book. 'In developing a moral culture a corporation must formulate clear ethical strategies and structures'. This is followed up in detail by Gael McDonald and Raymond Zepp in Chapter 13: 'Business ethics: practical proposals'. One justification for whistleblowing, discussed by Gene James in Chapter 7, stems directly from the need for an individual to have moral autonomy.

What is necessary for corporate moral excellence?
W. Michael Hoffman

I

There are some who would argue that this question doesn't even make sense, not at least until explanation is given as to how we can predicate moral properties such as moral responsibility to the corporation. Here we seem to run head-on into the controversial topic often called corporate moral agency, the debate over which has come almost to dominate (unwisely, I think) business ethics studies, especially among philosophers. One side, in its strongest formulation, seems to want to identify, ethically at least, corporations and persons. Peter French, for example, 'accepts corporations as members of the moral community, of equal standing with traditionally acknowledged residents – biological human beings' and as such 'they can have whatever privileges, rights, and duties as are, in the normal course of affairs, accorded to moral persons' [1]. On the other side, it is argued that only human individuals can be moral agents and, as Manuel Velasquez so shockingly puts it, this is 'why corporations are not morally responsible for anything they do' [2]. To make moral judgements of a corporation, then, is really only a shorthand way of speaking about certain individuals in the corporation.

Both of these positions go to what I see as mistaken extremes because of legitimate worries over where to place praise or blame when dealing with organized collectives. To say that only human individuals are morally responsible is to fail to recognize that collective entities like corporations, armies, nation states, faculties and committees do bring things about in ways that are not just reducible to or explainable by aggregates of individual actions. The whole of the collective entity is more than just the sum of its parts because the individuals who make up the collective (and whose actions are clearly necessary for the collective to act) are organized around cooperative purposes, goals, strategies, mission statements, policies, charters or whatever you call that which gives the collective its identity and spells out its function. People act on behalf of the collective purpose and according to collective directives. It is the collective relations that channel the actions of its individuals, giving the collective itself a kind of casual efficacy. This is why it makes sense to hold a corporation, say Ford for the making of its Pinto gas tank [3], not only legally but also morally responsible. Furthermore, to isolate just certain individuals within Ford as morally culpable, if that is even possible, seems to imply that by punishing or getting rid of those bad apples, the corporation will be fine in the future without any careful examination and change of the goals, strategies and environment for decision-making out of which the corporation operates. This is surely a cause of worry. Individuals should not be singled out as scapegoats for corporate systemic failure.

On the other hand, there is the worry that attributing moral responsibility to collectives like corporations blocks us from going inside the organization to get at praiseworthy or blameworthy individuals who in the most fundamental sense intentionally caused the action to come about. If individuals within Ford freely and knowingly produced an unsafe car, then they should not be allowed to escape legal or moral judgement by hiding behind a veil of corporate agency. Furthermore, to view the corporation as some sort of large-scale moral organism with some kind of life of its own is not only anthropomorphism at its very worst, but also creates a situation where individual interest and autonomy can be easily be submerged under what is perceived as corporate good. Velasquez refers to this as organizational totalitarianism, and 'philosophers who subscribe to the theory that the corporation is a moral agent that is morally responsible for its wrongful acts are unwittingly allying themselves with this new form of totalitarianism' [4]. These, too, are legitimate concerns. Corporations should not be used to subordinate individual moral responsibility or individual autonomy.

My aim here is not to capture the richness and complexity of the corporate agency debate, nor will I take on the ambitious task of trying to resolve the issue. The literature is filled with such efforts to the extent that I suspect it is time for work in business ethics to move on to more fertile ground. This is not to say that the debate has been unfruitful; on the contrary, the harvest has been rich, and we should carry with us the best of the fruits of our labours. In keeping with this I suggest there is insight to be gained from both sides of the debate as well as extremes to be avoided.

I see no need further to clutter our metaphysical landscape by granting a kind of personhood to collectives like corporations, forcing us to search for something like a corporate mind. Nevertheless, we must recognize that the goals and strategies of an organization can lead to certain actions which are subject to moral judgement and that these actions are not, in many cases, attributable or distributable to individuals within the collective. Systems and structures can be morally good or bad, rather than just morally neutral, because they result in morally good or bad consequences when followed. There is surely some sense in which Lieutenant Calley was a victim of a system and that neither he nor any collection of individuals alone was responsible for the massacre at My Lai, even though it was Calley who pulled the trigger. Therefore, although it maybe tricky, both conceptually and practically, corporations and other collectives can – must, in fact – stand up to the demands of moral responsibility, even though their actions are carried out by individuals acting on their behalf [5]. We should note that it is possible for there to be a complete changeover in the membership of a corporation without changing the structure or character of the corporation itself [6]. The name

'Ford' or the 'US. Army' denotes something that is, in a very significant sense, indifferent to or independent of the particular constitution of its membership.

We must, however, recognize the importance of the individual, both ontologically and ethically, to and within the collective. While it is wrong – even dangerous – to say that corporations are not morally responsible for anything they do such that the only 'proper subject of a business ethic is the individual business person' [7], it is, nevertheless, individuals who create corporations, constitute their membership, and carry out their functions. Although corporations are more than the sum of its members, without individuals there would be no corporations nor any activities by corporations. We surely also want to recognize that individuals can be praiseworthy or blameworthy within both good and bad corporations and that it is certainly possible, although not necessary, for individuals to get swallowed up by the environments of corporations, thereby losing their autonomy.

Relating individual and corporate responsibility can happen in several ways. A corporation might be held morally responsible when no specific individual of the corporation is morally responsible, similar to Karl Marx's indictment of the capitalist system whose members are simply products and tools of it. A corporation can be morally responsible when certain individuals of the corporation are also morally responsible. To point a finger of blame at the policies and procedures of the US Army should not necessary absolve Lieutenant Calley of moral guilt, and perhaps Lee Iacocca and Henry Ford II should have been indicted along with Ford Motor Company. And a corporation might be morally responsible when each individual of the corporation is also morally responsible. Even while holding the Nazi regime morally responsible, Karl Jaspers [8] proclaims that:

> Every German is made to share the blame for the crimes committed in the name of the Reich . . . inasmuch as we let such a regime rise among us.

We must also make sure that, by granting moral status to organized collectives like corporations – a status which in many cases is distinct from the moral responsibility of its members – we don't turn the individual into just a pawn for the corporate purpose. Individuals should have the necessary room and knowledge to engage in critical reflection on the corporation for which they are acting out a particular role. It is possible for corporations in all sorts of ways to deny this to their individual members, resulting in rational stagnation and moral blindness for the entire collective [9]. In fact, some feel this has become today's reality. We listen to William Scott and David Hart [10] say that:

> In our time, the source of legitimacy for institutions is the organizational imperative, which requires individual obedience to it. What is more, such obedience is now a value in and of itself, supplanting the presumed ascendency of individuality.

And we read in *Business Week* where 60–70% of the managers of two major corporations feel pressure to sacrifice their own personal ethical integrity for corporate goals [11].

I believe these insights and concerns stemming out of both sides of the corporate agency debate help to point our way to what is necessary for corporate moral excellence. Talking about corporate moral excellence does make sense, and not just by way of talking about individual moral excellence. We are referring here to what could be called the character or culture of the corporation, which is formed by its goals and policies, its structures and strategies, which ultimately reflect its attitudes and values. It is the set of formalized relations among the individuals who make it up, and it may well outlast those individuals who originally created it [12]. This culture defines the corporation's way of doing business, and it is out of this culture that the actions and attitudes of corporate individuals are shepherded and shaped.

But it is individuals, of course, who create these goals, who nurture or change them, and who actively carry them out. Without individuals there would be no critical evaluation of corporate cultures and, therefore, no way for the corporation to move forward rationally and creatively. Here we are referring to what could be called the autonomy of the individual. A corporation is constituted both by its culture and by its individual members. The culture provides the relational framework of shared beliefs and values around which a collection of individuals is identified as a corporation. The morally excellent corporation is one that discovers and makes operational the healthy reciprocity between its culture and the autonomy of its individuals.

But this is no easy task. It is the age-old problem of the individual within a society. Social cultures formed around common goals give meaning and purpose to individuals, but at the same time they present the danger of robbing individuals of their autonomy. When individuals lose their autonomy, they cease to be individuals, yet to act without regard to the common goals of the society is to give up one's identity as a part of the culture and to fail to live up to one's duties as a part of the collective whole. In fact, John Dewey and James Tufts [13] have observed that: 'Apart from ties which bind [the individual] to others, [the individual] is nothing'. Individualism and collectivism are both abstractions. Neither social cultures nor individuals can exist without the other. Their respective being and value are irrevocably interwoven. Referring again to Dewey and Tufts, 'no question can be reduced to the individual on one side and the social on the other' [14]. And the question of what is necessary for corporate moral excellence is no exception. The trick is to find the proper weave.

II

For a corporation to be morally excellent, it must develop and act out of a moral corporate culture. Although Thomas Peters and Robert Waterman [15] in their book *In Search of Excellence* do not focus on morality as such, there are, nevertheless, many moral lessons to be learned from America's excellent companies. And surely this concept of the corporate culture is one of the most important:

> Every excellent company we studied is clear on what it stands for, and takes the process of value shaping seriously. In fact, we wonder whether it is possible to be an excellent company without the clarity on values and without having the right sorts of values.

What we would want to add to this statement by Peters and Waterman is that morally excellent corporations must include ethical values in the shaping of their cultures. Or, better yet, their cultures must be shaped from a moral point of view.

Of course, there are those who argue that this whole tack is wrong. Corporations are amoral entities and urging them to develop a conscience or a moral perspective is to turn them away from their legitimate function – namely, to be efficient machines for production and profit. The result, so it is argued, will be bad for business and thereby bad for the common social good. Morality for business ought to be externally established by the government and the courts and/or by the market, but not internally by the corporation itself. Enough arguments have already been put forward to defeat this position. And, I think, most of us, including corporations, are now sufficiently convinced that corporations can and must morally regulate themselves with the help of external forces. Society expects it and morality demands it. I might only add here that, rather than being bad for business, the lessons learned from the best run companies singled out by Peters and Waterman strengthen the belief many have in the connection between business excellence and a morally sensitive corporate culture.

But what steps must be taken in developing a morally sensitive corporate culture? What elements go into making up a moral point of view for corporate culture? I suggest that we follow Christopher Stone's advice [16] and try to understand what moral responsibility entails 'in the ordinary case of the responsible human being'. After all, corporations are made up of human beings and act through human beings and are designed ultimately to serve the interests of human beings. Furthermore, I suggest that we can profit from Kenneth Goodpaster's 'projection' of the elements and steps involved in moral responsibility for the individual on to the corporation [17]. Borrowing from W.K. Frankena, Goodpaster isolates two basic components of the moral point of view: rationality and respect. The former involves the objectives and systematic reasoning out of one's purposes and the strategies for achieving them; the latter involves a concern for the intrinsic value of other human beings and a sensitivity towards their rights, needs and interests. Using rationality and respect as moral guides, three steps can be identified in the moral decision-making process: perception, reflection and action.

First, one must be able to perceive or recognize an ethical issue as ethical and thereby deserving of moral attention. And what we see, in many cases, depends on what we are looking for – on how and why we gather and categorize our data. If we are not sensitive to or interested in finding something, then we may very well filter it out of our conscious awareness, becoming blind to it, if you will. So it is with moral perception. If we are not wearing moral glasses, so to speak, we will not see or look for things from a moral viewpoint. In developing a moral culture a corporation must be on the watch for ethical situations.

Using moral glasses the corporation should cast its information net as wide as the effects of its activities on the quality of life. According to Ken Andrews [18], for the multinational corporation such a net would include the world within which it operates, the nation to which it belongs, the local community within which it is housed, the industry out of which it functions and the internal workings of the firm itself. Moral awareness takes concentrated effort and a commitment of vision which eventually develops into an habitual way of seeing, gathering, interpreting and processing data. Moral blindness does not excuse corporations from culpability. Corporations, like individuals, have the responsibility to pay attention to and seek out ethical facts.

Second, moral perception must then be synthesized through thinking. A moral point of view must bring rational principles and procedures to bear upon the moral data in order to arrive at a moral conclusion. In developing a moral culture a corporation must formulate clear ethical strategies and structures, taking into account opportunities and risks, resources and competencies, personal values and preferences, and economic and social responsibilities [19]. Such a moral corporate thinking process might include ethical codification, management and worker ethical training programmes, broad-based board representation, internal ethical audits, clear and open avenues for information flow to provide for ongoing communication and consultation at all levels, and the hiring and directing of top corporate officers to develop corporate ethical policies and management strategies for the carrying out of such policies. Moves such as these and others will enable the corporation systematically to reflect upon the moral data of which it becomes aware in an effort to arrive at a moral position for decision-making.

But such moral reflection would be incomplete without coordinating moral demands with other demands, interests and constraints. Just as one can be morally blind, one can also be morally foolish or quixotic. Surely morality doesn't demand that one plunge into a raging ocean to try vainly to save a life if one can't swim, or give all of one's earnings to charity, resulting in one's own destitution. Only when one sees one's total environment as consisting of many different and often conflicting demands, interests and constraints will alternatives be sought. One might then throw out a life preserver to save the drowning victim and work for charity drives in order to procure more funds from a wider distribution.

Corporations are no different. They too face many conflicting demands, interests and constraints. Corporations are designed for economic purposes and face pressures from laws and government regulations and from competitors in the market. I am reminded of a story told by George Cabot Lodge [20] where a business went bankrupt by unilaterally pouring millions of dollars into pollution equipment. As a result the river was no cleaner and 400 people were put out of work. I suggest this was no action from a moral point of view because no rational effort at coordinating the intersecting pressures, needs and goals was made. If such an effort had been made, then perhaps an alternative would have emerged, such as bringing all the polluting companies together to discuss ways of cleaning up the river. Such coordination is frustrating, complex and difficult to manage, especially in organizational structures; but it is the culmination of moral thinking and necessary to decision-making from a moral point of view. Without thoughtful coordination of all its goals, corporations, like individuals, will lack in coherent functioning and character, resulting in failure of moral excellence.

Finally, through moral awareness and moral thinking, decisions must be put in action. Good intentions and public relation statements are not enough for moral responsibility. To be morally excellent, corporations, like individuals, must demonstrate their characters through good deeds. For example, on the world level, the corporation might undertake partnership ventures with organizations of other countries rather than setting up operations with full controlling interests, and in other ways cooperate with governments of other countries to improve the dignity and quality of life for their people. On the national level, the corporation might demonstrate its ethical commitment through philanthropic contributions and use of its expertise and resources on our numerous social problems such as waste removal, health care, opportunities for women and the handicapped, minorities, education, housing, care of the elderly, crime, prison reform, care of our environment, etc.

In the communities within which the corporation does its business steps might be taken to minimize disruptive and harmful effects from pollution to pullouts and to maximize benefits and service to all its immediate neighbours. Within its own industry the corporation might initiate and cooperate in joint projects to further fair and healthy competition, to ensure quality and safe products, and to avoid pollution and other effects of doing business which are injurious to the quality of life. And, within the firm itself, the corporation may act in any number of ways to implement its moral responsibilities: institutionalizing compliance steps for its ethical codes; hiring ombudspeople with responsibilities for ethical oversight; forming ethical committees within the board of directors; fostering ethical discussion and communication at all levels; and providing positive incentives for employee pursuit of ethical goals such as affirmative action, worker health, product safety, environmental protection, truth in advertising and community service. Obviously moral action at various levels is necessary for a corporation to be morally responsible, but only after it has perceived the moral situations within its environment and thought out its moral demands, coordinating those demands with its other demands, interests and constraints. Moral action, without the other steps necessary for a fully mature moral point of view, would be implemented blindly and irrationally, yielding ineffectual or perhaps even dangerous consequences.

Through the development of a moral point of view as outlined above, a moral corporate culture will begin to emerge. Definite ethical goals, structure and strategies will be formally institutionalized and a moral framework of meaning and purpose will be created within which individuals of the corporation can develop ethical beliefs and attitudes and achieve a sense of ethical integrity. It is not necessary that everyone agrees with all the decisions and actions emanating from the corporate moral point of view for a corporation to be morally excellent. There might be disagreement from both inside and outside the corporation. Just as individuals can think and act out of moral points of view, yet come to radically different ethical conclusions, so it is too with corporations. It is the structure and process of the moral point of view that is essential, and more often than not, the thought and action stemming from it will command our respect, if not also our agreement.

Furthermore, a corporate moral culture is not a fixed thing such that once it is established it becomes complete. It is true that it consists of goals, structures and strategies but, as it is with individual moral character, it must be constantly nurtured and self-evaluated. This means that the corporate moral point of view, focusing on rationality and respect in each of its stages, must operate not only on new situations but on its own character as well. Only through such a moral dynamics, which requires the effort and commitment of all corporate members, will the corporation maintain a culture necessary for moral excellence.

III

For a corporation to be morally excellent it must allow for the moral autonomy of the individual within its culture. We find this theme throughout the pages of Peters and Waterman's *In Search of Excellence* [21]:

> Virtually all of the excellent companies are driven by a few key values, and then gives lots of space to employees to take initiatives in support of those values – finding their own paths, and so making the task and its outcome their own.
> There was hardly a more pervasive theme in the excellent companies than *respect for the individual*. That basic belief and assumption was omnipresent.

A corporation is made up of individuals and thinks and acts through them. For the corporation to deny those individuals the freedom to determine their own moral integrity within the company, to turn them into mere functionaries for the corporate purpose, is to fail to respect them as ends in themselves and to lose the ability rationally to evaluate its own moral character. In short, it would result in the abandonment of a moral point of view necessary for corporate moral excellence.

Can there be a corporate community that respects and fosters the development of individual autonomy? It might be argued that the work of the corporation can be carried out efficiently, smoothly and quickly only if each member of the corporation accepts his or her assigned role on the team and pulls in unison towards the corporate goal. All the excellent corporations singled out by Peters and Waterman have strong corporate cultures providing a distinctive identity and shared meaning of the group. This clearly poses a threat to individual expression and is why some have commented that, while admiring the excellent companies, they wouldn't work for one. As the Delta psychologist states of his stewardess interviews: 'I try to determine their sense of cooperativeness or sense of team work. At Delta, you don't just join a company, you join an objective' [22].

This surely calls forth images of William Whyte's organization man marching in step in his grey flannel suit singing company songs [23]. Scott and Hart [24] more recently observed that: 'Obedience is the cornerstone of an organisational edifice because it's essential to the chains of command', and, according to them, it is occurring even more viciously today. Individuality is not being abolished through coercion but rather converted into an individual commitment freely to adopt the demands of the organizational imperative and to be willing to substitute organizational values for personal values.

While the above corporate picture is surely possible, and even real in many cases, it is not inevitable. Having a strong corporate culture does not necessarily eliminate individual autonomy. Depending upon the nature of the culture, it can even enhance and encourage autonomy. Peters and Waterman found that their research of the excellent companies testifies to this [25]:

> In the very same institutions in which culture is so dominant, the highest levels of true autonomy occur. The culture regulates rigorously the few variables that do count, and it provides meaning. But within those qualitative values (and in almost *all* other dimensions), people are encouraged to stick out, to innovate.

For example, Hewlett-Packard, having one of the strongest cultures, referred to as 'the HP way', is proud of its people-oriented philosophy. The introduction to its revised corporate objective statement concludes [26]:

> Hewlett-Packard [should not] have a tight, military-type organization but rather ... give people the freedom to work toward [overall objectives] in ways they determine best for their own areas of responsibility.

It seems, then, that one of the essential features of the cultures of the excellent corporations is the respect that is given and the space that is allowed for personal expression and initiative. Rather than the culture snuffing out the individual autonomy, the culture itself is actually built on and around such autonomy.

This happens in a number of ways in the excellent companies. No one in an organization can have a real sense of freedom and power if kept in the dark concerning one's environment. In the excellent companies, intense effort is made at open communication throughout by way of all sorts of informal devices – from omnipresent blackboards to daily coffee 'klatches' to 'town meetings' and 'open forums' to army mess tables in the company dining room. The excellent companies go to extreme lengths to avoid the problem of NEMTA (Nobody Ever Tells Me Anything), even to GM's bringing financial information down to the shop floor and Delta's top-management open-door policy to all employees.

Another feature important to autonomy inside an organization is having enough room and acceptance to try new projects and fail. The excellent companies not only provide room and encouragement for autonomy and entrepreneurship, but these policies work because they also provide a climate within which failure is allowed. They all seem to follow 3M's Fletcher Byrom's ninth commandment: 'Make sure you generate a reasonable number of mistakes'; some even treat failures with celebratory style.

Also, bigness can thwart individual freedom and lead to a feeling of impotence. The excellent companies handle this by breaking themselves up into smaller units – by decentralizing and divisionalizing. Blue Bell kept its manufacturing units down to 300 people, Dana reduced the layers in its organization from eleven to five, and Johnson & Johnson broke up its 5 billion-dollar business into 150 divisions. 3M and HP hive off new productive units when divisions grow too big and most of the excellent companies have some form of 'skunk works' teams of eight to ten people initiating new projects.

Finally, although many other steps for ensuring individual autonomy could be mentioned, people should feel that they are a meaningful part of the activities of the organization, that they matter. Out of respect for this, the excellent companies try hard not to follow rigidly a chain of command and to avoid over formalization. Rene McPherson at Dana discarded 22½ inches of policy manuals in favour of a one-page statement of philosophy involving people. Sam Walton of Wal-Mart visits all 320 of his stores every year, listening to his employees (whom he calls his 'associates') and says: 'It's terribly important for everyone to get involved. Our best ideas come from clerks and stockboys' [27].

Although these lessons on individual autonomy from the excellent companies relayed to us by Peters and Waterman are directly connected to productivity gains, they are also lessons for understanding corporate moral excellence. Sufficient space should be given to every person in the corporation to initiate moral action within their own areas of responsibility, to make the corporate moral objectives their own. Failure to provide such space is failure to respect them as persons; the freedom to develop their moral integrity is essential to their humanity.

Avenues of communication concerning moral issues should be open to everyone and everyone should play a meaningful role in corporate ethical goal formation and decision-making. After such goals are set and decisions made, they should be clearly explained to each and every individual and how they affect his or her own function area.

Room should be made for rational disagreement and protest, and every attempt should be made to allow individuals moral alternatives to such goals and decisions if they find it impossible to coordinate them with their own moral points of view. If this proves to be impossible, then support should be given to their withdrawal from the activities of the organization.

Corporate bureaucracy and chains of command should be kept to an absolute minimum and large corporations should divide into smaller independent units with responsibility for moral decision-making within the guidelines of the overall moral corporate culture. Encouragement should be made not only to initiate moral action but understanding should be given when such action fails to achieve the moral objectives sought.

The morally excellent corporation must pursue the moral excellence of each of its individual members which demands a culture conducive to the pursuit of individual moral autonomy. In fact, it would seem impossible for the corporation to develop and maintain a moral culture independent of the moral autonomy of its members. The ideal of corporate moral excellence is that when the corporation is deserving of moral praise, so too is each of its members because, in a very real and concrete way, they have freely made that which was morally praiseworthy their own. What else could be meant by taking moral pride in a society to which one belongs?

IV

The weaving together of a moral culture and the moral autonomy of the individuals within it is the difficult challenge necessary for the attainment of corporate moral excellence. There is clearly an essential tension here, as there is with the individual in any society. The culture of an organization can dominate the individual freedom and expression of its members. It can become a Dostoevskian 'Crystal Palace' destroying a human being's right and desire to assert his or her individuality, where life becomes like an oversized anthill with clearly fixed functions and duties, where no one stands out or makes one's self. On the other hand, culture does provide meaning, direction, security and purpose for individuals. To stand out too much, outside the frameworks of social organizations, leads to separation, loneliness and isolation. The responsibility of societies and individuals is to avoid both extremes. We need to mould the above-mentioned tensions into a creative one rather than a destructive one.

Many of the best-run productive corporations have already taken giant steps towards the development of this creative tension – steps which are enlightening for the coming-to-be of the morally excellent corporation. In the words of Peters and Waterman [28]:

The companies provide the opportunity to stick out, yet combine it with a philosophy and system of beliefs . . . that provide the transcending meaning – a wonderful combination.

The nature of the moral corporate culture is the key. It must be created in such a way that definite ethical goals, structures and strategies are clearly put forward to form a conceptual and operational framework for moral decision-making. It must be made clear to all its individual members that it values and will not tolerate any deviation from the moral point of view. But at the same time, this moral culture, which gives meaning, identity and integrity to the whole corporate collective, must also value and encourage the moral autonomy of each of its individual members. To deny such moral autonomy is to cut off the possibility of rationally developing and examining the ethical principles of the culture itself and to fail to respect the persons making up the culture itself – both being violations of the moral point of view to which the moral culture is committed.

I am in total agreement with the following statement by Richard DeGeorge [29]:

Since human beings are social beings, they cannot be understood without understanding society. Since society is composed of human beings, it cannot be understood without understanding them. Both must be understood together, and to do this they must be understood in their relations.

For business ethics to focus on just corporate goals and structures or to focus on just individual moral responsibility results in the dangerous abstractions. We might say moral culture provides the form and individual moral autonomy provides the content for the morally excellent corporation. Such is the necessary reciprocity for an evolving corporate collection of human beings working towards the actualization of moral excellence.

References and notes

1 French, Peter, 'Corporate Moral Agency'. In: *Business Ethics: Readings and Cases in Corporate Morality*, Hoffman, W. Michael and Moore, Jennifer Mills (eds) New York: McGraw-Hill, 1984, p. 163. French has also said that the corporation 'denotes an entity that is itself an individual, in fact, I think that in the relevant moral senses, it may be shown to be a person'. See: 'Crowds and Corporations'. *American Philosophical Quarterly* 1982; **19**: 276.
2 Velasquez, Manuel 'Why Corporations Are Not Morally Responsible for Anything They Do'. *Business and Professional Ethics Journal* 2: Spring 1983, 1.
3 See Hoffman, W. Michael 'The Ford Pinto'. In: *Business Ethics: Readings and Cases in Corporate Morality*, New York: McGraw-Hill, 1984, pp. 412–420.
4 Velasquez, p. 16.
5 Patricia Wehane calls such corporation actions 'secondary actions'. See: 'Corporations, Collective Action, and Institutional Moral Agency'. In: Hoffman, W.

Michael, Moore, Jennifer Mills and Fedo, David A. (eds) *Corporate Governance and Institutionalizing Ethics: Proceedings of the Fifth National Conference on the Business Ethics*, Lexington, MA: Lexington Books, 1984. Larry May calls them 'vicarious actions'; see: 'Vicarious Agency and Corporate Responsibility'. *Philosophical Studies* 1983: **43**: 69–82.

6 See French, P. 'Crowds and Corporations'. *American Philosophical Quarterly* 1982; **19**: 271–278.

7 Velasquez, p. 1.

8 Jaspers, Karl 'Differentiation of German Guilt'. In Morris, H. (ed) *Guilt and Shame*, Belmont, CA: Wadsworth, 1971, p. 40. For further development of these distinctions, see Cooper, David Responsibility and the 'system'. In: French, Pete (ed) *Individual and Collective Responsibility*, Cambridge, MA: Schenkman, 1974, pp. 83–100.

9 See Ewing, David *Freedom Inside the Organization*, New York: McGraw-Hill, 1977; and *Do It My Way or You're Fired*, New York: Wiley, 1983.

10 Scott, William and Hart, David *Organizational America*, Boston, MA: Houghton Mifflin, 1979, p. 62.

11 *Business Week*, 31 January 1977, p. 107.

12 See DeGeorge, Richard 'Social Reality and Social Relations'. *Review of Metaphysics* 37: September 1983 8. Although DeGeorge doesn't refer to culture, much of what he develops along the lines of social institutions can be applied to my development of corporate culture.

13 Dewey, John and Tufts, James H. 'The Individual and the Social'. In: Struhl, Paul and Struhl, Karsten (eds) *Philosophy Now*, 3rd edn, New York: Random House, 1980, p. 315.

14 *Ibid.*, p. 314.

15 Peters, Thomas and Waterman, Robert *In Search of Excellence: Lessons from America's Best-Run Companies*, New York: Harper & Row, 1982, p. 280.

16 Stone, Christopher *Where the Law Ends*, New York: Harper & Row, 1975, p. 111.

17 See Goodpaster, Kenneth 'The Concept of Corporate Responsibility'. *Journal of Business Ethics*, 2: 7–16 February 1983. Goodpaster identifies four steps: (1) perception: (2) reasoning: (3) coordination: and (4) implementation. I have combined (2) and (3) under what I call 'reflection' since they are both really a part of moral thinking. However, my development of the moral decision-making process has been greatly influenced by Goodpaster's keen analysis.

18 Andrews, Kenneth *The Concept of Corporate Strategy*, revised edn, Homewood, IL: Irwin, 1980, pp. 92–95.

19 *Ibid.*, pp. 100–101.

20 Lodge, George Cabot 'The Connection Between Ethics and Ideology'. In: Hoffman, W. Michael (ed) *Business Values and Social Justice: Proceedings of the First National Conference on Business Ethics*, (Waltham, MA: The Centre for Business Ethics at Bentley College, 1977, pp. 78–80.

21 Peters, T. and Waterman, R. pp. 72–73 and 238.

22 *Ibid.*, p. 253.

23 Whyte, William, *The Organization Man*, London: Cape, 1957.

24 Scott, W. and Hart, D. pp. 62–65. Also see Sethi, S. P., Namiki, Nobuaki and Swanson, Carl *The False Promise of the Japanese Miracle*, Boston MA: Pitman, 1984.

25 Peters, T. and Waterman, R. p. 105.

26 *Ibid.*, p. 245.

27 *Ibid.*

28 *Ibid.*, p. 81.
29 DeGeorge, R. p. 20.

Additional reading

John D. Bishop in 'The moral responsibility of corporate executives for disasters' (*Journal of Business Ethics* 1991; **10**: 377–383) advances the discussion about responsibility by looking at a specific application. He analyses whether an executive can be held morally responsible for a disaster when the information that could have prevented it was known within the company but failed to reach the top. The required information flow is usually prevented by 'negative information blockage' – a phenomenon caused by differing roles of constraints and goals within the organization. Bishop concludes that executives are professionally responsible for meeting their moral obligation to prevent disasters.

Russel P. Boisjoly, Ellen Foster Curtis and Eugene Mellican investigate the relationship between individual and organizational responsibility in their paper 'Roger Boisjoly and the Challenger disaster: the ethical dimension' (*Journal of Business Ethics*) 1989; **8**: 217–230). By looking at the attempts by Roger Boisjoly to prevent the ill-fated launch of the Challenger, the authors address two key issues: the ethical ambiguity of the relationship between individual and organizational responsibility, and the importance of individual responsibility within large organizations.

Another analysis of the Challenger disaster is by Patricia H. Werhane: 'Engineers and management: the challenge of the Challenger incident' (*Journal of Business Ethics* 1991; **10**: 605–616). Werhane discusses what contributed to the failure (organizational structure, corporate culture, engineering and managerial habits and role responsibilities) and who was responsible for the failure.

For readings on corporate culture and ethics, see the listing after Chapter 5.

Questions for discussion

● When a significant mistake is made within your organization, how is blame apportioned between individuals, groups, departments, etc.? Is this allocation ethical? Is this allocation productive for the company: in the short term? in the long term?
● Is a sincere effort made to learn from any ethical mistakes made?
● Do individuals have moral autonomy within your company? If not, should they? How should this be brought about?

Chapter 4

An integrative model for understanding and managing ethical behaviour in business organizations

Managing ethical behaviour is felt by many experts to be the most formidable challenge of the 1990s. One UK company, for instance, privately concedes that a series of questionable – but not illegal – decisions may have cost it £1 billion in less than five years.

Employees' decisions to behave ethically or unethically are influenced by a myriad of individual and situational factors. Background, personality, decision history, managerial philosophy and reinforcement are but a few of the factors that have been identified by researchers as determinants of employees' behaviour when faced with ethical dilemmas.

Following a review of ethical behaviour data, Stead, Worrell and Stead here propose a model for understanding ethical behaviour in business organizations. The conclusion is that managing ethics requires that managers engage in a concentrated effort which involves espousing ethics, behaving ethically, developing screening mechanisms, providing ethical training, creating ethics units and reinforcing ethical behaviour.

In our work in the practical application of business ethics, at Integrity Works, we have found the use of the schematic shown in this chapter of particular value. It provides an easily understood description of the sometimes complex web of interrelationships which bear upon the nature of ethical behaviour in organizations.

The authors are at pains to explain that their work is based upon studies of available research; in our experience with companies we find it does reflect many of the realities that exist in business today. This is clearly of significant importance as business people are often reluctant to espouse theoretical models unless they are clear about the likely benefits, and unless they feel that the advice offered relates to the problems they face. This is especially the case when economic conditions are difficult; and when every item of investment must be scrutinized to ensure that the return on that investment is adequate.

The importance of the need for the highest quality of ethical leadership in organizations cannot be overstated. There is an old saying that 'a fish rots from the head down'. This is borne out in all cases that we have examined. Staff often look no further than the behaviour of their immediate manager in determining the ethos of an organization. Managers, in turn, are very much guided by the actions of their supervisory management. Few employees, when confronted by managerial actions which run counter to even skilfully conceived internal communications messages, will long believe the communications.

Again, our practical experience in the field of implementing ethics codes in companies also makes clear that for many employees a company's approach to human resource issues such as reward and remuneration is a key element in deciding whether ethics messages receive a fair hearing.

Ethics codes do have to be meaningful. They should not be a set of restrictions drawn up solely by a select group of senior executives. In most cases these codes carry strong enforcement messages, but give little scope for empowerment.

The key to a successful and effective ethics process in a company rests upon a combination of compliance and commitment. Compliance or enforcement on its own is not enough. It is essential that commitment and empowerment are embodied in any corporate ethics process.

Likewise, it is important that most levels in a company are consulted before any form of ethics code is issued. Not only does this often improve the language used; it also identifies the different ethical issues that affect different parts of the organization.

Enforcement is, in particular, an essential factor in corporate ethics processes. Management must underscore the central place of ethics by ensuring that unethical practices are never rewarded, even if the perpetrator is otherwise an excellent performer.

Training in ethical awareness is also a critical component in raising the ethical tone in an organization. Moreover, by sharing in discussions regarding ethical problems, staff are given an insight into the complexity of decision-making, and are more aware of the dangers in sacrificing integrity for short-term advantage.

Organizations seeking to make ethics a cornerstone of their operations in today's fast-changing world need, as the authors say, to put in place a structure for dealing with ethical problems, including, perhaps an ethics committee.

One far-sighted British company has enacted an ethics index which allows its board to assess its corporate ethical performance in a measured way. As a result, it seeks to determine the ethical behaviour of each of its major divisions and can compare their past and present ethical status. It can also measure how its level of corporate integrity compares with that of the industry at large.

The basic rule in ethics, as in every other aspect of business operations, is 'that which gets measured gets managed'. It is pointless putting in place an ethics code, then trusting to good fortune that all elements of the company are adhering to its requirements.

An integrative model for understanding and managing ethical behaviour in business organizations
W. Edward Stead, Dan L. Worrell and Jean Garner Stead

'The question of ethics in business conduct has become one of the most challenging [corporate issues] in this era', is the conclusion of a recent Business Roundtable report [1]. Indeed, support for this point abounds . . . [Examples] of unethical behaviour in business appear daily in the national and local media. In the last couple of years, virtually every major business and news periodical . . . has depicted the business ethics of the 1980s as greedy, selfish distortions of the free enterprise system with excessive emphasis on personal wealth and fame. Of the 1082 respondents to a 1988 Touche Ross survey [2] of business executives, directors and business school deans, 94% said that the business community as a whole is troubled by ethical problems. Some 68% of the respondents said they did not believe these problems were overblown in the press. In their book, Freeman and Gilbert [3] strongly contend that all strategies have some ethical foundation, and that managers must recognize that they do not operate in an ethical vacuum. They say that strategic decision-makers must address the issues facing them in moral terms or risk moral decay.

Managing ethical behaviour is thus no doubt a critical social problem for business organizations. It is also a very complex problem which requires an in-depth understanding of the many factors which contribute to employees' decisions to behave ethically or unethically. The purpose of this article is to develop an integrative model of ethical behaviour based on an extensive review of empirical and conceptual literature related to this issue. This model provides some important clues as to how ethical behaviour can be effectively managed in business organizations.

Understanding ethical behaviour in organizations

Current behavioural research strongly supports a person–situation interaction explanation of human behaviour in which both individual and situational factors influence the behavioural choices made by individuals [4–7]. In this section, we will focus on discussing the individual and situational factors identified in the current literature which seem to influence employees' decisions to behave ethically or unethically at work.

Individual personality and socialization factors

There is little doubt that personality and background will influence a person's ethical system – his or her system of ethical philosophies and behavioural patterns. Researchers have suggested three personality measures that may influence ethical behaviour – ego strength, machiavellianism and locus of control [7–9]. Ego strength is defined as an individual's ability to engage in self-directed activity and to manage tense situations [10]. Machiavellianism is a measure of deceitfulness and duplicity [11]. Locus of control is a measure of whether or not a person believes that his or her outcomes in life are determined by his/her own actions (internal) or by luck, fate or powerful others and institutions (external) [12].

Socialization also seems to influence a person's ethical system. Researchers have identified sex role differences, religious beliefs, age, work experience and nationality as factors which may influence the ethical decisions made by individuals [8,9].

A critical socialization factor for business managers is the influence of significant others. Research in social learning theory strongly supports the idea that we learn appropriate behaviour by modelling the behaviour of persons we perceive as important – parents, siblings, peers, teachers, public officials, etc. [4,5]. Managers no doubt represent significant others to employees, and thus the ethical behaviour of managers will certainly influence the ethical behaviour of employees.

Ethical philosophies and decision ideologies

As we discussed above, a person's personality and socialization will likely influence his or her ethical system. Both the content of an individual's ethical system – the norms that guide his or her ethical behaviour – and the individual's perception about when and how to apply these ethical norms will likely vary according to differences in personality and socialization factors. For example, it has been found that machiavellians are likely to believe that ethics are situational rather than absolute [13].

The content of one's ethical system, the network of ethical norms and principles one holds, constitutes a person's ethical philosophy. Social psychologists have contended for years that these normative structures influence the behavioural decisions made by individuals [14]. Thus, an individual's ethical philosophy will likely influence his or her ethical decisions.

Cavanagh *et al.* [15] identified three basic ethical philosophies, each of which represents a unique part of the total ethical situation faced by individuals in business organizations. The first is utilitarianism. The central concept of utilitarianism is a belief that ethics is best applied by considering the greatest good for the greatest number. The second philosophy is individual rights. This philosophy focuses on protecting individual rights such as the right to be informed, the right of free consent, the right to due process, etc. The third ethical philosophy is justice. Such an ethical system stresses social justice and the opportunity for all to pursue meaning and happiness in life. Researchers have concluded that these philosophies accurately represent the ethical normative structures of individuals [16]. Most individuals allow one of these philosophies to dominate their ethical decisions, with the utilitarian philosophy being dominant among business managers [17].

As mentioned above, when and how persons apply their ethical philosophies will also vary from individual to individual. Forsyth [18] contends that individuals differ in terms of the moral judgements they make, and that the actions they take resulting from these moral judgements also differ. He refers to these differences as ethical decision ideologies and says that these are based on two dimensions. First is idealism – the degree to which an individual believes that ethical behaviour always results in good outcomes. Second is relativism – the degree to which an individual believes that moral rules are situational. Persons high in both idealism and relativism are called sit-uationists. They reject the use of universal or individual moral principles, preferring to analyse each situation and to determine appropriate moral behaviour based on this analysis. Subjectivists are individuals low in idealism and high in relativism. They base their moral judgements on individual rather than universal principles. Absolutists are individuals low in relativism but high in idealism. They believe that they achieve the best outcomes in life by following strict, universal moral codes. Finally, exceptionists, those low in both dimensions, believe in universal moral rules as guides, but are open to practical exceptions. Researchers have found that persons with different ethical decision-making ideologies vary in terms of how they integrate ethical information, how they judge their own ethical dilemmas, and how they judge the moral decisions of others [19–21]. They also differ in terms of their sense of moral obligation, responsibility and caring for other people [22].

Ethical decision history

Social learning theorists contend that past decisions play a key role in current and future decisions. Once reinforced, a decision made by an individual will influence future decisions that he or she makes [4,5]. Thus as ethical decisions are made and reinforced over time, the individual develops an ethical decision history. Through this process ethical philosophies and decision ideologies are likely to become relatively enduring.

Decision history is unique in the sense that it is both situational, because of its reinforcement foundation, and individual, because of the influence of the person's own ethical systems and unique behavioural history. The fact that it is both individual and situational may explain why researchers have found that decision history has a strong direct influence on ethical decisions made by individuals [23].

Organizational factors

Another set of factors influencing the ethical behaviour of employees exists in the organizational context. Researchers have concluded that a variety of organizational variables influence ethical behaviour among employees. Further, because of their immediate situational impact on employee behaviour, these variables, as with decision history, have been shown to have a strong direct influence on specific ethical decisions made by employees, usually overwhelming individual variables such as personality and socialization [7, 8, 23].

The philosophies of top managers as well as immediate supervisors represent a critical organizational factor influencing the ethical behaviour of employees. Copious research over a period of more than 25 years clearly supports the conclusion that the ethical philosophies of management have a major impact on the ethical behaviour of employees [2, 8, 24–31].

Another organizational factor is managerial behaviour. According to Nielsen [32], managers behaving unethically contrary to their ethical philosophies represents a serious limit to ethical reasoning in the firm. Much of the research cited in the above paragraph implicitly or explicitly states that ethical philosophies will have little impact on employees' ethical behaviour unless they are supported by managerial behaviours which are consistent with these philosophies. If normative structures help explain behaviour patterns, as social psychologists contend [14], then, conversely, norms not supported by appropriate behaviours are not likely to be accepted as legitimate by employees. One of the keys to understanding the influence of managerial philosophy and behaviour on the ethical behaviour of employees lies in a point made earlier that managers represent significant others in the organizational lives of employees and as such often have their behaviour modelled by employees.

One of the most basic of management principles states that if you desire a certain behaviour, reinforce it. Another critical organizational variable that influences behaviour is the firm's reinforcement system. Research in ethical behaviour strongly supports the conclusion that if ethical behaviour is desired, the performance measurement, appraisal and reward systems must be modified to account for ethical behaviour [7,8,28,31]. According to Nielsen [32] (p. 730),

> In many cases, managers choose to do, go along with or ignore the unethical . . . because they want to avoid the possibility of punishments [or] to gain rewards.

Several dimensions of the job itself may also influence the ethical behaviour of employees. Researchers believe that the more centrally located a job is in the communication network of the firm, the more ethical decisions will likely have to be made by the occupant of that job [7]. Also jobs involving external contacts are believed to have more potential for ethical dilemmas than jobs with purely internal contacts [30]. Further, management often responds less severely to breaches of ethics by employees on whom they rely for technical expertise, because these employees represent a scarce resource for the firm [33].

External forces

There are a variety of external factors which will likely influence the ethical philosophies and behaviour of managers, the reinforcement system established to control employee behaviour, the discretion given employees to behave ethically or unethically, etc. Two-thirds of the respondents to the Touche Ross survey [2] believed that the most threatening condition to American business ethics today is the decay in political, social and cultural institutions.

Two-thirds of the respondents to the Touche Ross survey also believed that competitive pressures represent a significant threat to American business ethics. Two key competitive factors which affect ethics were mentioned by these executives. One was the ever increasing competitive pressure to concentrate on short-term earnings. Another was related to the current multinational business environment with its varying ethical standards from country to country . . . .

Volatile economic conditions, resource scarcity and pressure from stakeholders may also serve to undermine ethical behaviour in organizations. The ethical trap provided by external factors such as these is obvious. It places the firm in a position of having to choose between being an ethical role model for its industry and the environment in general or succumbing to the situational pressures and engaging in unethical practices. While it is certainly encouraging that 65% of the Touche Ross survey respondents believed that high ethical standards strengthened the firm's competitive position, it is somewhat discouraging that 35% of those respondents believed that high ethical standards either weakened or had no effect on the firm's competitiveness [2].

This discrepancy in the opinions of the respondents to the Touche Ross survey as to whether high ethical standards enhance or detract from a firm's competitive position probably reflects the fact that ethical decisions have several potential competitive outcomes. Being ethical may directly increase a firm's profitability (i.e. reducing costs by reducing employee theft) or it may directly decrease a firm's profitability (i.e. increasing costs by installing an expensive pollution control system or ensuring a safe workplace). Further, ethical actions may have a less direct but none the less real effect on a firm's competitiveness. For example, decisions to recall a defective product (i.e. Tylenol) or to withdraw from a market for moral reasons (i.e. South Africa) may have immediate costs but may also enhance a firm's image and thus its long-term profitability. In their casebook, Matthews, Goodpaster and Nash [34] present several cases which clearly demonstrate each of these potential competitive outcomes.

A model of ethical behaviour in organizations

The model depicted in Figure 4.1 conceptually demonstrates the relationships among the factors discussed above. Hopefully, the model will help to improve managers' understanding of both why employees behave ethically or unethically in business organizations and what managers can do to influence this behaviour.

The initial linkage in the model reflects the relationship between the individual factors and the development of the person's ethical philosophy and decision ideology. Essentially, this linkage demonstrates that the ethical beliefs one holds and how and when these beliefs are applied are strongly influenced by personality and background.

The interactions between one's ethical philosophy and decision ideology will likely influence the ethical decisions a person makes. These decisions are usually reinforced – rewarded, punished, etc. Over time, the individual's ethical choices and the nature of the reinforcement that accompanies these choices lead to his or her ethical decision history.

As the individual enters and gains experience in an organization, his or her ethical behaviours are influenced by managerial philosophy and behaviour, the reinforcement system and the characteristics of the job itself. This work experience with its reinforcement and significant influence by management in turn become critical socialization forces influencing the individual.

Of course, these organizational factors do not exist in isolation, but are instead heavily influenced by outside forces such as competitive pressures, economic conditions, resource needs, stakeholder demands, etc. As mentioned above, maintaining high ethical standards may directly increase or decrease a firm's competitiveness, or it may have both these outcomes over

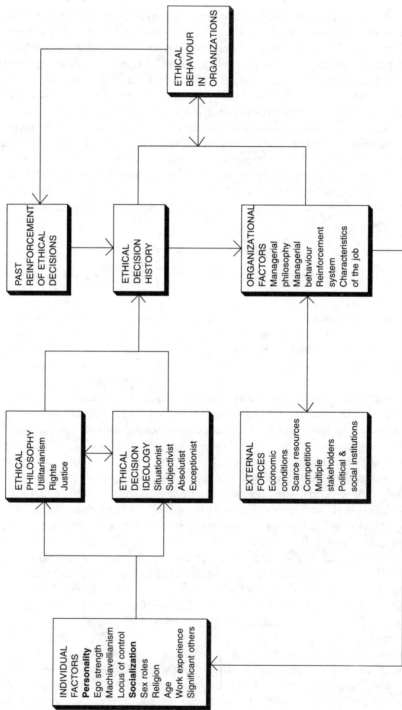

Fig. 4.1   *Model of ethical behaviour*

time. However, Goodpaster and Matthews [35] (p. 139) contend that if 'moral demands are viewed as containments – not replacements – for self-interest' then firms can for the most part be competitive while maintaining moral responsibility. This will not always be the case, of course, but the cases in which being ethical requires self-sacrifice are rare [35].

Note that the model depicts a direct relationship between decision history and organizational factors and the ethical choices made by the individual in the organization. These factors have consistently overshadowed personality and socialization factors in research. Also note that as the ethical choices the employee makes are reinforced over time by the organization, they become a part of the employee's decision history which in turn can influence the ethical culture of the organization.

Conclusions and recommendations

Our position, of course, is that ethical behaviour needs managing and can be managed in business organizations. However, influencing ethical behaviour in business organizations is a multifaceted problem with many traps and pitfalls. In developing a system for managing ethical behaviour, a firm may have to modify its structure, selection and training procedures, reporting system, reward system, communication system and internal auditing procedures. These modifications cannot be made in an organization unless those who spearhead the effort have adequate leadership skills, a reasonable period of time, and support from the organization's authority structure and culture [36]. Thus, implementing the ethical management suggestions discussed in this section will require the firm to have total commitment and cooperation from top to bottom.

As the model and research indicate, decision history and organizational factors have the most significant impacts on the ethical behaviour of employees. Thus, managers do not have to rely on the integrity of the employee alone. They have the power to structure the organizational context to promote ethical behaviour. If managers are willing to take the actions necessary to support ethical behaviour, then employees, when faced with ethical dilemmas such as improper gifts, kickbacks, improper pricing, nepotism, favouritism, etc., may be encouraged to make the right choices. Some of the things firms can do to manage ethical behaviour are presented below.

Behave ethically yourself

This is first and foremost in influencing ethical organizational behaviour. As Ranken [37] points out, it is not the corporation itself that exerts moral responsibility, but rather the individual members of the corporation. There-fore, the institutionalization of high ethical standards in corporations 'stems from the character of persons who occupy the relevant positions (p. 634).' Managers cannot expect ethical behaviour from employees if they do not behave ethically themselves. Managers are the most significant role models in the organizational setting; thus they have a major socializing influence on lower-level employees. The key to being an effective ethical role model for employees is to demonstrate consistency between one's ethical philosophy and ethical behaviour.

None of the other suggestions made in this section are likely to have much influence on ethical behaviour if managers do not behave ethically. This is especially true of top managers. Remember, as stated above, that ethical management systems in organizations require the support of the organiza-tional culture and authority structure [35]. The dominant core values of the firm's culture are formulated at the top, and the authority structure of the firm begins at the top. Thus, ethical behaviour must begin at the very top.

Managers who wish to influence ethical behaviour without the support from the top will likely have to do so by initiating individual action against unethical behaviour in the organization. Behaving ethically may mean that a manager refuses to carry out unethical policies, threatens to blow the whistle, or actually blows the whistle. Individuals who take such actions often risk high anxiety and loss of potential livelihood. Thus, engaging in ethical behaviour may require a great deal of courage for the individual [36].

Screen potential employees

Since individuals are likely to face ethical issues most of their lives, there is little doubt that potential employees have significant ethical decision histories when they apply. Thus the first line of defence against unethical behaviour in the organization is the employment process. There are several methods available to organizations for ethical screening. These techniques vary widely in terms of costs and benefits. Further, these techniques may vary widely also in terms of their legality and may themselves have ethical implications.

Paper-and-pencil honesty tests are one technique which may be used for ethical screening in organizations. These tests seem to be reasonably valid, with low costs and short time periods involved in administration [38].

Background investigations, which can range in scope from simply checking résumé information, calling references and requiring transcripts to hiring investigators, can be valuable tools in screening employees. Of course, full-blown investigations can be very expensive and time-consuming and thus are cost-effective only in cases of very sensitive positions. Further, before conducting such an investigation, the organization should inform the applicant and get his/her permission. On the other hand, since researchers have found that between 30 and 80% of all credentials may contain at least some misstatement of fact [39], it seems that firms would be well-advised to require official transcripts, call references and former employers, etc. These methods are not very costly, and can help the company in avoiding problems down the road. Interestingly, relatively few firms seem to bother to invoke these simple procedures.

Other means for screening the ethics of employees were revealed in the Business Roundtable report [1]. For example, Chemical Bank requires all potential employees to read and sign a statement obligating them to abide by the company's values and ethical standards as part of the application process; Johnson & Johnson includes its code of ethics in all its recruiting material; and Norton specifies honesty and integrity as characteristics it wants search firms to screen for when finding applicants for positions with the firm.

As mentioned above, there are both legal and ethical issues involved in screening employees. For example, one screening mechanism, the much maligned polygraph (often referred to as twentieth-century witchcraft), is no longer available for employee screening except for a few sensitive government positions. Its use in employment decisions has been seriously restricted by [American] legislation. Also, firms must be careful to consider the privacy rights of both potential and former employees when checking references, conducting background investigations, etc.

Develop a meaningful code of ethics

Codes of ethics are probably the most visible sign of a company's ethical philosophy. In order for a code of ethics to be meaningful, it must clearly state its basic principles and expectations; it must realistically focus on the potential ethical dilemmas which may be faced by employees; it must be communicated to all employees; and it must be enforced. Further, a meaningful code of ethics cannot rely on blind obedience. It must be accepted and internalized by the employees who are required to implement it. This means that managers must attend not only to the content of the code but also to the process of determining that content. To be most effective, a code should be developed and disseminated in an open, participative environment involving as many employees as possible.

All ten firms in the Business Roundtable report [1] had strict codes of ethics. These firms stressed several factors related to successful institutionalization of their codes, including giving codes to new employees as part of their selection and orientation, conducting seminars on the codes, and requiring communication of the codes to all levels. This last factor seemed to be of particular importance to these firms. They stressed that communication of their codes takes place in open discussion environments where employees are encouraged to ask questions and make suggestions concerning the codes. For example, many of these companies encouraged separate units to develop their own specific codes which dealt with the unique ethical dilemmas they faced. They believe that participative methods like this improve the potential that the codes will play a central role in the management of ethical behaviour within their organizations.

On the other hand, it appears that not all firms stress their ethical codes to this degree, and that many of the codes themselves ignore certain crucial ethical issues. The conclusions of one study indicated that very few [American chartered accountants] have a good working knowledge of [their professional] code of ethics [40]. William Frederick has found that many codes of ethics seem to be little more than lip-service documents which focus primarily on profit-oriented issues while often ignoring other critical issues such as personal character matters and environmental problems [41].

Provide ethics training

Employees need to have an experiential awareness of the types of ethical dilemmas they may face, and they need to know what actions to take in these dilemmas. Providing ethics training for employees is one key to increasing this awareness.

Ethics training normally begins with orientation sessions and open discussion of the firm's code of ethics. Employees should be encouraged to participate at a high level in these sessions as well as in other training that follows. This is often followed by the use of fictitious ethical scenarios which simulate situations that employees may face on the job. Providing salespeople with scenarios involving improper gifts or kickback offers gives employees a chance to make ethical decisions in realistic situations and to discuss these decisions openly with peers, supervisors, etc. Organizations such as McDonnell Douglas and General Dynamics have used scenario training to transform their codes of ethics from simple documents to tools for training, education and communication about ethical standards [42].

Neilsen [32] believes that this traditional approach to ethics training may not be completely effective because it relies too heavily on ethical reasoning as an action (praxis) strategy for managing unethical behaviour. He states that traditional training approaches may improve an employee's intellectual understanding of what ethics is. However, there are many limitations (i.e. bounded rationality and time constraints) which can impede the employee's ability to translate this intellectual understanding into practice. He suggests an alternative approach in which the actual ethical experiences, values and intuitions of the participants become the primary elements of ethics training.

He believes that such an approach may achieve a better balance between experiential and abstract classroom learning than traditional methods.

Reinforce ethical behaviour

The reinforcement system of the company must support ethical behaviour. Employees should be rewarded for behaving ethically, and they should be punished for behaving unethically. This is not as simple as it sounds, however. It involves developing a clear understanding of how ethical behaviour is defined by the organization, developing a system to measure and report ethical behaviour, and developing a performance and appraisal system that includes ethical behaviour. Chemical Bank, for example, has a comprehensive internal and external audit system in place, and its employees are encouraged and provided with mechanisms to report any suspected improprieties. General Mills uses integrity and social responsibility as a key factor in its performance appraisal and reward distribution decisions [1].

Effective reinforcement also involves being willing to make tough decisions in situations involving unethical behaviour. Remember, employees in positions to make ethical decisions are often those who play a central role in the organization or on whom the organization relies for technical expertise, etc. Disciplining employees who are critical for the organization's success is not easy. And yet, successful management of ethical behaviour requires the resolve on management's part to be willing to severely punish unethical performance. There was consensus among the firms in the Business Roundtable [1] on this point. Most said that ethics violators would be fired summarily and prosecuted for their actions if possible. They also said that punishment for unethical behaviour must be followed up by immediately spreading the news of the offence and the punishment through the firm's grapevine.

Create positions, units and other structural mechanisms to deal with ethics

As noted above, no cooperative effort for influencing ethical behaviour from within an organization is going to be successful unless it is supported by the authority structure and culture of an organization [36]. One way to operationalize such support for ethical behaviour is by creating structural mechanisms for managing ethics. A variety of structural mechanisms designed to advise management about ethics, monitor ethical behaviour among employees, communicate ethical policies, serve as ombudsmen for reporting ethical violations, etc. can be put in place in business organizations. Raelin [43] calls for a professional ethical aide-de-camp for top managers. Xerox has established an internal audit committee to monitor ethics; Norton has established an ethics committee of the board of directors. Employee newspapers and magazines are frequently used to publish codes of ethics, ethical policies, etc.[1].

In sum, ethical behaviour in business organizations is a complex multi-faceted problem with significant individual and situational dimensions. Effective management of ethical behaviour requires that organizations espouse ethics, expect ethical behaviour from managers, screen potential employees effectively, provide meaningful ethical training for employees, create ethics units, measure ethics, report ethics, reward ethics and make the tough decisions when none of this works. Developing systems with these character-istics requires sound leadership and support from organizational culture and authority. Managers must often be willing to take risks in effectively implementing such a system. Yes, managing ethical behaviour in business organizations is possible, but it is no easy task.

References and notes

1 Business Roundtable *Corporate Ethics: A Prime Business Asset*. New York: 1988.
2 Touche Ross *Ethics in American Business: An Opinion Survey*, Touche Ross, 1988.
3 Freeman, E. and Gilbert, D. *Corporate Strategy and the Search for Ethics*, Englewood Cliffs, NJ: Prentice-Hill, 1988.
4 Jones, E.E. 'Major Development in Social Psychology During the Past Five Decades'. In: Lindzey, G. and Aronson, E. (eds) *The Handbook of Social Psychology*, New York: Random House, 1985, pp. 47–107.
5 Luthans, F. and Krietner, R. *Organizational Behaviour Modification and Beyond: An Operant and Social Learning Approach*. Glenview, IL: Scott Forsman, 1985.
6 Terborg, J.R. 'Interaction Psychology and Research on Human Behaviour in Organizations'. *Academy of Management Review* 1981; **6**: 569–576.
7 Trevino, L.K. 'Ethical Decision Making in the Organizations: A Person–Situation Interactionist Model'. *Academy of Management Review*, **11**, (3) 1986; 601–617.
8 Hegarty, W. and Sims, H. Jr, 'Some Determinants of Unethical Decision Behaviour: An Experience'. *Journal of Applied Psychology*, **63**, (4) 1978; 451–457.
9 Preble, J.F and Miesing, P. 'Do Adult MBA and Undergraduate Business Students Have Different Business Philosophies?' *Proceedings of the National Meeting of the American Institute for Decision Sciences* 1984; 346–348.
10 Crandall, R. 'The Measurement of Self-Esteem and Related Constructs'. In: Robinson, J.P. and Shaver, P.R. (eds) *Measures of Social Psychological Attitudes*, Ann Arbor, MI: Institute for Social Research, 1973; pp. 45–167.
11 Robinson, J. 'General Attitudes Toward People'. In: Robinson, J.P. and Shaver, P.R. (eds) *Measures of Social Psychological Attitudes* Ann Arbor, MI: Institute for Social Research, pp. 587–627.
12 Levenson H. 'Activism and Powerful Others: Distinctions Within the Concept of Internal–External Control'. *Journal of Personality Assessment*, **38**; 1974; 377–383.

13 Leary, M.R., Knight, P.D. and Barnes, B.D. 'Ethical Ideologies of the Machiavellian'. *Personality and Social Psychology Bulletin*, **12,** (1) 1986; 75–80.

14 Hogan R. 'Moral Conduct and Moral Character: A Psychological Perspective'. *Psychological Bulletin*, **79:** (4) 1973.

15 Cavanagh, G., Moberg, D. and Velasquez, M. 'The Ethics of Organizational Politics'. *Academy of Management Review*, **3,** 1981; 363–374.

16 Boal, K.B. and Peery, N. 'The Cognitive Structure of Corporate Social Responsibility'. *Journal of Management*, **11,** (3) 1985; 71–82.

17 Fritzche, D. and Becker, H. 'Linking Management Behaviour to Ethical Philosophy: An Empirical Investigation'. *Academy of Management Journal*, **1,** 1984; 166–175.

18 Forsyth, D.R. 'A Taxonomy of Ethical Ideologies'. *Journal of Personality and Social Psychology*, **39,** (1) 1980; 175–184.

19 Forsyth, D.R. 'Moral Judgement: the Influence of Ethical Ideology'. *Personality and Social Psychology Bulletin*, **7,** (2) 1981; 218–223.

20 Forsyth, D.R. 'Individual Difference Information Integration During Moral Judgment'. *Journal of Personality and Social Psychology*, **49,** (1) 1985; 264–272.

21 Forsyth, D.R. and Pope, W.R. 'Ethical Ideology and Judgements of Social Psychological Research: Multidimensional Analysis'. *Journal of Personality and Social Psychology*, **46,** (6) 1984; 1365–1375.

22 Forsyth, D., Nye, J. and Kelley, K. 'Idealism, Relativism and the Ethic of Caring'. *Journal of Psychology*, **122,** (3) 1988; 243–248.

23 Stead, W.E., Worrell, D.L., Spalding J.B. and Stead, J.G. 'Unethical Decisions: Socially Learned Behaviours'. *Journal of Social Behaviour and Personality*, **2,** (1) 1987; 105–115.

24 Arlow, P. and Ulrich, T.A. 'Auditing Your Organization's Ethics'. *Internal Auditor*, **39,** (4) 1980; 26–31.

25 Baumhart, R. 'How Ethical are Businessmen?' *Harvard Business Review*, **39;** (4) 1961; 26–31.

26 Brenner, S. and Molander, E. 'Is the Ethics of Business Changing?' *Harvard Business Review*, **55:** (1) 1977; 55–71.

27 Carroll, A.B. 'Linking Business Ethics to Behaviour in Organizations'. *Advanced Management Journal*, **43;** (3) 1978; 4–11.

28 Hegarty, W.H. and Sims, H.P. Jr 'Organizational Philosophy, Policies and Objectives Related to Unethical Decision Behaviour: A Laboratory Experiment'. *Journal of Applied Psychology*, **64;** (3) 1979; 331–338.

29 Posner, B. and Schmidt, W. 'Values and the American Manager: An Update'. *California Management Review*, **24,** (3) 1984; 206–216.

30 Vitell, S. and Festervand, T. 'Business Ethics: Conflicts, Practices and Beliefs of Industrial Executives'. *Journal of Business Ethics*, **6,** 1987; 111–122.

31 Worrel, D.L., Stead, W.E., Stead, J.G. and Spalding, J.B. 'Unethical Decisions: The Impact of Reinforcement Contingencies and Managerial Philosophies'. *Psychological Reports*, **57,** 1985; 355–365.

32 Nielsen, R.P. 'Limitations of Ethical Reasoning as an Action (Praxis) Strategy'. *Journal of Business Ethics*, **7:** 1988; 725–733.

33 Rosen, B. and Adams, J.S. 'Organizational Coverups: Factors Influencing the Disciplining of Information Gatekeepers'. *Journal of Applied Psychology*, **4,** (4) 1974; 375–384.

34 Matthews, J.B., Goodpaster, K.E. and Nash, L.L. *Politics and Persons: A Casebook in Business Ethics*, New York: McGraw-Hill, 1985.

35 Goodpaster, K.E. and Matthews, J.B. Jr 'Can a Corporation Have a Conscience?' *Harvard Business Review*, **60,** (1) 1982; 132–141.

36 Nielsen, R.P. 'Changing Unethical Organizational Behaviour'. *Academy of Manage-*

ment Executive, **3**, (2) 1989; 123–130.

37 Ranken, N.L. 'Corporations as Persons: Objections to Goodpaster's Principle of Moral Projection'. *Journal of Business Ethics*, **6**, 1987; 633–637.

38 Sackett, P.R. and Harris, M.M. 'Honesty Testing for Personnel Selection: A Review and Critique'. *Personnel Psychology*, **37**, (2) 1984; 221–245.

39 Bayes, P. and McKee, T. 'Do CAP Firms Have Adequate Internal Control Over Hiring?' Unpublished manuscript.

40 Davis, R.R.'Ethical Behaviour Reexamined'. *CPA*, **54**, *Journal* 1984; 33–36.

41 Wartzman, R. 'Nature or Nurture? Study Blames Ethical Lapses on Corporate Goals'. *Wall Street Journal*, 9 October 1987, p. 31.

42 Otten, A.L. 'Ethics on the Job: Companies Alert Employees to Potential Dilemmas'. *Wall Street Journal*, 14 July 1986, p. 23.

43 Raelin, J.A. 'The Professional as the Executive's Ethical Aide-de-Camp'. *Academy of Management Executive*, **1**, (3) 1987; 171–182.

Additional reading

According to Steven N. Brenner, 'All organizations have ethics programs, but most do not know they do. This is because such programs are frequently not explicitly created, but inherent in the culture and process of the organization'. In his article 'Ethics programs and their dimensions' (*Journal of Business Ethics* 1992; **11**, 391–399), Brenner identifies explicit and implicit programme components and provides a structural and behavioural classification scheme to help measure their impact. He also suggests fifteen propositions about the influences on the programmes. These relate to founder values, competitive pressures, leadership and organizational problems.

Ronald R. Sims states that ethical behaviour can be improved through 'The institutionalization of organizational ethics' (*Journal of Business Ethics* 1991; **10**, 493–506). This can be done by managing the psychological contract that exists between employees and organizations; reinforcing an employee's commitment to the organization; and encouraging an ethically oriented culture.

There is a strong body of literature on the topic of ethics codes – one example being Joanne Ciulla's 'Breathing new life into corporate codes of ethics' in *Business Ethics in a New Europe*, edited by Jack Mahoney and Elizabeth Vallance (Kluwer Academic Publishers, Dordrecht, Netherlands, 1992). Ciulla describes how she helped a large multinational company set up an ethics programme and discusses relevant issues such as incentive systems and corporate communication.

Questions for discussion

● Cite specific examples of organizational factors that support ethical behaviour; support unethical behaviour.

- Which ethical decision ideology do you follow? Which ideology do those you work closely with follow? What are the ramifications of any matches or mismatches?
- If you were to advise your company on what could or should be done to improve ethical behaviour, what specific actions would you recommend?

Chapter 5

Ethics as an integrating force in management

In this classic contribution, Professor Mark Pastin looks at ethics as a key integrating force in management. Some experts argue that this is of paramount importance as companies move rapidly to decentralize their operations with the aim of achieving maximum profitability and flexibility.

The comments in this chapter about the difference between goals and purpose are reflected in the present importance attached to developing corporate vision and mission statements.

We suspect that the most successful companies in the future will be those able to deal best with the question: Why is the existence of my company worthwhile and why should I perform this task or seek this goal with maximum commitment?

Pastin's comments about the importance of a clear sense of corporate purpose are of major importance. Too often, companies put their goals in place for all stakeholders to see, and then find it very difficult to motivate staff to achieve them. Perhaps Professor Pastin's story about woodcutting, told elsewhere [1], serves to illustrate the point:

The head forester gives our team of woodcutters an order: cut down 50% of the trees in six months. We follow the order. Wielding our axes, we chop down trees every day for three months straight. At the start of the fourth month we stand bleary-eyed, looking at the trees stretching endlessly ahead, and we do not care to see another tree. Even if the head forester wants 50% of the forest cleared in six months, we do not want to do it.

What is lacking?

We have been set clear goals. What could be clearer than cutting down 50% of the trees in six months? But a faint suspicion lurks at the back of our minds. Even if we were to cut down 50% of the forest, chances are we will merely be moved to a different forest and told to cut down 50% of the trees there.

We are getting tired of goals.

We must discover what is missing; what is the fuel that drives us to accomplish goals? We seek answers to a few basic questions: why should I do a good job? Why should I care if this organization continues to exist? Why should I exemplify integrity in what I do? Why should our various publics tolerate or support our existence?

The most basic question of all, if answered honestly, could have resounding repercussions throughout the organization: Why does what I do matter?

It is hard to find a word that answers these questions. The answers are complex and strike at the very heart of an organization and our relationship to it. The best word, according to Professor Pastin, is probably purpose. What is lacking in the woodcutting example is purpose, he claims. Purpose need not be grandiose. You may simply want to be the best woodcutter ever. If that is your purpose, then you relish the endless chopping down of trees. He feels that, when your task matches your purpose, you have a framework that helps to answer the questions posed above.

Reference

1 *Hard Problems of Management*, San Francisco: Jossey-Bass, 1986.

Ethics as an integrating force in management
Mark Pastin

One of the curious phenomena of the . . . industrial scene is the uncomfort-ableness with which questions of ethics are generally treated. Managers, on one hand, bristle at the suggestion that they are not highly ethical or that, excepting a few aberrations, the management of major business organizations is not in the hands of people with ethical values. On the other hand, a dichotomous mentality places ethics outside the decision-making process, suggesting that one makes decisions independently of ethics and *then* examines the ethical implications. This attitude imposes a kind of stupidity on management thinking that must be remedied for both economic and ethical reasons.

The current crop of writing on business ethics is, for the most part, not helping. Critics of business use ethics as a fortress from which to attack. Management theorist Peter Drucker rightly observes that those who promote a special ethics for business often harbour antibusiness sentiments. These critics believe it will take special medicine to make this sickly patient well. Professional ethicists are not much help either. All too often they get lost in each other's convoluted reasoning – as if it makes no difference whether ethics could be applied. In the world of academe, business professors pontificate on how to get 'me-generation MBA students' to be as enlightened as their professors.

Although authors of ethics articles may advocate different approaches to ethics in business, their discussions converge in viewing ethics as an 'add-on' to the decision-making process rather than as an integral, facilitating element. The reasons why ethics continue to be viewed as an add-on are complicated and diverse. They range from the inaccessible character of ethical theories to the belief – mistaken or not – that efficiency is the golden idol and that values and efficiency do not mix.

Unfortunately, there are no statistics on economic losses resulting from the failure of business to treat ethics as a cementing mechanism that holds the fabric of economic decision-making together. Speculation suggests, however, that it is enormous. For example, while it is a mistake to fix exclusively on human factors in explaining declining rates of productivity improvement in recent years, there is a sense that the absence of an ethics of interdependence among workers, management, company and society is a significant contribut-ing factor.

The current interest in such slightly disguised ethical topics as organizational culture, superordinate goals and individual versus collective responsibility (e.g. in the USA and Japan) indicates that managers are beginning to believe that ethics has a bottom-line impact.

If we could but harness ethics as an integrating force, with its own tools to aid decision-making, we could plug it in at the outset of the decision-making process. Ethics then could serve as a catalyst to operate between and among more familiar tools of analysis, hopefully with synergistic results. To the extent that ethics can serve as an integrating force, it will be viewed as a mainstream tool of analysis. I believe that this type of integration is possible and that it can be expected to produce more effective and innovative decision-making.

There is, of course, no guarantee that incorporating ethics in the decision-making process will enhance profitability. But there are distinct advantages, which can be converted into economic and ethical gains, to a decision-making process that integrally includes ethics.

Ethical considerations systematically remind the decision-maker of his or her basic goals, those of coworkers, and, crucially, the company's goals. These considerations force the decision-maker to rethink – and possibly reject or revise – basic assumptions about other employees at the company, the company itself and the relationships between the company, its environment and the decision-maker.

Ethical decision-making requires that one ask the right questions at the right times. The decision-maker who looks at problems in ethical terms is likely to see alternatives not visible to ethics-blind competitors. New competitive edges are revealed during the process of looking at problems in a way that differentiates one's thinking from that of competitors . . . .

Many ethical concepts could be used to illustrate a business decision-making process integrally, including ethics. This article focuses on one key idea, the concept of *the good* or, less archaically, *the valuable*. This concept is especially important to business decision-making because it uncovers the confusion that permeates strategic thinking and generates questions that are central to any complex management decision.

The purpose of ethical behaviour

Goals are the intended output of strategic thinking. However, the role of goals in strategic thinking is often confused, as evidenced by inflated jargon, such as goals and objectives, and undermined confidence in strategic thinking. This confusion is best unravelled by contrasting goals with purposes.

A goal is a more or less specific target towards which one aims. A goal can be achieved and is exhausted when reached. Suppose my company sets a goal of having [£5] million in sales by the end of [this year]. It now has the opportunity of reaching that goal or not. If sales reach [£5] million by the end of [the year], that goal is met and new objectives must be set.

Goal-setting helps answer several important business questions, including, 'Why are you doing that?' 'Where do you expect this company to be in one year?' And, 'Where do you expect this company to be in five years?' Although goals typically are economic in form and include a target date (15% return on investment by a certain year, etc.), they do not always need to be economic and quantifiable. Minnesota Mining and Manufacturing has succeeded through product innovation as a leading goal.

Non-economic, non-quantified goals, however, should be translatable into specific economic-temporal terms. 3M translates its goal of succeeding through product innovation into the more specific goal of achieving 25% of its profits from new products each year.

The contribution of superordinate goals to organizational performance recently has received considerable attention. R.H. Waterman, Thomas J. Peters and Julien Phillips have said that 'by "superordinate goals," we mean guiding concepts – a set of values and aspirations, often unwritten – that go beyond the conventional formal statements of corporate objectives. Super-ordinate goals are the fundamental ideas around which a business is built'. Although these authors are talking about goals, they are confusing the concept of a *purpose* with that of a goal. If an organization is built on goals (rather than *on* values or *for* purposes) and the goals are achieved, or not achieved, then what? If we want more goals, where will they come from? Consultants? Management retreats?

Organizations often avoid thinking about superordinate goals or they formulate unreachable or hopelessly vague goals to avoid asking, 'Then what?' The answer to the 'Then what?' question is not, however, a bigger, more distant or fuzzier goal. It is a *purpose* or *value*. A purpose is a way of *being* or *functioning* viewed by an individual or an organization as valuable-in-itself.

A purpose makes a value specific or operational. If my goal is to sell insurance aggressively and honestly, then this purpose makes the values of being aggressive and honest concrete for me. While the concept of a purpose is hard to separate from the notion of a goal, a clear grasp of purposes and of the differences between purposes and goals is essential to constructive strategic thinking.

If purposes and goals are not distinguished, the process of setting goals will require that these objectives be wished into existence from nothing. As a result, goal implementation will become difficult because it is unclear where the goals to be implemented came from and why anyone should care whether or not they are met.

Suppose you have the individual purpose of realizing your potential. It is your conviction that each person has nothing better to do than to discover and develop his or her intellectual and personal abilities. If you are intelligent and curious, you might realize your potential by pursuing a challenging research problem. For example, you might adopt the goal of discovering a cure for lung cancer within five years.

While this goal is specific, the background purpose – realizing oneself – resists specification in economic, temporal or other terms. Contrasting this goal and the background purpose reveals some surprises. For instance, one might consistently and fully satisfy or live up to one's purpose over the next five years and not achieve the desired goal. You might set out to discover a cure for lung cancer but instead discover a cure for cerebral palsy.

On the other hand, you might achieve your goal without living up to your purpose. If you discover a cure for lung cancer through a fluke – a child scribbles a formula and insists that you try it – you have not realized your intellectual abilities. If your goals are not arbitrary, you have chosen them on the basis of purposes. But the connections between goals and background purposes are not simple.

Another difference between goals and purposes is that goals are *exhausted* at a specific time, whereas purposes are not. One may not discover a cure for lung cancer in the next five years. If one does, the goal is achieved and exhausted. If the goal is not achieved, one must adopt a revised goal – differing, say, only in target date – or abandon this line of action. The original goal no longer exists.

Purposes persist. Even if you have satisfied a purpose up to a given time, it is neither exhausted nor non-existent. If you have fully exercised your intellectual abilities up to a given time, the purpose of realizing yourself is not exhausted. Purposes are not completed; they are either being satisfied or not – lived up to or not – at any point in time. Achieving a particular goal does not diminish the value of further successes from the perspective of a purpose.

For example, an intellectual achievement does not diminish the value of later achievements for someone whose purpose is to realize his or her intellectual abilities. Purposes undergo transformation over time but are not lightly changed or abandoned. Since purposes define who you are, shifts in purpose threaten loss of identity.

Establishing corporate goals and purposes

Setting corporate goals can help answer important questions concerning a company's future, including, 'Where is my company headed and when do we intend to be there?' Purposes, on the other hand, help decision-makers answer the question: 'Why is the existence of my company worthwhile and why should I perform this task or seek this goal with maximum commitment?'

If these questions seem philosophic, the need to address them is quite concrete. Purposes give a company a sense of what it is, where its goals come from and why it should attempt difficult undertakings. Purposes provide *continuity* for an organization despite the inevitable changes in goals, people, operations, structure, markets and success.

For example, a large electronics manufacturer tried to institute a programme of shared company values or purposes. Despite a strong commitment to the programme by top executives, a supporting training and communications plan, a complementary reward structure and a general sense that shared values would be good for all, the programme bogged down after two years. An outside consultant was called in to determine what the problem was. A study of the leading values of managers and employees revealed three kinds of values – product values ('given a quality product, everything else follows'), human values ('committed, capable people are the source of success') and economic values ('it all boils down to a return on net assets').

Low-level employees favoured product values, top managers favoured economic values and mid-managers were 'conflicted'. Although the process of trying to establish values heightened awareness of the role of values in the company, discouragement and an adversarial attitude ('this too will pass') set in.

The problem deepened when the company adopted as its leading goal beating, or 'crushing', foreign competition by [19●●]. This goal had been highly publicised and a war-campaign atmosphere was consciously generated. The problem was: How do product quality, committed employees and maximum return on net assets fit with beating foreign competition by 19●●? What really counts?

This company could not align itself behind a goal because it was running its goals and purposes together. Each constituency in the company had identified as the leading value that which was closest to the goals it was used to seeking. There was no sense that any purpose was central, no rationale for backing a particular purpose and no sense that any of this truly mattered.

It also wasn't clear whether the company genuinely cared about values or whether these values would be junked if something better served the goal of beating foreign competition. What if these values were just the latest corporate weapons? In this particular instance, values or purposes were being measured against goals. However, the reason for having values is to provide a framework for choosing and assessing goals. This was a confused company and it showed – in economic performance, product quality and bewildered employees.

Is the moral of this tale that companies should skip purposes altogether to avoid such difficulties? Having no purpose is *exactly* as feasible as having no strategy. To have no strategy is to have the strategy of letting the company drift at the whim of external forces, internal politics and chance. To have no purpose is to have the company stand for nothing. The zero option in strategy or values is not attractive.

Further, there are powerful advantages in having clearly subscribed-to purposes or values. Purposes provide the continuity that companies need to succeed in the long run. A company that knows what it stands for can effectively evaluate strategies, goals and employees. In fact, this is the key to the recalcitrant problem of evaluating employees in the face of changing goals and shifting perceptions of what matters.

Virtually every action of a manager or employee is discretionary. A company with clear purposes can expect a higher percentage of discretionary actions to align with its interests. If purposes tie the company to an encompassing community, they also can produce a generally higher level of motivation. The true moral is that a company setting out to adopt, create or entrench purposes or values must understand what it is up to. It must respect the differences between purposes and goals. These concerns, by themselves, are not sufficient to produce a purposeful or 'value-driven' company. But integrating the distinction between what you stand for (purposes) and where you want to go (goals) into management thinking is a precondition of success.

Establishing a value framework

The concept of an organizational purpose – what the organization stands for – is a central and traditional ethical concept. By pursuing purposes through the root ethical concept of the valuable, or good, we uncover questions that must be part of any effective management decision-making process.

Purposes are concerned with that which is good – or valuable – *in itself*. They also encompass not only definitive ends but ways of doing things ('If we can't win *just by being the best* in a market, then we won't compete in that market') and ways of being ('We don't treat people that way around here'). Purposes establish the framework of values within which specific questions of ends and means are discussed.

How do you establish a value framework? One standard recipe says that the assessment of what is valuable in itself depends on three factors: the individuals who fall within the scope of assessment, the time over which the assessment is to be maintained, and the standards by which the assessment is made. For instance, we might say that a commitment to advancing technologies is valuable for a firm having certain employees – such as scientists – and markets – such as medical providers – for the foreseeable future judging by the joint best interests of the firm, its customers and suppliers.

When trying to determine what is valuable to a company, decision-makers can ask three questions. They are:

1 *Who counts?* That is, who should be considered in this choice or policy?
2 *When counts?* That is, what time period should be considered in this choice or policy?
3 *How do you count?* That is, what principles or methods should be used to critique the value implications of this choice or policy?

The full benefit of integrating a concern for the valuable in decision-making is contained in the process of thinking through these questions. It is, obviously, implausible to imagine managers explicitly raising these questions in the course of the work day. Therefore, there is all the more reason to raise these concerns when we reflect on the work environment. We should become as familiar with these focusing questions as we are with procedural questions. Eventually, we should be able to integrate these questions in decision-making so that they cease to require special attention.

Answering the question of 'Who counts?'

When we think about purposes, we are thinking about ways of being and functioning that are valuable. To think about what is valuable for ourselves and our company is, in part, to think about whom we affect and take into our domain of concern. Indeed, an important advantage of incorporating consideration of the valuable in decision-making is that it forces us to think about who is truly relevant to our decisions instead of whom we usually consider or who makes the most noise.

Disagreements about whether or not a policy of action is valuable or good often mask different assessments of *who counts* in the issue. When consumer groups argue that it would be good to put dates on frozen foods, they probably are considering this policy in terms of members of their own group plus other consumers whom they think they represent. In arguing against product dating, a company representative probably considers management, stockholders, other companies in the industry, the press and 'typical' consumers.

If the consumer group's claim implicitly identifies *one* group as relevant, while the company's claim implicitly identifies a *different* group as relevant, it is clear that this rather typical value dispute hinges on the answer to the 'Who counts?' question.

In any consequentional decision, an effective manager should pointedly ask: 'Who counts?' Fellow-managers, employees and stockholders surely count. Do customers count in this decision? Non-customers? All non-customers? Should I consider what will happen to competitors? Should I care if they fail?

In trying to organize these questions, our attention naturally turns to decision models – including cost-benefit analysis – based on John Stuart Mill's utilitarian maxim, which said, 'Maximize the balance of benefits over costs for everyone'. While considering everyone is a worthy idea, Mill's axiom offers little practical guidance, unless we so delimit 'everyone' that considering everyone is feasible!

In a practical context, of course, it is impossible to consider everyone who might conceivably be affected to any degree by our company's actions. Rather than trying to define a particular subgroup that has special claim to consider in our decision-making, we can require that our decision-making move towards the ideal of taking into account all groups that have or claim a significant stake in our decisions.

No extant decision-making approach aspires to encompass all significantly affected constituencies. Some approaches are better than others. Participatory decision-making processes have the spirit of inclusiveness that a concern for the valuable imposes on decision-making – the more so the broader decision-making participation.

Participatory approaches currently in favour emphasize participation by *internal* constituencies. Some of these approaches, such as those purportedly rooted in Japanese management practices, are based on the belief that internally directed participation builds team and organizational identity. But a value-informed decision process must also take account of significantly affected external constituencies, including customers, suppliers, competitors and regulators.

While allowing decision-making participation by external groups, such as customers and suppliers, is a radical idea, economic considerations converge with the 'Who counts?' question in commending this idea for consideration. An ongoing study of successful [American] companies (New York Stock Exchange industrial corporations that have paid a dividend for at least 100 years consecutively) shows that a key factor in these companies' success comes from their view of themselves as an intermediary between suppliers and customers. The chief executives of these firms also believe that to be successful in the long run, a company must be in dialogue with society at large on every topic of mutual concern to the two entities.

The 'Who counts?' component of value assessment gives the manager a criterion of adequacy for any decision-making process in place or under consideration. This question consistently turns management attention outward, to see which groups or persons will be significantly affected. If decision-making at Ford had been measured against this criterion, I doubt that the disastrous Pinto would ever have surfaced . . . .

How do you count?

Once your company has determined who should be considered in a decision and the time period to consider, it still is necessary to determine how to reconcile these factors in a critically acceptable choice or policy.

The response to the 'How do you count?' question would seem to be a set of principles for making a rational choice. It is widely assumed that ethics, including the study of what is valuable, should focus on the principles of rational choice for individuals and groups. Hence, the great, if barely comprehensible, systems of ethics offer broad principles. Unfortunately, these principles simply do not apply to real world problems.

When we look at some principles of choice, it is important to note how much of the *practical* core of ethical thinking is included in the 'Who counts?' and 'When counts?' questions. Principles turn out to be needed not so much to settle what to choose as to anchor the process of sharply criticizing the choice options.

In business, a rational choice is usually understood as an economically rational decision – a decision that maximizes some economic variable, such as profit, return on investment or return on net assets, over a specified time. Such concepts of economic rationality, however, are only marginally applicable in actual situations of limited time, partial information and little desire to take risks to maximize when one already has enough.

Acceptable minimum concepts of economic rationality are only slightly less idealized with their limitation to a few favoured variables. Concepts of economic rationality presuppose a specified time period over which perform-ance is measured. But how long a manager's time perspective *should be* is not a matter of economic rationality. To claim that one should have a time perspective of x months or years is to assume that one knows the correct time period for assessing the rationality of setting time periods. A small but vicious circle results. Concepts of economic rationality can be applied only if a broader concept of rationality allows us to determine the relevant time period of application.

Theoretical discussions view general concepts of rational choice as a function of what one *believes* and *desires*. What you choose in a situation depends on what you want out of the situation and what you believe you will get from the options available for choice. Whether or not the choice you make is rational depends on whether the relevant beliefs are warranted and the relevant desires are considered. For example, I am 5 feet 6 inches tall and 36 years old. My desire to be a centre in [professional basketball] is not considered; my belief that I could succeed is unwarranted. If I chose to pursue a career in [basketball], my choice would be irrational.

Thus, the theories of rationality offer various principles for determining whether beliefs are warranted and desires are considered. Such discussions produce controversy, scholarly articles and virtually no consensus.

Our strategy is not to seek principles which determine whether any given belief is warranted or desire is considered. We seek a procedure, consisting of a core idea and a set of questions, for assessing the warrant of a belief. For example, an analogous strategy is used in jurisprudence, where the system does not settle every case but sets procedures for fair case settlement and in negotiating systems that first seek agreement on procedures for resolving disputes.

The idea behind the proposed procedure is this: a person, or an organization, is warranted in holding a belief to the extent that it can be tested and rejected. What separates warranted belief from superstitious belief is the decision-maker's willingness to challenge the belief no matter how dearly it is held. I think this is political economist George Gilder's point in arguing that capitalism is as much a way of knowing as a form of economy – the market serves as a powerful belief-challenging mechanism.

Questions that challenge beliefs

Our procedure consists of a set of questions that provide a strong basis for testing management beliefs. The first question, which we'll call the Systems Question, asks, 'Is this belief part of a system that provides a *coherent* picture of the choice situation and is it *comprehensive* enough to encompass the variables relevant to the choice?' This question draws attention to the need for an explanatory picture of the choice situation – a picture that gives a credible account of what is going on without leaving out critical variables.

This question helps companies avoid using the 'management gizmo', which can be defined as an idea intended to solve a defined problem. The gizmo may be effective within the domain of a defined problem. All too often, however, it is mistaken for an all-purpose remedy and may rest on assumptions that are inconsistent with generally effective management. For example, the portfolio matrix is a proven analysis tool. If it is used as part of a general management system, however, it becomes a gizmo because it excludes many variables relevant to a company's long-term performance.

Wholesale use of Japanese-style management techniques often qualifies as gizmos, too. When managers borrow helter-skelter from their Japanese counterparts, they frequently fail to ask whether these purloined techniques fit in a comprehensive picture of their own management problems. In using such techniques, executives should ask whether top-level managers will yield comfortable decision-making power to make participation democratic enough to succeed. The Systems Question directs the manager's attention to the interrelationships among a given choice, other problems, individuals, the company and other companies.

The second question, the Options Question, asks: 'Is there an alternative belief system which can provide another belief that is equally or more comprehensive and coherent than the belief being tested?'

The more familiar and accepted a belief is, the more likely we are to have constructed a good 'story' around it. But no matter how good a story we tell, it merely rationalizes a belief if we do not seek competing stories. This can cause problems. In a . . . symposium, Paul R. Lawrence, author of *Renewing American Industry*, and William Ouchi, author of *Theory Z*, emphasized that managers construct good stories around untested beliefs during boom years only to find out later that these beliefs do not hold true in bust years.

For example, a good story backs the belief that success in the automotive industry depends mainly on marketing. But a better story would include the competing belief that product factors, such as quality, durability and simplicity, are the main success factors. Oil companies argue persuasively that there is no such thing as an excess profit. But a look at alternative belief systems that reject this favoured notion would advance the thinking of executives in this industry. It would enable them to see why their critics are not moved by their arguments and speak to their critics' premises.

The last question decision-makers can ask, the Sunk Ego question, focuses on the psychic investment in the belief. This question asks, 'Which of my/our interests would be threatened if this belief were abandoned?' It forces us to consider whether we maintain a belief just because we wish to avoid the cost of *admitting* error. All too often, parties in negotiations will hold on to positions that no longer serve them or their constituents, rather than admitting that they were wrong in the first place.

This phenomenon of ego attachment to a belief also is represented in other areas of business thinking. The Cummins Engine Company earned an advantage over its competitors by abandoning the standard diesel engine industry belief that clean air regulations were unnecessary. By supporting intelligent regulations rather than opposing all regulations, Cummins gained both a time and product-fit edge over competitors.

Awareness of one's investment in a belief allows a person or company to hold notions that serve *actual* interests rather than the interests of a calcified beliefs system.

There also is a procedure that allows us to assess the *desires* that go into making a choice. Considered desires grow out of a range of options, a sound view of the rewards, the costs of pursuing these options and an awareness of the interest of others. Thus, a union representative may want a fixed schedule of wage increases because he or she thinks union members can benefit from higher wages. The representative may alter the wage demand, however, if he or she considers the issue of job security over wage increases and is aware of the possibilities and consequences of layoffs that might result from higher salaries.

Since the 'How do you count?' question focuses attention on rationality, I have explored a concept that encompasses both ethical and economic rationality. The importance of non-ethical as well as ethical benefits to management decision-making has been emphasized. It is important to remember that a concern for the valuable does not exhaust the topic of ethics. Integrating other aspects of ethical thinking in decision-making may prove less conciliatory.

The 'How do you count?' question reveals that a concern for the valuable mandates a stance of systematically questioning personal and organizational beliefs and desires in light of a broad range of alternatives and the interests of others. While strongly challenging beliefs and laundering desires is, at best, an uncomfortable process, there is no reason why managers should fear incorporating these procedures in the practice of decision-making.

Final questions to ask

The idea of integrating ethics in management decision-making will remain an interesting topic unless we can confront the issue of operationalizing ethics, specifically including a concern for the good or the valuable, in decision-making. We do not propose a new system of management-by-ethics, although such a system would make more economic and ethical sense than many others.

The great positivist philosopher of science, Otto Neurath, compared the task of ridding science of metaphysics with the task of rebuilding a raft while one is afloat on it. No matter what revolutionary idea comes along, the executive or manager is always rebuilding a system, hoping all along to keep it afloat. The suggestions in this article are offered in the raft-building spirit. We offer questions that managers can ask to seed the decision-making process with both ethical and economic rationality.

Our aim has been to take some first steps towards the integration of ethics, particularly the concept of the good or the valuable, in management thinking and decision-making. The proposals offered are intended to be both implementable and beneficial to the quality of decision-making. At the outset, we observed that there is no guarantee that ethics pays. But there is no guarantee that non-ethics pays, either.

With the integrity and health of ourselves and our organizations at stake, it is surely worth trying to bind the components of decision-making together with some glue – the glue of ethics.

Additional reading

Moving on from this contribution by Pastin to the topic of corporate culture and business ethics (discussed in detail by Pastin in *Hard Problems of Management*, referred to in the introduction), Amanda Sinclair's article 'Approaches to organisational culture and ethics' (*Journal of Business Ethics* 1993; **12**, 63–73) is a mine of information. Sinclair examines two competing notions of what organizational culture is in order to determine if it can be used to enhance business ethics. The first model holds 'that creating a unitary cohesive culture around core moral values is the solution to enhancing ethical behaviour'. The second approach questions whether organizational culture even exists. Instead, organizations are portrayed as 'nothing more than shifting coalitions of subcultures'. Improved ethical behaviour may then result from the diversity and debate of opinions held. Sinclair discusses the risks of each approach along with the different kind of ethics that each promises.

R. Eric Reidenbach and Donald P. Robin contribute to the topic through their paper 'A conceptual model of corporate moral development' (*Journal of Business Ethics* 1991; **10,** 272–284). They identify five levels of corporate moral development (amoral, legalistic, responsive, emerging ethical and ethical) and argue that moral development is determined by the corporate culture and, in turn, helps define this culture.

Questions for discussion

● Select a specific business transaction/case that you are familiar with and that was considered to be an ethical problem. Ask the questions that help determine what is valuable in a company:

  1 Who was considered in this choice or policy?
  2 What time period was considered?
  3 What principles or methods were used to critique the value implications of this choice?

● With the benefit of hindsight, do you disagree with any of the answers to the above questions? If so, would different answers have led to a better handling of the ethical problem?

Chapter 6

The moral muteness of managers

Arguably the greatest obstacle in the way of stimulating a serious debate of ethics in business is the moral muteness exhibited by many managers when the subject is raised. In this seminal contribution, Bird and Waters discuss this issue and its ramifications.

A long experience of working with manager and employee groups on ethical issues has shown us that ethics is unquestionably a subject which generates strong feelings. It straddles all functions and all levels in organizations, and it can give rise to the most heated debate. We have encountered very few employees who, deep down, are 'agnostic' about corporate ethics. Most staff, in interviews with us, have a clear perception of the standards of ethical behaviour in the organizations of which they are a part. Why then do we rarely hear morality and ethics discussed except when there is a crisis? The authors discuss this in detail.

They point out how ethical discussions are often seen as a threat to harmony and efficiency, and a blow against the image of power and effectiveness cherished by many managers. This latter point may strike some women executives as a peculiarly male perspective of what is important in organizations.

On this note, some experts see growing evidence of a trend towards the feminization of management, with more emphasis on *process* rather than *task*.

Moreover, it could be argued that the move towards more networked operations, inside and outside companies, will strengthen these changes. As companies become 'de-layered', that is, increasingly strip out layers of management, they will seek the provision of some essential services from outside. And the requirement which conditions the effective operation of networks, in our experience, is fairness.

Fairness brings stability to network arrangements. All parties need to know that business transactions will be handled honourably. Many business observers feel that future business success depends crucially upon the recruitment and retention of the very best staff and suppliers. Therefore sustaining relationships will be an essential skill. This being so, it has been argued that women managers may have a significant business edge in the future.

It is clear that it will be essential for all managers, of whatever gender, to rid themselves of moral muteness to ensure that processes under their control operate fairly.

It is, of course, very difficult to achieve any of this when the moral and ethical issues cannot be raised. For those managers attempting to tackle ethical problems, there is little doubt that a general debate on ethical issues in an unpressured environment would make them better able to tackle such problems when suddenly confronted with them in practice.

The moral muteness of managers
Frederick B. Bird and James A. Waters

Many managers exhibit a reluctance to describe their actions in moral terms even when they are acting for moral reasons. They talk as if their actions were guided exclusively by organizational interests, practicality, and economic good sense even when in practice they honour morally defined standards codified in law, professional conventions and social mores. They characteristically defend morally defined objectives such as service to customers, effective cooperation among personnel, and utilization of their own skills and resources in terms of the long-run economic objectives of their organizations. Ostensibly moral standards regarding colleagues, customers, and suppliers are passed off as . . . 'ways to succeed' [1].

Many observers have called attention to this reluctance of managers to use moral expressions publicly to identify and guide their decision-making even when they are acting morally. A century and a half ago, de Tocqueville noted the disinclination of American business people to admit they acted altruistically even when they did [2]. More recently, McCoy has observed that managers are constantly making value choices, privately invoking moral standards, which they in turn defend in terms of business interests [3]. Silk and Vogel [4] note that many managers simply take for granted that business and ethics have little relation except negatively with respect to obvious cases of illegal activities, like bribery or price-fixing. Solomon and Hanson [5] observe that, although managers are often aware of moral issues, discussion of these issues in ethical terms is ordinarily neglected.

Current research based on interviews with managers about how they experience ethical questions in their work reveals that managers seldom discuss with their colleagues the ethical problems they routinely encounter [6]. In a very real sense, 'Morality is a live topic for individual managers but it is close to a non-topic among groups of managers' [7].

This article explores this phenomenon of moral muteness and suggests ways in which managers and organizations can deal openly with moral questions.

Actions, speech and normative expectations

To frame the exploration of moral muteness, it is useful to consider in general terms the relationships between managers' actions, their communicative exchanges, and relevant normative expectations. Normative expectations are standards for behaviour that are sufficiently compelling and authoritative that people feel they must comply with them, make a show of complying with them, or offer good reasons why not.

While normative expectations influence conduct in many areas of life from styles of dress to standards of fair treatment, in most societies certain types of activities are considered to be morally neutral. Choices of how to act with respect to morally neutral activities are considered to be matters of personal preference, practical feasibility or strategic interest [8].

Although managers often disagree regarding the extent to which business activities are morally neutral, their interactions in contemporary industrial societies are influenced by a number of normative expectations. These expectations are communicated by legal rulings, regulatory agencies' decrees, professional codes, organizational policies and social mores [9]. Considerable consensus exists with respect to a number of general ethical principles bearing upon management regarding honest communication, fair treatment, fair competition, social responsibility, and provision of safe and worthwhile services and products [10].

Through verbal exchanges people identify, evoke and establish normative expectations as compelling cultural realities. Moral expressions are articulated to persuade others, to reinforce personal convictions, to criticize and to justify decisions. Moral expressions are also invoked to praise and to blame, to evaluate and to rationalize. Moral discourse plays a lively role communicating normative expectations, seeking cooperation of others and rendering judgements.

For those decisions and actions for which moral expectations are clearly relevant, it is possible to conceive of four different kinds of relationship between managers' actions and their verbal exchanges. These are depicted in Figure 6.1. One pattern (quadrant I) identifies those situations in which speaking and acting correspond with each other in keeping with moral expectations. A second congruent pattern (quadrant III) is the mirror image of the first: no discrepancy exists between speech and action, but neither is guided by moral expectations.

The other two patterns represent incongruence between speech and action. In quadrant II, actual conduct falls short of what is expected. Verbal exchanges indicate a deference for moral standards that is not evident in actual conduct. Discrepancy here represents hypocrisy, when people intentionally act contrary to their verbalized commitments [11]. Discrepancy may also assume the form of moral backsliding or moral weakness. In this case, the failure to comply with verbalized commitments occurs because of moral fatigue, the inability to honour conflicting standards or excusable exceptions [12]. Because they are intuitively understandable, none of these three patterns are our concern in this article.

Rather, our focus is on the more perplexing fourth pattern (quadrant IV) which corresponds with situations of moral muteness: managers avoid moral

	Actions follow normative expectations	Actions do not follow normative expectations
Moral terms used in speech	I Congruent moral conduct	II Hypocrisy, moral weakness
Moral terms not used in speech	IV Moral muteness	III Congruent immoral or amoral conduct

Fig. 6.1 *Relations between moral action and speech*

expressions in their communicative exchanges but would be expected to use them because their actual conduct reveals deference to moral standards, because they expect others to honour such standards or because they privately acknowledge that those standards influence their decisions and actions. In other words, with respect to those instances where the managers involved feel that how they and others act ought to be and is guided by moral expectations, why do they avoid moral references in their work-related communications?

For example, a given manager may argue that the only ethic of business is making money, but then describe at length the non-remunerative ways she fosters organizational commitment from her coworkers by seeking their identification with the organization as a community characterized by common human objectives and styles of operation. In another example, managers may enter into formal and informal agreements among themselves. In the process they necessarily make promises and undertake obligations. Implicitly, they must use moral terms to enter and confirm such understandings even though explicitly no such expressions are voiced. This discrepancy occurs most pervasively in relation to countless existing normative standards regarding business practices that are passed off as common sense or good management, e.g. taking care of regular customers in times of shortage even though there is opportunity to capture new customers, respecting the bidding process in purchasing even though lower prices could be forced on dependent suppliers, and ensuring equitable pricing among customers even though higher prices could be charged to less knowledgeable or less aggressive customers.

Causes of moral muteness

Interviews with managers about the ethical questions they face in their work indicate that they avoid moral talk for diverse reasons [13]. In the particular pattern of moral muteness, we observe that in general they experience moral talk as dysfunctional. More specifically, managers are concerned that moral talk will threaten organizational harmony, organizational efficiency and their own reputation for power and effectiveness.

Threat to harmony

Moral talk may, on occasion, require some degree of interpersonal confrontation. In extreme cases, this may take the form of blowing the whistle on powerful persons in the organization who are involved in illegal or unethical practices and may involve significant personal risk for the whistleblower [14]. Even in less extreme cases, moral talk may involve raising questions about or disagreeing with practices or decisions of superiors, colleagues or subordinates. Managers typically avoid any such confrontation, experiencing it as difficult and costly – as witnessed, for example, by the frequent avoidance of candid performance appraisals. Faced with a situation where a subordinate or colleague is involved in an unethical practice, managers may 'finesse' a public discussion or confrontation by publishing a general policy statement or drawing general attention to an existing policy.

In the case of moral questions, managers find confrontations particularly difficult because they experience them as judgemental and likely to initiate cycles of mutual finger-pointing and recrimination. They are aware of the small and not-so-small deceits which are pervasive in organizations, e.g. juggling budget lines to cover expenditures, minor abuses of organizational perks, favouritism, nepotism, and fear that if they 'cast the first stone' an avalanche may ensue [15].

Many managers conclude that it is disruptive to bring up moral issues at work because their organizations do not want public discussion of such issues. We interviewed or examined the interviews of sixty managers who in turn talked about nearly 300 cases in which they had faced moral issues in their work. In only 12% of these cases had public discussion of moral issues taken place and more than half of these special cases were cited by a single executive. Give-and-take discussions of moral issues typically took place in private conversations or not at all.

Threat to efficiency

Many managers avoid or make little use of moral expressions because moral talk is associated with several kinds of exchanges that obstruct or distract from responsible problem-solving. In these instances, moral talk is viewed as being self-serving and obfuscating. Thus, for example, while moral talk may be legitimately used to praise and blame people for their conduct, praising and blaming do not facilitate the identification, analysis and resolution of difficult moral conundrums. Similarly, while moral talk in the form of ideological exhortations may function to defend structures of authority and to rally support for political goals, it does not facilitate problem-solving among people with varied ideological commitments [16].

Because of the prevalence of such usages, many managers are loathe to use moral talk in their work. Blaming, praising and ideological posturing do not help to clarify issues. Moreover, such moral talk frequently seems to be narrowly self-serving. Those who praise, blame or express ideological convictions usually do so in order to protect and advance their own interests.

In addition, managers shun moral talk because such talk often seems to result in burdening business decisions with considerations that are not only extraneous, but at times antagonistic to responsible management. Moral talk may distract by seeking simplistic solutions to complicated problems. For example, discussions of justice in business often divert attention to theoretical formulas for distributing rewards and responsibilities without first considering how resources as a whole might be expanded and how existing contractual relations might already have built-in standards of fair transactions and allocations.

Moral talk may also be experienced as a threat to managerial flexibility. In order to perform effectively, managers must be able to adapt to challenges in their organizations and environments. They are correspondingly wary of contractual relations that seem to be too binding, that too narrowly circumscribe discretionary responses. They therefore seek out working arrangements, when they legally can, that are informal, flexible, and can be amended easily. They assume that if the stipulations are formally articulated in terms of explicit promises, obligations and rights, then flexibility is likely to be reduced. In order to preserve flexibility in all their relations, managers frequently seek verbal, handshake agreements that make minimal use of explicit moral stipulations [17].

Many managers also associate moral talk with rigid rules and intrusive regulations. Too often, public talk about moral issues in business is felt to precede the imposition of new government regulations that are experienced as arbitrary, inefficient and meddlesome. Complaints about particular immoral practices too often seem to lead to government harassment through procedures and rules that make little economic sense. Managers may therefore avoid using moral expressions in their exchanges so that they do not invite moralistic criticisms and rigid restrictions [18].

Threat to image of power and effectiveness

Ambitious managers seek to present themselves as powerful and effective. They avoid moral talk at times because moral arguments appear to be too idealistic and utopian. Without effective power, the uses of moral expressions are like empty gestures. Many managers experience futility after they attempt unsuccessfully to change corporate policies which they feel are morally questionable. They privately voice their objections but feel neither able to mount organized protests within their organization nor willing to quit in public outcry. *De facto* they express a loyalty they do not wholeheartedly feel [19].

This sense of futility may even be occasioned by management seminars on ethics. Within these workshops managers are encouraged to discuss hypothetical cases and to explore potential action alternatives. Many find these workshops instructive and stimulating. However, when managers begin to consider problems that they actually face in their organizations, then the character of these discussions often changes. Moral expressions recede and are replaced by discussions of organizational politics, technical qualifications, competitive advantages as well as costs and benefits measured solely in economic terms. In the midst of these kinds of practical considerations, moral terms are abandoned because they seem to lack robustness. They suggest ideals and special pleadings without too much organizational weight.

Managers also shun moral talk in order not to expose their own ethical illiteracy. Most managers neither know nor feel comfortable with the language and logic of moral philosophy. At best they received instruction in juvenile versions of ethics as children and young adults in schools and religious associations. They have little or no experience using ethical concepts to analyse issues. They may more readily and less self-consciously use some ethical terms to identify and condemn obvious wrong-doings, but do not know how to use ethical terms and theories with intellectual rigour and sophistication to identify and resolve moral issues.

Finally the 'value of autonomy places great weight on lower managers' ability to solve creatively all their own problems they regularly face' [20]. They

Moral talk is viewed as creating these negative effects . . .	. . . because of these assumed attributes of moral talk
Threat to harmony	Moral talk is intrusive and confrontational and invites cycles of mutual recrimination
Threat to efficiency	Moral talk assumes distracting moralistic forms (praising, blaming, ideological) and is simplistic, inflexible, soft and inexact
Threat to image of power and effectiveness	Moral talk is too esoteric and idealistic, and lacks rigour and force

Fig. 6.2 *Causes of moral muteness*

observe how this valuing of autonomy actually decreases the likelihood that managers will discuss with their superiors the ethical questions they experience.

Figure 6.2 summarizes these three causes of moral muteness.

Consequences of moral muteness

The short-term benefits of moral muteness as perceived by managers (i.e. preservation of harmony, efficiency and image of self-sufficiency) produce significant long-term costs for organizations. These costly consequences include:

1 Creation of moral amnesia.
2 Inappropriate narrowness in conceptions of morality.
3 Moral stress for individual managers.
4 Neglect of moral abuses.
5 Decreased authority of moral standards.

Moral amnesia

The avoidance of moral talk reinforces a caricature of management as an amoral activity, a condition we describe as moral amnesia. Many business people and critics of business seem to be unable to recognize the degree to which business activities are in fact regulated by moral expectations. Critics and defenders of current business practices often debate the legitimacy of bringing moral considerations to bear as if most business decisions are determined exclusively by considerations of profit and personal and organizational self-interest. In the process they ignore the degree to which actual business interactions are already guided by moral expectations communicated by law, professional codes, organizational conventions and social mores.

When particular business practices seem not to honour particular standards, then it may be wrongly assumed that such actions are guided by no normative expectations whatsoever. Actually, specific business practices which are not, for example, guided primarily by particular standards such as social welfare and justice may in fact be determined in a large part by other moral expectations such as respect for fair contractual relations, the efficient and not wasteful use of human and natural resources, and responsiveness to consumer choices and satisfactions. Often when businesses act in ways that are judged to be immoral, such as the unannounced closure of a local plant, they may well be acting in keeping with other normative standards, regarding, for example, organizational responsibility. To assume that conduct judged to be unethical because it is counter to particular standards necessarily springs solely from amoral consideration is to fail to grasp the extent to which such conduct may well be guided and legitimated by other conflicting norms.

The moral amnesia regarding business practices is illustrated by the debate occasioned by an article by Friedman entitled 'The social responsibility of business is to increase its profit' [21]. To many, Friedman seemed to conclude that business people had no moral responsibility other than to use any legal means to increase the returns on the investments of shareholders. He did argue that business people were ill-equipped to become social reformers and that such moral crusading might well lead them to do harm both to those they sought to help and to their own organizations. Both defenders and critics assumed that Friedman was defending an amoral position. However, although cloaked in the language of economic self-interest, Friedman's article alluded in passing to eight different normative standards relevant for business practices: namely, businesses should operate without fraud, without deception in interpersonal communications, in keeping with conventions regarding fair competition, in line with existing laws, with respect to existing contractual agreements, recognizing the given rights of employees and investors, seeking to maximize consumer satisfactions, and always in ways that allow for the free choices of the individual involved. It can be argued that Friedman invited misunderstanding by polarizing issues of profit and social responsibility. It cannot be argued that according to his position profits can be pursued without any other moral criteria than legality.

It is characteristic of this moral amnesia that business people often feel themselves moved by moral obligations and ideals and find no way to refer explicitly to these pushes and pulls except indirectly by invoking personal preferences, common sense and long-term benefits. They remain inarticulate and unselfconscious of their convictions.

Narrowed conception of morality

In order to avoid getting bogged down in moral talk which threatens efficiency, managers who are convinced they are acting morally may argue that their actions are a morally neutral matter. They 'stonewall' moral questions by arguing that the issues involved are ones of feasibility, practicality and the impersonal balancing of costs and benefits and that decisions on these matters are appropriately made by relevant managers and directors without public discussion.

We interviewed a number of managers who made these kinds of claims with respect to issues that others might consider contentious. A utilities executive argued, for example, that studies had exaggerated the impact of steam plants on water supplies. He also contended that no moral issues were relevant to the decisions regarding the domestic use of nuclear power. A pharmaceutical company manager criticized those who attempted to make a moral issue out of a leak in a rinse water pipe. An accountant criticized a colleague for arguing that the procedure recently used with a customer involved moral improprieties. These managers attempted to treat issues that had been questioned as if they were not publicly debatable.

In so far as it is thought that moral issues are posed only by deviance from acceptable standards of behaviour, then managers have a legitimate case to shun moral discussions of their actions which are neither illegal nor deviant. However, while appropriately claiming that their actions are not morally improper, managers stonewall whenever they insist, in addition, that their actions are constituted not only by deviance, but also by dilemmas (when two or more normative standards conflict) and by shortfalls (from the pursuit of high ideals). In the examples cited above, the managers were correct in asserting that no illegal nor blatantly deviant actions were involved. However, they were incorrect to argue that these actions were morally neutral.

Moral muteness in the form of stonewalling thus perpetuates a narrow conception of morality, i.e. as only concerned with blatant deviance from moral standards. Most importantly, moral muteness in this case prevents creative exploration of action alternatives that might enable the organization to balance better conflicting demands or to approximate better the highest ideals.

Moral stress

Managers experience moral stress as a result of role conflict and role ambiguity in connection with moral expectations [22]. They treat their responsibility to their organizations as a moral standard and, when confronted with an ethical question, they frequently have difficulty deciding what kinds of costs will be acceptable in dealing with the question (e.g. it costs money to upgrade toilet facilities and improve working conditions). Moreover, moral expectations (for example, honesty in communications) are often very general and the manager is frequently faced with a decision on what is morally appropriate behaviour in a specific instance. He or she may have to decide, for example, when legitimate entertainment becomes bribery or when legitimate bluffing or concealment of basic positions in negotiations with a customer or supplier becomes dishonesty in communication.

A certain degree of such moral stress is unavoidable in management life. However, it can be exacerbated beyond reasonable levels by the absence of moral talk. If managers are unable to discuss with others their problems and questions, they absorb the uncertainty and stress that would more appropriately be shared by colleagues and superiors. In the absence of moral talk, managers may cope with intolerable levels of moral stress by denying the relevance or importance of particular normative expectations. This may take the form of inappropriate idealism in which the legitimacy of the organization's economic objectives is given inadequate attention. Conversely, and perhaps more frequently, managers may cope with excessive moral stress by treating decisions as morally neutral, responding only to economic concerns and organizational systems of reward and censure. In either case, moral muteness eliminates any opportunity that might exists for creative, collaborative problem-solving that would be best for the manager, as well as for the organization and its stakeholders.

Neglect of abuses

The avoidance of moral talk by managers also means that many moral issues are simply not organizationally recognized and addressed. Consequently, many moral abuses are ignored, many moral ideals are not pursued, and many moral dilemmas remain unresolved. Managers we interviewed readily cited moral lapses of colleagues and competitors [23]. The popular press continually cites examples of immoral managerial conduct, often failing in the process to credit the extent to which managers actually adhere to moral standards.

Just as norms of confrontation contribute to moral muteness, in circular fashion that muteness reinforces those norms and leads to a culture of neglect. Organizational silence on moral issues makes it more difficult for members to raise questions and debate issues. What could and should be ordinary practice – i.e. questioning of the propriety of specific decisions and actions – tends to require an act of heroism and thus is less likely to occur.

Decreased authority of moral standards

Moral arguments possess compelling authority only if the discourse in which these arguments are stated is socially rooted. It is an idealistic misconception to suppose that moral reasons by virtue of their logic alone inspire the feelings of obligation and desire that make people willingly adhere to moral standards. Blake and Davis refer to this assumption as the 'fallacy of normative determinism' [24]. The pushes and pulls which lead people to honour normative standards arise as much, if not more, from social relationships as from verbal communication of moral ideas. The articulations of moral ideas gain compelling authority to the degree that these expressions call to mind existing feelings of social attachments and obligations, build upon tacit as well as explicit agreements and promises, seem to be related to realistic rewards and punishments, and connect feeling of self-worth to moral compliance [25]. That is, moral expressions become authoritative, and therefore genuinely normative, to the degree that they both arouse such feelings and reveal such agreements, and also connect these feelings and recollections with moral action.

Moral ideas communicated without being socially rooted simply lack compelling authority. Such expressions are like inflated currency: because they possess little real authority, there is a tendency to use more and more of them in order to create hoped-for effects. Such language, unless it has become socially rooted, is experienced as disruptive, distracting, inflexible and overblown. Simply attempting to talk more about moral issues in business is not likely to make these conversations more weighty and authoritative. What is needed is to find ways of realistically connecting this language with the experiences and expectations of people involved in business.

Indeed, in an even more general effect, the resolution of organizational problems through cooperation becomes more difficult to the extent that managers shun moral talk. Cooperation may be gained in several ways. For example, it may be inspired by charismatic leadership or achieved by forceful commands. Charisma and command are, however, limited temporary devices for gaining cooperation. Many managers do not have the gift for charismatic leadership. In any case, such leadership is best exercised in relation to crises and not ordinary operations. Commands may achieve compliance, but a compliance that is half-hearted, foot-dragging and resentful. Cooperation is realized more enduringly and more fully by fostering commitments to shared moral values. Shared values provide a common vocabulary for identifying and resolving problems. Shared values constitute common cultures which provide the guidelines for action and the justifications for decisions [26].

It is impossible to foster a sense of ongoing community without invoking moral images and normative expectations. Moral terms provide the symbols of attachment and guidelines for interactions within communities [27]. In the absence of such images and norms, individuals are prone to defend their own interests more aggressively and with fewer compromises. Longer-range and wider conceptions of self-interest are likely to be abandoned. Without moral appeals to industry, organizational well-being, team work, craftsmanship and service, it is much more difficult to cultivate voluntary rather than regimented cooperation [28].

The nature of change interventions

Several factors must be taken into account by those who wish to reduce this avoidance of moral talk by managers. Those who wish to 'institutionalize ethics' in business, 'manage values in organizations', or gain 'the ethical edge' [29] must take into account the factors which give rise to this avoidance. It is impossible to foster greater moral responsibility by business people and organizations without also facilitating more open and direct conversations about these issues by managers.

First, business people will continue to shun open discussions of actual moral issues unless means are provided to allow for legitimate dissent by managers who will not be personally blamed, criticized, ostracized or punished for their views. From the perspective of the managers we interviewed, their organizations seemed to expect from them unquestioning loyalty and deference. Although many had privately spoken of their moral objections to the practices of other managers and their own firms, few had publicly voiced these concerns within their own organizations. Full discussions of moral issues are not likely to take place unless managers and workers feel they can openly voice arguments regarding policies and practices that will not be held against them when alternatives are adopted.

Business organizations often do not tolerate full, open debate of moral issues because they perceive dissent as assuming the form either of carping assaults or of factional divisiveness. Carping is a way of airing personal grievances and frustrations, often using moral expressions in order to find fault [30]. Ideally, managers ought to be able openly to voice dissent and then, once decisions have been made contrary to their views, either respectfully support such choices or formally protest. However, business organizations that stifle open discussions of moral concerns invite the carping they seek to avoid by limiting debate in the first place. Managers are most likely to complain, to express resentment, and to find personal fault in others if they feel they have no real opportunities to voice justifiable dissents.

Legitimate expressions of dissent may be articulated in ways that do not aggravate and reinforce factional divisiveness. Before considering recommendations for organizational change (about which various managers and workers are likely to have vested interests), it is useful to set aside time for all those involved to recognize the degree to which they both hold similar long-run objectives and value common ethical principles [31]. These exercises are valuable because they help to make shared commitments seem basic and the factional differences temporary and relative. In addition, factional differences are less likely to become contentious if these factions are accorded partial legitimacy as recognized functional subgroups within larger organizations. Finally, legitimate dissent is less likely to aggravate factional divisiveness if ground rules for debate and dissent include mutual consultations with all those immediately involved. These rules can help reduce the chances of discussions turning into empty posturing and/or irresolute harangues.

Second, if business people are going to overcome the avoidance of moral talk, then they must learn how to incorporate moral expressions and arguments into their exchanges. Learning how to talk ethics is neither as simple nor as difficult as it seems to be to many managers. Initially, managers must learn to avoid as much as possible the ordinary abuses of moral talk. In particular, efforts must be made to limit the degree to which moral talk is used for publicly extolling the virtues or excoriating the vices of other managers. Evaluations of personal moral worth ought to remain as private as possible. Furthermore, the use of moral expressions to rationalize and to express personal frustrations ought to be censored. In addition, the use of moral expression to take ideological postures ought to be minimized. Moral talk ought to be used primarily to identify problems, to consider issues, to advocate and criticize policies, and to justify and explain decisions.

Managers should recognize and learn to use several of the typical forms in which moral arguments are stated. An elementary knowledge of moral logics as applied to business matters is a useful skill not only for defending one's own argument, but also for identifying the weaknesses and strengths in the arguments of others. It is important, however, to recognize that verbal skill at talking ethics is primarily a rhetorical and discursive skill and not a matter of philosophical knowledge. Like the skill of elocution, learning how to talk ethics involves learning how to state and criticize moral arguments persuasively. What is critical is that managers are able to use moral reasoning to deal with issues they actually face in their lives and to influence others to consider carefully their positions.

Managers must regularly and routinely engage with each other in reflection and dialogue about their own experiences with moral issues. The attempt to overcome the avoidance of moral talk by managers by introducing them to formal philosophical language and logics not rooted in their social experiences is likely to fail. Philosophical ethics is indeed an instructive and critical tool that can be used to analyse moral arguments of business people and to propose creative solutions to perceived dilemmas. It is improbable, however, that many managers are likely to adopt philosophical discourse on a day-to-day basis to talk about moral issues. At best, this language might serve as a technical instrument, much like the specialized languages of corporate law and advanced accounting used by specialized experts in consultation with executives. Such technical use does not overcome the moral amnesia that infects ordinary communications among managers. To be compelling, moral discourse must be connected with, express, foster and strengthen managers' feelings of attachment, obligation, promises and agreements.

Moral ideas rarely possess compelling authority unless some group or groups of people so closely identify with these ideas as to become their articulate champions. Moral ideas are likely to gain widespread following by business people as smaller groups of managers and workers so closely identify with these ideas – which in turn express their own attachments, obligations and desires – that they champion them. This identification is most likely to occur where business people with existing feelings of community, due to professional, craft or organizational loyalties, begin to articulate their moral convictions and to discuss moral issues. It is precisely in these sorts of subgroups of people who have to work with each other as colleagues that managers will be willing to risk speaking candidly and see the benefits of such candour in fuller cooperation.

The role of senior managers in fostering such good conversation among managers in an organization cannot be overemphasized [32]. If they seek to provide moral leadership to an organization, senior managers must not only signal the importance they place on such conversations, but also demand that they take place. They need also to build such conversations into the fabric of organizational life through management mechanisms such as requiring that managers include in their annual plans a statement of the steps they will take to ensure that questionable practices are reviewed, or that new business proposals include an assessment of the ethical climate of any new business area into which entry is proposed [33].

Finally, interventions require patience. Open conversations of the kind we have been describing will, in the short run, be slow and time-consuming and thus reduce organizational efficiency. They will, in the short run, be awkward and fumbling and appear futile and thus they will be quite uncomfortable for managers used to smooth control of managerial discussions. Patience will be required to persevere until these short-run problems are overcome, until new norms emerge which encourage debate without carping and acrimony, until managers develop the skills necessary for efficient and reflective problem-solving with respect to moral issues, until moral voices and commitments are heard clearly and strongly throughout their organizations.

References and notes

1 Barnard, Chester *The Function of the Executive*, Cambridge, MA: Harvard University Press, 1938, p. 154; Breen, George E. 'Middle Management Morale in the 80s', *An AMA Survey Report*, New York, NY: The American Management Association, 1983; McCormick, Mark H. *What they don't teach you at Harvard Business School*, Toronto: Bantam Books, 1984, chapter 2.
2 de Tocqueville, Alexis *Democracy in America*, vol 2., translated by Reeve, Henry revised by Bowen, Francis, New York, NY: Mentor Books, 1945, pp. 129–132.
3 McCoy, Charles *Management of Values: The Ethical Differences in Corporate Policy and Performance*, Boston, MA: Pitman, 1985, pp. 8, 9, 16, 98.
4 Silk, Leonard and Vogel, David *Ethics and Profits: The Crisis of Confidence in American Business*, New York, NY: Simon and Schuster, 1976, chapter 8.
5 Solomon, Robert C. and Hanson, Kristine R. *It's Good Business*, New York, NY: Atheneum, 1985, p. xiv; see also Pastin, Mark *The Hard Problems of Management: Gaining the Ethics Edge*, San Francisco, CA: Jossey-Bass, 1986, Introduction, Part One.
6 Waters, James A., Bird, Frederick and Chant, Peter D. 'Everyday Moral Issues Experienced by Managers'. *Journal of Business Ethics*, 5, 1986; 373–384; Toffler, Barbara Lee, *Tough Choices: Managers Talk Ethics*, New York, NY: John Wiley,

1986; Kram, Kathy E., Yaeger, Peter C. and Reed, Gary 'Ethical Dilemmas in Corporate Context', paper presented at Academy of Management, August 1988; Derry, Robin 'Managerial Perceptions of Ethical Conflicts and Conceptions of Morality: A Qualitative Interview Study', paper presented at Academy of Management, August 1988.

7 Waters, James A. and Bird, Frederick B. 'The Moral Dimension of Organisational Culture'. *Journal of Business Ethics*, 1987; **6**, 18.

8 Habermas, Jurgen *The Theory of Communicative Action*, vol. I, translated by McCarthy, Thomas, Boston, MA: The Beacon Press, 1984, Part I, chapter 3.

9 Taylor, Mark L. *A Study of Corporate Ethical Policy Statements*, Dallas, TX: The Foundation of the Southwestern Graduate School of Banking, 1980.

10 Bird, Frederick and Waters, James A. 'The Nature of Managerial Moral Standards'. *Journal of Business Ethics*, 1987; **6**, 1–13.

11 Hegel, George Wilhelm Frederick *Philosophy of Right*, translated by Knox, T.M., London: Oxford University Press, 1967, pp. 93–103.

12 Aristotle, *The Nichomachean Ethics*, translated by Rhomson, J.A.R. Middlesex, UK. Penguin Books, 1953, Book VII; Winch, Peter *Ethics and Action*, London: Routledge and Kegan Paul, 1972, chapters 4 and 8.

13 Waters, Bird, and Chant, *op. cit.*; Bird, Frederick, Westey, Francis and Waters, James A. 'The Uses of Moral Talk: Why Do Managers Talk Ethics?' *Journal of Business Ethics*, **8**, 1989, pp. 75–89.

14 Nader, Ralph, Petkas, Peter and Blackwell, Kate (eds) *Whistle Blowing*, New York, NY: Grossman, 1972; Nielsen, Richard P. 'What Can Managers Do About Unethical Management?' *Journal of Business Ethics* 1987; **6**, pp. 309–320.

15 Kerr, Steven 'Integrity in Effective Leadership'. In: Srivastra, Suresh and Associates (eds) *Executive Integrity*, San Francisco, CA: Jossey-Bass, 1988.

16 Geertz, Clifford *The Interpretation of Cultures*, New York, NY: Basic Books, 1973, chapter 9.

17 Williamson, Oliver E. 'Transactional Cost Economics: The Governance of Contractural Relations'. *Journal of Law and Economics* 1980; 233–261.

18 Pastin, *op. cit.*, chapter 3; Silk and Vogel, *op. cit.*, chapter 2; Solomon and Hanson, *op. cit.*, p. 5; Kerr, *op. cit.*, p. 138.

19 Hirschman, Albert *Exit, Voice and Loyalty: Responses to Decline in Firms and States*, Cambridge, MA: Harvard University Press, 1970, chapter 7.

20 Kram, Yaeger, and Read, *op. cit.*, p. 28.

21 Friedman, Milton 'The Social Responsibility of Business is to Increase its Profit'. *New York Times Magazine*, 13 September 1970.

22 Waters and Bird, *op. cit.*, pp. 16–18.

23 Waters, Bird and Chant, *op. cit.*

24 Blake, Judith and Davis, Kingsley 'Norms, Values and Sanctions'. In: Wrong, Dennis and Gracey, Harry L. (eds) *Readings in Introductory Sociology*, New York, NY: Macmillan, 1967.

25 Durkheim, Emile *Suicide*, translated by Spaulding, John A. and Simpson, George New York, NY: The Free Press, 1974, chapter 2; Bird, Frederick 'Morality and Society: An Introduction to Comparative Sociological Study of Moralities', unpublished manuscript, 1988, chapter 4.

26 Weick, Karl E. 'Organisational Culture as a Source of High Reliability'. *California Management Review*, Winter 1987; **29**, 112–127.

27 Bernstein, Basil *Class Codes, and Control*, St Albans, NY: Palladin, 1973.

28 Westley, Frances and Bird, Frederick 'The Social Psychology of Organisational Commitment'. Unpublished paper, 1989.

29 Hanson, Kirk 'Ethics and Business: A Progress Report'. In: McCoy, Charles (ed)

Management of Values, Boston, MA: Pitman, 1985, pp. 280–288; Twining, Fred and McCoy, Charles 'How to Manage Values in Organisations', unpublished manuscript, 1987; Pastin, *op. cit.*
30 Bird, Westley and Waters, *op. cit.*
31 Twining and McCoy, *op. cit.*
32 Waters, James A. 'Integrity Management: Learning and Implementing Ethical Principles in the Workplace'. In: Srivastva, S. (ed) *Executive Integrity*, San Francisco, CA: Jossey-Bass, 1988.
33 Waters, James A. and Chant, Peter D. 'Internal Control of Management Integrity: Beyond Accounting Systems'. *California Management Review*, Spring 1982; **24**, 60–66.

Additional reading

For some excellent examples of positive results of managers not being morally mute, see Barbara Ley Toffler's *Tough Choices: Managers Talk Ethics* New York: John Wiley, 1986. Toffler interviews a series of high-ranking business people who openly discuss ethical issues.

Questions for discussion

● Referring to Figure 6.1, where would you place: yourself; your managing director; your subordinates? What problems, if any, are caused by the relations between moral action and speech in your organization?
● What problems has moral muteness caused in your organization?

Chapter 7

Whistleblowing: its moral justification

Few subjects are more calculated to raise corporate blood pressure more surely than whistleblowing, not least because it smacks of disloyalty. However, with today's management emphases on teamwork and cooperation it also reflects poorly on the quality of staff motivation.

The results of whistleblowing can be very damaging to a company and it may therefore come as no surprise to learn that none of our researches has uncovered a single case of a declared whistleblower avoiding reprisal of some kind.

It may be for this reason that a law has been enacted in the USA to protect whistleblowers; or it may also be, in part, a response to the concerns expressed in this chapter. We know of no such legislation in Europe at present.

As a result of the new US law, auditor Christopher Urda was awarded £3.75 million for disclosing that his company, the Singer Corporation, had cheated the Pentagon out of £38.5 million over eight years [1]. The award was made under legislation known as the Whistleblower's Charter, which rewards citizens who report corporate dishonesty. Mr Urda is quoted as saying: 'I was just an ordinary guy, but it was the right thing to do'.

In the UK, whistleblowing has received government 'blessing' when it is used for signalling health and safety concerns. However, leaving legal requirements aside, it is advisable for companies to take whistleblowing seriously. There can be few events which can be so jeopardizing to corporate careers, and so damaging in terms of executive time. In some cases, the result of whistleblowing has been to create a 'black hole' for management resources.

Most executives would prefer to avoid managing in public, which is the almost inevitable result of whistleblowing. Therefore it is important for prudent managers to study the ways that whistleblowing may come about, and to be aware of the principles that constitute a defence for whistleblowing.

I think it is important too that managers consider the implications of the guidance to whistleblowers included in this chapter – Not least because it may provide advice in the formulation of a 'safety valve' or internal whistleblowing mechanism, to help deal with ethical concerns before these result in the need to go outside the organization.

Reference

1 *London Evening Standard*, 6 August, 1992.

Whistleblowing: its moral justification
Gene G. James

Whistleblowing may be defined as the attempt by an employee or former employee of an organization to disclose what he or she believes to be wrong-doing in or by the organization. Like blowing a whistle to call attention to a thief, whistleblowing is an effort to make others aware of practices one considers illegal or immoral. If the wrong-doing is reported to someone higher in the organization, the whistleblowing may be said to be *internal*. If the wrong-doing is reported to outside individuals or groups such as reporters, public interest groups or regulatory agencies, the whistleblowing is *external*. If the harm being reported is primarily to the whistleblower alone, such as sexual harassment, the whistleblowing may be said to be *personal*. If it is primarily harm to other people that is being reported, the whistleblowing is *impersonal*. Most whistleblowing is done by people currently employed by the organization on which they are blowing the whistle. However, people who have left the organization may also blow the whistle. The former may be referred to as *current* whistleblowing; the latter as *alumni* whistleblowing. If the whistle-blower discloses his or her identity, the whistleblowing may be said to be *open*; if the person's identity is not disclosed, the whistleblowing is *anonymous*.

Whistleblowers almost always experience retaliation. If they work for private firms and are not protected by unions or professional organizations, they are likely to be fired. They are also likely to receive damaging letters of recommendation and may even be blacklisted so they cannot find work in their profession. If they are not fired, they are still likely to be transferred, given less interesting work, denied salary increases and promotions or demoted. Their professional competence is usually attacked. They are said to be unqualified to judge, misinformed, etc. Since their actions seem to threaten both the organization and their fellow employees, attacks on their personal lives are also frequent. They are called traitors, rat finks, disgruntled, known trouble-makers, people who make an issue out of nothing, self-serving and publicity seekers. Their lifestyles, sex lives and mental stability may be questioned. Physical assaults, abuse of their families, and even murder are not unknown as retaliation for whistleblowing. . . .

The moral justification of whistleblowing

Under what conditions, if any, is whistleblowing morally justified? Some people have argued that whistleblowing is never justified because employees have absolute obligations of confidentiality and loyalty to the organization for which they work. People who argue this way see no difference between employees who reveal trade secrets by selling information to competitors and whistleblowers who disclose activities harmful to others [1]. This position is similar to another held by some business people and economists that the sole obligation of corporate executives is to make a profit for stockholders. If this were true, corporate executives would have no obligations to the public. However, no matter what one's special obligations, one is never exempt from the general obligations we have to our fellow human beings. One of the most fundamental of these obligations is not to cause avoidable harm to others. Corporate executives are no more exempt from this obligation than other people.

Just as the special obligations of corporate executives to stockholders cannot override their more fundamental obligations to others, the special obligation of employees to employers cannot override their more fundamental obligations. In particular, obligations of confidentiality and loyalty cannot take precedence over the fundamental duty to act in ways that prevent unnecessary harm to others. Agreements to keep something secret have no moral standing unless that which is to be kept secret is itself morally justifiable. For example, no one can have an obligation to keep secret a conspiracy to murder someone, because murder is an immoral act. It is for this reason also that employees have a legal obligation to report an employer who has committed or is about to commit a felony. Nor can one justify participation in an illegal or immoral activity by arguing that one was merely following orders. Democratic governments repudiated this type of defence at Nuremberg.

It has also been argued that whistleblowing is always justified because it is an exercise of the right to freedom of speech. However, the right to free speech is not absolute. An example often used to illustrate this is that one does not have the right to shout 'Fire!' in a crowded theatre because it is likely to cause a panic in which people may be injured. Analogously, one may have a right to speak out on a particular subject, in the sense that there are no contractual agreements which prohibit one from doing so, but it nevertheless may be the case that it would be morally wrong for one to do so because it would harm innocent people, such as one's fellow workers and stockholders who are not responsible for the wrong-doing being disclosed. The mere fact that one has the right to speak out does not mean that one ought to do so in every case. But this kind of consideration cannot create an absolute prohibition against whistleblowing, because one must weigh the harm to fellow workers and stockholders caused by the disclosure against the harm caused to others by allowing the organizational wrong to continue. Furthermore, the moral principle that one must consider all people's interests equally prohibits giving priority to one's own group. There is, in fact, justification for not giving as much weight to the interests of the stockholders as to those of the public, because stockholders investing in corporate firms do so with the knowledge that they undergo financial risk if management acts in imprudent, illegal or immoral ways. Similarly, if the employees of a company know that it is engaged in illegal or immoral activities and do not take action, including whistleblowing, to terminate the activities, then they too must bear some of the guilt for the actions. To the extent that these conditions hold, they nullify the principle that one ought to refrain from whistleblowing because speaking out would cause harm to the organization. Unless it can be shown that the harm to fellow workers and stockholders would be *significantly greater* than the harm caused by the organizational wrong-doing, the obligation to avoid unnecessary harm to the public must take precedence. Moreover, as argued above, this is true even when there are specific agreements which prohibit one from speaking out, because such agreements are morally void if the organization is engaged in illegal or immoral activities. In that case one's obligation to the public overrides one's obligation to maintain secrecy.

The criteria for justifiable whistleblowing

The argument in the foregoing section is an attempt to show that, unless special circumstances hold, one has an obligation to blow the whistle on illegal or immoral actions – an obligation that is grounded on the fundamental human duty to avoid preventable harm to others. In this section I shall attempt to spell out in greater detail the conditions under which blowing the whistle is morally obligatory. Since Richard De George has previously attempted to do this, I shall proceed by examining the criteria he has suggested [2].

De George believes that there are three conditions that must hold for whistleblowing to be morally permissible and two additional conditions that must hold for it to be morally obligatory. The three conditions that must hold for it to be morally permissible are:

1 The firm, through its product or policy, will do serious and considerable harm to the public, whether in the person of the user of its product, an innocent bystander or the general public.
2 Once an employee identifies a serious threat to the user of a product or to the general public, he or she should report it to his or her immediate superior and make his or her moral concern known. Unless he or she does so, the act of whistleblowing is not clearly justifiable.
3 If one's immediate superior does nothing effective about the concern or complaint, the employee should exhaust the internal procedures and possibilities within the firm. This usually will involve taking the matter up the managerial ladder, and if necessary – and possible – to the board of directors.

The two additional conditions which De George thinks must hold for whistleblowing to be morally obligatory are:

4 The whistleblower must have, or have accessible, documented evidence that would convince a reasonable, impartial observer that one's view of the situation is correct and that the company's product or practice poses a serious and likely danger to the public or to the user of the product.

5 The employee must have a good reason to be believe that by going public the necessary changes will be brought about. The chance of being successful must be worth the risk one takes and the danger to which one is exposed [3].

De George intends for the proposed criteria to apply to situations in which a firm's policies or products cause physical harm to people. Indeed, the first criterion he proposes is intended to restrict the idea of harm even more narrowly to threats of serious bodily harm or death.

De George apparently believes that situations which involve threats of serious bodily harm or death are so different from those involving other types of harm that the kind of considerations which justify whistleblowing in the former situations could not possibly justify it in the latter. Thus, he states, referring to the former type of whistleblowing: 'As a paradigm, we shall take a set of fairly clear-cut cases, namely, those in which serious bodily harm – including possibly death – threatens either the users of a product or innocent bystanders' [4].

One problem in restricting discussion to clear-cut cases of this type, regarding which one can get almost universal agreement that whistleblowing is justifiable, is that it leaves us with no guidance when we are confronted with more usual situations involving other types of harm. Although De George states that his 'analysis provides a model for dealing with other kinds of whistleblowing as well' [5], his criteria in fact provide no help in deciding whether one should blow the whistle in situations involving such wrongs as sexual harassment, violations of privacy, industrial espionage, insider trading and a variety of other harmful actions.

No doubt, one of the reasons De George restricts his treatment the way he does is to avoid having to define harm. This is indeed a problem. For if we fail to put any limitations on the idea of harm, it seems to shade into the merely offensive or distasteful and thus offer little help in resolving moral problems. But on the other hand, if we restrict harm to physical injury, as De George does, it then applies to such a limited range of cases that it is of minimal help in most of the moral situations which confront us. One way of dealing with this problem is by correlated harm with the violations of fundamental human rights such as rights to due process, privacy and property, in addition to the right to freedom from physical harm. Thus, not only situations which involve threats of physical harm but also those involving actions such as sexual harassment which violates the right to privacy and causes psychological harm, compiling unnecessary records on people and financial harm due to fraudulent actions are situations which may justify whistleblowing.

A still greater problem with De George's analysis is that, even in cases where there is a threat of serious physical harm or death, he believes that this only makes the whistleblowing morally permissible, rather than creating a strong *prima facie* obligation in favour of whistleblowing. His primary reasons for believing this seem to be those stated in criterion 5. Unless one has reason to believe that the whistleblowing will eliminate the harm, and the cost to oneself is not too great, he does not believe that whistleblowing is morally obligatory. He maintains that this is true even when the person involved is a professional whose code of ethics requires her or him to put the public good ahead of private good. He argued in an earlier article [6], for example, that:

The myth that ethics has no place for engineering has . . . at least in some corners of the engineering profession . . . been put to rest. Another myth, however, is emerging to take its place – the myth of the engineer as moral hero . . . The zeal . . . however, has gone too far, piling the moral responsibility upon moral responsibility on the shoulders of the engineer. This emphasis . . . is misplaced. Though engineers are members of a profession that holds public safety paramount, we cannot reasonably expect engineers to be willing to sacrifice their jobs each day for principle and to have the whistle ever at their sides.

He contends that engineers only have the obligation 'to do their jobs as best they can' [7]. This includes reporting concerns about the safety of products to management, but does *not* include 'the obligation to insist that their perceptions or . . . standards be accepted. They are not paid to do that, they are not expected to do that, and they have no moral or ethical obligation to do that' [8].

To take a specific case, De George maintains that even though some Ford engineers had grave misgivings about the safety of the Pinto gas tanks and several people had been killed when tanks exploded after rear-end crashes, the engineers did not have an obligation to make their misgivings public. De George's remarks are puzzling because the Pinto case would seem to be exactly the kind of clear-cut situation which he says provides the paradigm for justified whistleblowing. Indeed, if the Ford engineers did not have an obligation to blow the whistle, it is difficult to see what cases could satisfy his criteria. They knew that if Pintos were struck from the rear by vehicles travelling thirty miles per hour or more, their gas tanks were likely to explode, seriously injuring or killing people. They also knew that if they did not speak out, Ford would continue to market the Pinto. Finally they were members of a profession whose code of ethics requires them to put public safety above all other obligations.

De George's remarks suggest that the only obligation the Ford engineers had was to do what management expected of them by complying with their job descriptions and that so long as they did that, no one should find fault with them or hold them accountable for what the company did. It is true that when people act within the framework of an organization, it is often difficult to assess individual responsibility. But the fact that one is acting as a member of an organization does not relieve one of moral obligations. The exact opposite is true. Because most of the actions we undertake in organizational settings have more far-reaching consequences than those we undertake in our personal lives, our moral obligation to make sure that we do not harm others is *increased* when we act as a member of an organization. The amount of moral responsibility one has for any particular organizational action depends on the extent to which the consequences of the action are foreseeable and one's own action or failure to act is a cause of consequences. It is important to include failure to act here, because frequently it is easier to determine what will happen if we do not act than if we do, and because we are morally responsible for not preventing harm as well as for causing it.

De George thinks that the Ford engineers would have had an obligation to blow the whistle only if they believed doing so would have been likely to prevent the harm involved. But we have an obligation to warn others of danger even if we believe they will ignore our warnings. This is especially true if the danger will come about partly because we did not speak out. De George admits that the public has a right to know about dangerous products. If that is true, then those who have knowledge about such products have an obligation to inform the public. This is not usurping the public's right to decide acceptable risk; it is simply supplying people with the information necessary to exercise that right.

De George's comments also seem to imply that in general it is not justifiable to ask people to blow the whistle if it would threaten their jobs. It is true that we would not necessarily be justified in demanding this if it would place them or their families' lives in danger, but this is *not* true if only their jobs are at stake. It is especially not true if the people involved are executives and professionals, who are accorded respect and high salaries, not only because of their specialized knowledge and skills, but also because of the special responsibilities we entrust to them. Frequently, as in the case of engineers, they also subscribe to codes of ethics which require them to put the public good ahead of their own or the organization's good. Given all this, it is difficult to understand why De George does not think the Ford engineers had an obligation to blow the whistle in the Pinto case.

The belief that whistleblowing is an act of disloyalty and disobedience seems to underlie De George's second and third criteria for justifiable whistleblowing. The whistleblower must have first reported the wrong-doing to his or her immediate superior and, if nothing was done, have taken the complaint as far up the managerial ladder as possible. Some of the problems with adopting these suggestions as general criteria for justified whistleblowing are:

1 It may be one's immediate supervisor who is responsible for the wrong-doing.

2 Organizations differ considerably in both their procedures for reporting and how they respond to wrong-doing.
3 Not all wrong-doing is of the same type. If the wrong-doing is of a type that threatens people's health or safety, exhausting channels of protest within the organization may result in unjustified delay in correcting the problem.
4 Exhausting internal channels of protest may give people time to destroy evidence needed to substantiate one's allegations.
5 Finally, it may expose the employee to possible retaliation against which he or she might have some protection if the wrong-doing were reported to an external agency.

His fourth criterion, that the whistleblower have documented evidence which would convince an impartial observer, is intended to reduce incidences of whistleblowing by curbing those who would blow the whistle on a mere suspicion of wrong-doing. It is true that one should not make claims against an organization based on mere guesses or hunches, because if they turn out to be false one will have illegitimately harmed the organization and innocent people affiliated with it. But De George also wishes to curb whistleblowing, because he thinks that if it were widespread, this would reduce its effectiveness. De George's fourth and fifth criteria are, therefore, deliberately formulated in such a way that if they are satisfied 'people will only rarely have the moral obligation to blow the whistle' [9].

De George's fear, that unless strict criteria of justification are applied to whistleblowing it might be widespread, is unjustified. If it is true, as he claims, that there is a strong tradition in America against 'ratting', that most workers consider themselves to have an obligation of loyalty to their organization, and that whistleblowers are commonly looked upon as traitors, then it is unlikely that whistleblowing will ever be a widespread practice. De George believes that if one is unable to document wrong-doing without recourse to illegal or immoral means, this relieves one of the obligation to blow the whistle. He argues [10]:

> One does not have an obligation to blow the whistle simply because of one's hunch, guess or personal assessment of possible danger, if supporting evidence and documentation are not available. One may, of course, have the obligation to attempt to get evidence if the harm is serious. But if it is unavailable – or unavailable without using illegal or immoral means – then one does not have the obligation to blow the whistle.

I have already indicated above that I do not think one has an obligation to blow the whistle on possible wrong-doing on the basis of a mere guess or hunch because this might harm innocent people. But if one has good reasons to believe that the wrong-doing is occurring even though one cannot document it without engaging in illegal or immoral actions, this does not relieve one of the obligation to blow the whistle. Indeed, if this were true one would almost never have an obligation to blow the whistle, because employees are rarely in a position to satisfy De George's fourth criterion that the whistleblower 'must have, or have accessible, documented evidence that would convince a reasonable, impartial observer that one's view of the situation is correct'. Indeed, it is precisely because employees are rarely ever in a position to supply this documentation without themselves resorting to illegal or immoral actions that they have an obligation to inform others who have the authority to investigate the possible wrong-doing. The attempt to secure such evidence on one's own may even thwart the gathering of evidence by the proper authorities. Thus, instead of De George's criterion being a necessary condition for justifiable whistleblowing, the attempt to satisfy it would prevent its occurrence. One has an obligation to gather as much evidence as one can so that authorities will have probable cause for investigation. But, if one is convinced the wrong-doing is occurring, one has an obligation to report it even if one is unable adequately to document it. One will then have done one's duty even if the authorities ignore the report.

The claim that it is usually necessary for the whistleblower to speak out openly for whistleblowing to be morally justified implies that anonymous whistleblowing is rarely, if ever, justified. Is this true? It has been argued that anonymous whistleblowing is never justified because it violates the right of people to face their accusers. But, as Frederick Elliston [11] has pointed out, although people should be protected from false accusations, it is not necessary for the identity of whistleblowers to be known to accomplish this. 'It is only necessary that accusations be properly investigated, proven true or false and the results widely disseminated'.

Some people believe that because the whistleblower's motive is not known in anonymous whistleblowing, this suggests that the motive is not praise-worthy and in turn raises questions about the moral justification of anonymous whistleblowing. De George apparently believes this, because in addition to stating that only public whistleblowing by previously loyal employees who display their sincerity by their willingness to suffer is likely to be effective and morally justified, he mentions, at several places, that he is restricting his attention to whistleblowing for moral reasons. For example, he states that 'the only motivation for whistleblowing we shall consider . . . is moral motivation' [12]. However, in my opinion, concern with the whistle-blower's motive is irrelevant to the moral justification of whistleblowing. It is a red herring which takes the attention away from the genuine moral issue involved: whether the whistleblower's claim that the organization is doing something harmful to others is true. If the claim is true, then the whistleblowing is justified regardless of the motive. If the whistleblower's motives are not moral, that makes the act less praiseworthy, but this is a totally different issue. As De George states, whistleblowing is a 'practical matter'. But precisely because this is true, the justification of whistleblowing turns on the truth or falsity of disclosure, not on the motives of the whistleblower.

Anonymous whistleblowing is justified because it can both protect the whistleblower from unjust attacks and prevent those who are accused of wrong-doing from shifting the issue away from their wrong-doing by engaging in an irrelevant *ad hominem* attack on the whistleblower. Preoccupation with the whistleblower's motive facilitates this type of irrelevant diversion. It is only if the accusations prove false or inaccurate that motives of the whistleblower have any moral relevance. For it is only then, and not before, that the whistleblower rather than the organization should be put on trial.

The view that whistleblowing is *prima facie* wrong because it goes against the tradition that 'ratting' is wrong is indefensible because it falsely assumes both that we have a general obligation not to inform others about wrong-doing and that this outweighs our fundamental obligation to prevent harm to others. The belief that whistleblowers should suffer in order to show their moral sincerity, on the other hand, is not only false and irrelevant to the issue of the moral justification of whistleblowing, but is perverse. There are *no* morally justifiable reasons why a person who discloses wrong-doing should be put at risk or made to suffer. The contradictory view stated by De George that 'one does not have an obligation to put oneself at serious risk without some compensating advantage to be gained' [13] is also false. Sometimes doing one's duty requires one to undertake certain risks. However, both individuals and society in general should attempt to reduce these risks to the minimum.

In the next section I consider some of the actions whistleblowers can take both to make whistleblowing effective and to avoid unnecessary risk. In the last section I briefly consider some of the ways in which society can reduce the need for whistleblowing.

Factors to consider in whistleblowing

Since whistleblowing usually involves conflicting moral obligations and a wide range of variables and has far-reaching consequences for everyone concerned, the following is not intended as a recipe or how-to-do list. Like all complicated moral actions, whistleblowing cannot be reduced to such a list. Nevertheless, some factors can be stated which whistleblowers should consider in disclosing wrong-doing if they are also to act prudently and effectively.

Make sure the situation is one that warrants whistleblowing

Make sure the situation is one that involves illegal or immoral actions which harm others, rather than one in which you would be disclosing personal matters, trade secrets, customer lists or similar material. If disclosure would involve the latter as well, make sure that the harm to be avoided is great enough to offset the harm from the latter.

Examine your motives

Although it is not necessary for the whistleblower's motive to be praiseworthy for whistleblowing to be morally justified, examining your motives can help in deciding whether the situation is one that warrants whistleblowing.

Verify and document your information

Try to obtain evidence that will stand up in court or regulatory hearings. If this is not possible, gather as much information as you can and indicate where and how additional information might be obtained. If the *only* way you could obtain either of these types of information would be through illegal procedures, make sure the situation is one in which the wrong-doing is so great that it warrants this risk. Although morality requires that in general we obey the law, it sometimes requires that we break it. Daniel Ellsberg's release of the Pentagon papers was a situation of this type, in my opinion. If you do have to use illegal methods to obtain information, try to find alternative sources for any evidence you uncover so that it will not be challenged in legal hearings. Keep in mind also that if you use illegal methods to obtain information you are opening yourself to *ad hominem* attacks and possible prosecution. In general, illegal methods should be avoided unless substantial harm to others is involved.

Determine the type of wrong-doing involved and to whom it should be reported

Determining the exact nature of the wrong-doing can help you both decide what kind of evidence to obtain and to whom it should be reported. For example, if the wrong-doing consists of illegal actions such as submission of false test reports to government agencies, bribery of public officials, racial or sexual discrimination, violation of safety, health or pollution laws, then determining the nature of the law being violated will help indicate which agencies have authority to enforce the law. If, on the other hand, the wrong-doing is not illegal but is nevertheless harmful to the public, determining this will help you decide whether you have an obligation to publicize the actions and if so, how to go about it.

The best place to report this type of wrong-doing is usually to a public interest group. Such an organization is more likely than the press to (1) be concerned about and advise the whistleblower how to avoid retaliation; (2) maintain confidentiality if that is desirable; and (3) investigate the allegations to try to substantiate them, rather than sensationalizing then by turning the issue into a personality dispute. If releasing information to the press is the best remedy for the wrong-doing, the public interest group can help with or do this.

State your allegations in an appropriate way

Be as specific as possible without being unintelligible. If you are reporting a violation of a law to a government agency and it is possible to do so, include technical data necessary for experts to verify the wrong-doing. If you are disclosing wrong-doing which does not require technical data to substantiate it, still be as specific as possible in stating the type of illegal or harmful activity involved, who is being harmed, and how.

Stick to the facts

Avoid name-calling, slander and being drawn into a mud-slinging contest. As Peter Raven-Hansen wisely points out [14]: 'One of the most important points . . . is to focus on the disclosure . . . This rule applies even when the whistleblower believes that certain individuals are responsible . . . The disclosure itself usually leaves a trail for others to follow to the miscreants'. Sticking to the facts also helps the whistleblower minimize retaliation.

Decide whether the whistleblowing should be internal or external

Familiarize yourself with all available internal channels for reporting wrong-doing and obtain as much data as you can both on how people who have used these channels were treated by the organization and what was done about the problems they reported. If people who have reported the wrong-doing in the past have been treated fairly and the problems corrected, use internal channels. If not, find out which external agencies would be the most appropriate to contact. Try to find out also how these agencies have treated whistleblowers, how much aid and protection they have given them, etc.

Decide whether the whistleblowing should be open or anonymous

If you intend to blow the whistle anonymously, decide whether partial or total anonymity is required. Also, document the wrong-doing as thoroughly as possible. Finally, since anonymity may be difficult to preserve, anticipate what you will do if your identity becomes known.

Decide whether current or alumni whistleblowing is required

Sometimes it is advisable to resign one's position and obtain another before blowing the whistle. This is because alumni whistleblowing helps protect one from being fired, receiving damaging letters of recommendation, or even being blacklisted in one's profession. However, changing jobs should not be thought of as an alternative to whistleblowing. If one is aware of harmful practices, one has a moral obligation to try to do something about them, which cannot be escaped by changing one's job or location. Many times people who think the wrong-doing involved is personal, harming only them, respond to a situation by simply trying to remove themselves from it. They believe that 'personal whistleblowing is, in general, morally permitted but not morally required' [15]. For example, a female student subjected to sexual harassment and fearful that she will receive low grades and poor letters of recommendation if she complains, may simply change departments or schools. However, tendencies towards wrong-doing are rarely limited to specific victims. By not blowing the whistle the student allows a situation to exist in which other students are likely to be harassed also.

Make sure you follow proper guidelines in reporting the wrong-doing

If you are not careful to follow any guidelines that have been established by organizations or external agencies for a particular type of whistleblowing, including using the proper forms, meeting deadlines, etc., wrong-doers may escape detection or punishment because of technicalities.

Consult a lawyer

Lawyers are advisable at almost every stage of whistleblowing. They can help determine if the wrong-doing violates the law, aid in documenting it, inform you of any laws you might break in documenting it, assist in deciding to whom to report it, make sure reports are filed correctly and promptly and help protect you from retaliation. If you cannot afford a lawyer, talk with an appropriate public interest group that may be able to help. However, lawyers frequently view problems within a narrow legal framework and decisions to blow the whistle are moral decisions, so in the final analysis you will have to rely on your own judgement.

Anticipate and document retaliation

Although not as certain as Newton's law of motion that for every action there is an equal reaction, whistleblowers whose identities are known can expect retaliation. Furthermore it may be difficult to keep one's identity secret. Thus, whether the whistleblowing is open or anonymous, personal or impersonal, internal or external, current or alumni, one should anticipate retaliation. One should, therefore protect oneself by documenting every step of the whistle-blowing with letters, tape recordings of meetings, etc. Without this documentation, the whistleblower may find that regulatory agencies and courts are of little help in preventing or redressing retaliation.

Beyond whistleblowing

What can be done to eliminate the wrong-doing which gives rise to whistleblowing? One solution would be to give whistleblowers greater legal protection. Another would be to try to change the nature of organizations so as to diminish the need for whistleblowing. These solutions of course are not mutually exclusive.

Many people are opposed to legislation to protect whistleblowers because they think it is unwarranted interference with the right to freedom of contract. However, if the right to freedom of contract is to be consistent with the public interest, it cannot serve as a shield for wrong-doing. It does this when threat of dismissal prevents people from blowing the whistle. The right of employers to dismiss at will has been previously restricted by labour laws which prevent employers from dismissing employees for union activities. It is ironic that we have restricted the right of employers to fire employees who are pursuing their economic self-interest, but allowed them to fire employees acting in the public interest. The right of employers to dismiss employees in the interest of efficiency should be balanced against the right of the public to know about illegal, dangerous and unjust practices of organizations. The most effective way to achieve this goal would be to pass a federal law protecting whistleblowers.

Laws protecting whistleblowers have also been opposed on the grounds that: (1) employees would use them as an excuse to mask poor performance; (2) they would create an 'informer ethos'; and (3) they would take away the autonomy of business, strangling it in red tape.

The first objection is illegitimate because only those employees who could show that an act of whistleblowing preceded their being penalized or dismissed, and that their employment records were adequate up to the time of the whistleblowing, could seek relief under the law.

The second objection is more formidable but nevertheless invalid. A society that encourages snooping, suspicion and mistrust is not most people's idea of the good society. Laws which encourage whistleblowing for self-interested reasons, such as the federal tax law which pays informers part of any money that is collected, could help bring about such a society [16]. However, laws protecting whistleblowers from being penalized or dismissed are quite different. They do not reward the whistleblower; they merely protect him or her from unjust retaliation. It is unlikely that federal or state laws of this type would promote an informer society.

The third objection is also unfounded. Laws protecting whistleblowers would not require any positive duties on the part of organizations – only the negative duty of not retaliating against employees who speak out in the public interest.

However, not every act of apparent whistleblowing should be protected. If the whistleblower's accusation turn out to be false and it can be shown that she or he had no probable reasons for assuming wrong-doing, then the individual should not be shielded from being penalized or dismissed. Both of these conditions should be satisfied before this is allowed to occur. People who can show that they had probable reasons for believing that wrong-doing existed should be protected even if their accusations turn out to be false. If the accusation has not been disproved, the burden of proof should be on the organization to prove that it is false. If it has been investigated and proven false, then the burden of proof should be on the individual to show that she or he has probable reasons for believing wrong-doing existed. If it is shown that the individual did not have probable reasons for believing the wrong-doing existed, and the damage to the organization from the false charge is great, it should be allowed to sue or seek other restitution. Since these provisions would impose some risks on potential whistleblowers, they would reduce the possibility of frivolous action. If, on the other hand, it is found that the whistleblower had probable cause for the whistleblowing and the organization has penalized or fired him or her, then that person should be reinstated, awarded damages or both. If there is further retaliation, additional sizeable damages should be awarded.

What changes should be made in organizations to prevent the need for whistleblowing? Some of the suggestions which have been made are that organizations develop effective internal channels for reporting wrong-doing, reward people with salary increases and promotions for using these channels, and appoint senior executives, board members, ombudspersons, etc. whose primary obligations would be to investigate and eliminate organizational wrong-doing. These changes could be undertaken by organizations on their own or mandated by law. Other changes which might be mandated are requiring that certain kinds of records be kept, assessing larger fines for illegal actions, and making executives and other professionals personally liable for filing false reports, knowingly marketing dangerous products, failing to monitor how policies are being implemented, and so forth. Although these reforms could do much to reduce the need for whistleblowing, given human nature it is highly unlikely that this need can ever be totally eliminated. Therefore, it is important to have laws which protect whistleblowers and for us to state as clearly as we can both the practical problems and moral issues pertaining to whistleblowing.

References and notes

1 For a more detailed discussion of this argument, see James, G.G. 'Whistleblowing: Its Nature and Justification'. *Philosophy in Context*, 1980; **10**.
2 See De George, Richard T. *Business Ethics*, 2nd edn, New York: Macmillian, 1986. Earlier versions of De George criteria can be found in the first edition (1982), and in 'Ethical Responsibilities of Engineers in Large Organizations'. *Business & Professional Ethics Journal*, Fall 1981; **1**.
3 De George, Richard T. *Business Ethics*, *op. cit.*, pp. 230–234.
4 *Ibid.*, p. 223.
5 *Ibid.*, p. 237.
6 De George, Richard T. 'Ethical Responsibilities of Engineers in Large Organizations'. *Business and Professional Ethics Journal*, 1981; **1**, 1.
7 *Ibid.*, p. 5.
8 *Ibid.*
9 De George, Richard T. *Business Ethics*, *op. cit.*, p. 235.
10 *Ibid.*, p. 234.
11 Elliston, Frederick A. 'Anonymous Whistleblowing'. *Business & Professional Ethics Journal*, Winter 1982; **1**.
12 De George, Richard T. *Business Ethics*, *op. cit.*, p. 235.
13 *Ibid.*, p. 234.
14 Raven-Hansen, Peter 'Dos and Don'ts for Whistleblowers: Planning for Trouble'. *Technology Review* May 1980; 30. My discussion in this section is heavily indebted to this article.
15 De George, Richard T. *Business Ethics*, *op. cit.*, p. 222.

16 People who blow the whistle on tax evaders in fact rarely receive any money because the law leaves payment to the discretion of the Internal Revenue Service.

Additional reading

Marcia P. Miceli and Janet P. Near have published an authoritative book on the subject entitled *Blowing the Whistle: Organizational and Legal Implications for Companies and Employees* (New York: Lexington Books, 1992). It is written for both managers who want to respond to employees' concerns and employees who are considering blowing the whistle. The authors present a model of the whistleblowing process and discuss the relevant variables. The consequences of whistleblowing and practical implications are discussed.

One article which is particularly well-suited to group discussions is 'The case of the willful whistle-blower' by Sally Seymour (*Harvard Business Review*, **66**, January-February 1988 pp. 103–9). An employee of a firm that designs nuclear reactors blows the whistle about a flaw that had been known by the company for years but hidden away. The company is forced to explain its past actions and to deal with the whistleblower. In addition to the case details, five experts comment on what they would have done.

A more philosophical approach to the topic is taken by Mike W. Martin in his paper 'Whistleblowing: professionalism, personal life, and shared responsibility for safety in engineering' (*Business & Professional Ethics Journal*, **11**, 1992; 21–40. He discusses the moral relevance of personal life to professional duty.

Also see the paper by Boisjoly *et al.* 'Roger Boisjoly and the Challenger disaster: the ethical dimension' discussed at the end of Chapter 3.

Questions for discussion

- With reference to a whistleblowing case that you are familiar with (e.g. one within your organization or one covered in the media): Was blowing the whistle the best action that the employee could take? Was the organization's response ethical? Did the whistleblowing result in an overall net benefit for society?
- In your organization, what norms support the need for whistleblowing? What should be done by the organization to eliminate the need for whistleblowing?

Chapter 8

The ethics of advertising and sponsorship

Anyone who has worked in business organizations or who has helped them deal with ethical issues soon learns that the specific challenges thrown up in the marketing area are amongst the most taxing. In particular, discussions on the ethics of advertising generally give rise to strong feelings.

Professor Mahoney points out that Dr Johnson once wrote that 'Promise, large promise, is the soul of an advertisement'. He feels this should alert us, as well as any other description of advertising, to what might be regarded as the major ethical aspects of advertising: should advertising make the promises it does make? And does it deliver on its promises?

It is important that special attention is given to particular aspects of commercial operations in any discussion of business ethics.

In most companies, special attention would normally be given to areas such as purchasing, auditing and marketing in any arrangements for dealing with ethical behaviour. Purchasing, because its practitioners are exposed to blandishments from unscrupulous suppliers often aimed at clouding their professional judgement. Auditing, and for that matter accountancy, where practitioners may be encouraged to be 'creative' in order to avoid, and in some regrettable cases, evade taxation.

By the way, it is becoming more common for conflicts of interest to place an executive in the extremely difficult position of having to choose between the dictates of his/her profession and those of management.

Many years of working with business executives have shown that marketing managers are exposed to specific ethical pressures which can pose special difficulties. For example, it is not unusual to find marketing managers agreeing with the suggestion that if a competitor's marketing plans should come into their possession anonymously, they would have no compunction in using this data. Indeed, some have gone so far in interviews as to declare that their job requires that they should make full use of such information.

Yet the same individuals claimed they would be very suspicious if a sum of money arrived on their desks in the same way, and most would report it.

Perhaps the principal message in Professor Mahoney's paper is that marketing professionals and their supervisors occupy a special role that requires them to pay particular attention to the ethics of what they do; not least because it is entirely possible for advertising to be completely legal and yet highly questionable at the same time.

So much of advertising and sponsorship can take place in that grey area of corporate operations where unethical behaviour may be rewarded, or at least condoned, because it may generate short-term benefits. This means that marketing executives carry a particular responsibility for safeguarding the ethos of the organization.

Advertising and sponsorship
Jack Mahoney

Dr Johnson once wrote: 'Promise, large promise, is the soul of an advertisement'. And I suppose that alerts us as well as any other description of advertising to what might be regarded in summary as the major ethical aspects of advertising: should advertising make the promises it does make? And does it deliver on its promises?

The economic case for advertising is fairly clear when it is considered as a necessary component of the competitive market system. It draws attention to goods and services which are available, and by stimulating purchases it contributes to a return on costs, increases the market share of products, leads to increased production and reduction of unit costs, and in general contributes to a better material standard of living all round. In this sense advertising may be considered inherently good, and a valuable element of the conduct of business in a free society.

From a fuller human perspective advertising also contributes to an expansion of human freedom, by increasing the scope and the range of people's choices, and enabling them to satisfy their desires and to enhance the quality of their living. When the Berlin wall was broken through and East Berliners flocked wide-eyed into the glitter of West Berlin and its shop-windows, they became aware of the sheer poverty of choice under which they had laboured for years, and of the diminished freedom, not just economic but also in human terms, from which they were breaking free. I do not wish to be considered starry-eyed about either the capitalist system or the conditions of the market economy, and I shall shortly turn to consider the failings of advertising as it is sometimes or frequently practised. My main introductory point, however, is to propose that in principle advertising is a desirable and valuable feature of society, in bringing together demand and supply by means of communication and in enabling individuals to exercise their freedom of choice and enhance their personal freedom in many new and often different ways.

I have referred to advertising as a communication and that is what it basically is. It is not, of course, disinterested communication, in terms of truth for truth's sake, or the dissemination of information in purely altruistic terms; and therein lie many of the ethical issues involved in advertising. It is communication with a vested interest, presenting information with a view to sales, and in legal terms setting up the situation for a contract in commutative justice.

As such a relationship between persons, either in their own capacity or as agents for others, the communication involved in advertising is therefore subject to various ethical conditions which affect the way in which people treat each other. And one important ethical condition is the way in which people respect each other's freedom, including their freedom to make rational and informed choices.

In the particular communication of advertising the basic tension may be considered to be that the potential customer seeks information in order to make a choice, while the potential seller seeks to persuade in order to make a sale. The danger is then that the seller's motive to exercise influence, with a view to competing with other sellers or just to increasing turnover, may lead him or her to short-change the potential customer in one of two ways; either in the information provided or in the pressure brought to bear in various ways on the customer. I propose to consider each of these ideas of information and pressure in turn.

If we consider information, then what this brings out is that human freedom, to be truly human, has to be informed, or knowledgeable, freedom. It is not simply the exercise of arbitrary decisions; it is based on factual and rational considerations. In the field of medicine, for example, signing a consent form for treatment is not, or should not be, merely a bureaucratic formality. It involves the basic idea of informed consent; consent, that is, which shows an awareness of what is involved in the treatment, of what is the hoped-for outcome, and of what are the likely hazards which may also be encountered along the way.

Similar conditions affect the buying of other goods and services in society. And this is where the whole question of truth comes into the picture of advertising, as a necessary condition of our choices not being vitiated by ignorance or biased by deception. I need not labour the general point about the need for claims about a product to be accurate and truthful and not to suffer from lying or misrepresentation. At the level of application, however, to particular cases or practices in advertising several counterclaims have to be considered. For instance, there may be a grey area in the distinction between, on the one hand, misrepresentation, or making claims which are false, and on the other hand omitting certain facts about the product, or being, in the now-famous phrase, 'economical with the truth'. While singing the praises of a product, does one necessarily need to point out all its failings and weaknesses? Perhaps it may suffice to say, in general terms, that ethically the potential customer has a right to whatever information is considered relevant and necessary for him or her to make a free and rational choice; and that this will include being made aware of those particular features which, were they known, would materially affect that choice: for instance, that the machinery is dangerous, or that spare parts will shortly go out of production, or that the rate of interest can be changed at will by the creditor, or that between the luxury time-sharing block of flats and the glistening sands there are plans to build a new eight-lane motorway.

Exaggerations and unwarranted claims about the efficacy of the product also fall into consideration in assessing the truth factor in advertising, whether those claims have to do with one's health, or one's sex appeal, or one's social status, or one's general well-being in society. The counter to such considerations may often be that there's nothing wrong with a little harmless exaggeration, that no one is really fooled by it, and that in any case there is considerable scepticism which has to be taken into account. A too punctilious or solemn approach to advertisements would take all the fun and attractiveness out of them, reducing them to a mere scrupulous cataloguing of sales features. Surely no one is fooled by the pictorial element in advertisements, whether it be the use of mashed potatoes in place of the icecream which would melt under the arc-lights, or the sight of a new razor in action effortlessly removing the surface from a sheet of sandpaper.

It must be acknowledged that there are certain conventions in this form of communication, as in every other, whether it be bluffing in the course of agreeing a price or a wage rate, or obviously outlandish suggestions that drinking a special brand of vodka will transport one into a fairyland or harem of delights. The unspoken presupposition here, of course, is that the potential customer will be not only resistant but also sensible and reasonable in assessing the claims for various goods and services and will not take it all absolutely literally. The problem lies with the concept or the criterion of the 'reasonable consumer' which is appealed to. Certain levels of intelligence may no doubt be taken for granted in some cases, but there are particular problems, at least in the case of some groups in society, such as young children, adolescents and others who may feel socially inadequate, people in poor health, or individuals suffering from addictions of various kinds. In all of these and others there is an element not just of needs to be met or wants to be satisfied, but of vulnerability, which is exploited by inflated claims for what a particular product will deliver.

It is in such areas particularly that regulation and monitoring of advertisements have an important social function by protecting the vulnerable in society from being exploited. But in ethical terms what should be most to the fore on the part of advertisers is not just compliance with the letter of the law or regulation, perhaps coupled with attempts to get round it or slip past it, but the spirit of the law. And that is based on a fundamental respect for consumers as primarily human beings and not just potential customers, an awareness of their need for relevant information in order to exercise their freedom of choice, and an alertness to their human vulnerability, as contrasted with their rational needs and desires.

The second, and perhaps more ethically interesting sphere in which advertising needs to be scrutinized, is the area of pressure on individuals to make particular choices, to which I now turn. For not only is freedom dependent on accuracy of information in the ways in which I have been suggesting; it is also dependent on immunity from undue pressure.

And in that simple phrase 'undue pressure', there are many important considerations to be unpacked and analysed.

The ultimate assault on the freedom of a potential customer is generally agreed to be the activity of subliminal persuasion, and it is interesting to explore just why such extreme advertising techniques are considered ethically wrong. In part it appears to be because the approach slips through the consciousness of subjects, as it were, so that, in the popular phrase, they are 'being got at' without their permission. In that sense subliminal advertising may be considered an invasion of psychic privacy. Additionally, however, what is also involved in such techniques is that they bypass one's exercise of rationality and seek to influence one's choices by a direct appeal to feelings and emotions. We may recall Aristotle's comment that human beings are characteristically rational animals, and if that is so, then we may conclude in general that any attempt to influence people's choices in irrational or non-rational ways is ultimately demeaning to them and to their dignity as rational human beings.

Feelings and emotions do, of course, have a place in ordinary human decisions. We are not calculators, nor do we always fulfil the economic expectation of being entirely intellectual and predictable in our choices. And this raises the ethical question of how far advertising can justifiably play on our feelings and emotions in order to influence our choices. As Dr Johnson observed, in my opening quotation, 'Promise, large promise, is the soul of an advertisement'. And you may recall Vance Packard's remark in his perhaps over-sensational study of *The Hidden Persuaders* that shoe-shops do not sell ladies' shoes; they sell 'beautiful feet'. What Packard and others object to is not persuasion on the part of the sales force, but hidden persuasion, of which the potential customer is unaware.

There appears to be nothing wrong with persuasion as such: most of us are doing it much of the time in our attempts to bring others round to our way of thinking. In the introduction to his famous *Essay on Liberty*, John Stuart Mill attacked the idea of compelling others to behave in certain ways because it would make them happier or better or wiser people, or even right, and he explained, 'there are good reasons for remonstrating with him, or reasoning with him, or persuading him, or entreating him, but not for compelling him', although he carefully made exceptions in the case of minors and 'backwards states of society'. I suppose the point here is that, for persuasion to be legitimate, it must be rational or at least amenable to rational consideration. And in this context it seems ethically permissible to attempt to persuade others by appealing not only to individual arguments leading to choices but also to individuals' motives in approaching their choices.

One of the problems, however, remains to what extent such appeal to personal motivation actually is amenable to rational consideration, and for that we have to be conscious of such appeals rather than let them slip under our guard.

Ultimately perhaps this is the difference between persuasion and manipulation, in what I suggest may be a sliding scale of information, suggestion, persuasion and manipulation. Information here may be seen as simply the offering of the possibility of satisfying a person's felt and acknowledged want: You want a mousetrap? I sell mousetraps. Suggestion may be more a matter of helping the customer to articulate his or her desire: Wouldn't it be nice to get away from it all? Have you considered whether you need a weekend break? Persuasion may consist in marshalling the arguments for buying the latest encyclopaedia or shares in the new government privatization. All of these include the element of rational consideration, although of course it need not be in verbal propositions; it can also be conveyed more subtly and attractively in visual terms. And inevitably all of these also contain a strong element of attraction, since in our choices of goods and services we are aiming not just at what is true and appeals to our mind, but primarily at what is good and what we should like to have or obtain. By contrast with all of these, manipulation consists in getting people to make decisions and choices without their actually being aware of why they decide or choose in this manner.

There is one final and underlying consideration concerning the ethics of advertising which I want to look at briefly before turning to the question of sponsorship, and that is to what extent advertising responds to demand or, on the contrary, actually creates demands. The thesis is well-known that the purpose of advertising is to create dissatisfaction, so that potential customers who may have been blithely unaware of the range of products and services available are enticed into purchasing them without actually needing them. Perhaps the most obvious instance here, apart from so-called 'luxury goods', are various addictive or dependence-inducing substances such as tobacco and alcohol. And national and European regulations limiting advertising in these areas appear partly directed at preventing the market from growing by stimulating sales. More serious perhaps is the creation of new customers for the arms trade.

Part of an answer to this charge against advertising is economic in nature, that costs have to be recovered, or that a given volume of sales is essential to justifying research and development, as in the development of new armaments, and that the only way of achieving this is by increasing the market. In more psychological terms, however, the charge presumes that new human needs should not be created, and that we should all be content with satisfying our basic requirements in society. It is not easy, however, to distinguish between human needs, wants and desires. Perhaps needs are deepest, and are expressed or consciously articulated in wants, while desires refer to less significant or less profound experiences. Perhaps also this is where the distinction which I have already suggested between information and suggestion is important, in so far as suggestion can articulate in terms of wants what is already an underlying unconscious need.

More fundamentally, however, the attempt to distinguish between basic needs and perhaps induced needs, while important when sheer human survival is concerned, becomes less successful when quality of life and human culture are concerned. I have always remembered a TV play of Marghanita Laski called, if I recall, *The Offshore Island*, in which Britain had been devastated by nuclear disaster and a mother was concerned not only to feed her children but also to teach them to sing the theme from Beethoven's Choral Symphony, so that good music would not be entirely lost. Part of human culture, then, consists in inducting people into new experiences, perhaps largely of an aesthetic kind and to do with the human senses, and in the process creating habits and even needs which then fail to be satisfied. If this is the case, the conspiracy charge against advertising in general must be considered not proven, even if in particular instances it may well be sustained.

Perhaps, however, a final general point may be raised about advertising in general, and that concerns the values which it promotes, either covertly or even overtly. The cultural stereotypes of gleaming fitted kitchens, or of female or male sex-objects, are not only holding out promises of a vague kind; they are also inculcating views of life and of human relationships in society which often give serious cause for ethical questioning, if not disquiet. It may be easy here, of course, to confuse taste with ethics, but the depiction of reality in shocking or seductive or otherwise offensive terms may be matter for considering whether mental or cultural health warnings should sometimes accompany some advertisements.

My title also includes the ethics of sponsorship, and here there has, I think, been rather less thought given to the subject than in the case of advertising. In general terms sponsorship is often expressed as the exercise of corporate responsibility or of corporate generosity towards the community, and there appears nothing exceptionable in this, and much to commend it. Again, of course, it can scarcely be termed purely altruistic, since the company expects some return in good will and popularity, and even in some cases gratitude, if the event or the institution might not otherwise exist or be provided. The standard arguments against corporate giving can apply here, to the extent that individual shareholders might prefer to make their own philanthropic decisions rather than have them made for them by others. But I suppose one counter-argument, at least so far as the beneficiaries are concerned, is that the amount contributed will be the greater if it is exercised at corporate level. Another difficulty can concern the choice of 'good causes' as the recipients of corporate generosity; on what criteria are they decided, by whom, and with what background of expertise and experience to exercise discrimination?

It is also noteworthy, of course, that some sponsorship is actually advertising by association on the part of companies whose direct advertising of particular products may be limited or curtailed.

This is where the difference between advertising particular products and drawing public attention to the company's image as a whole by sponsorship is ethically relevant, for such indirect advertising may be an attempt to evade laws or regulations according to their letter, although it clearly contravenes the spirit and the social purpose of such enactments. Again, some sponsorship may be an attempt to make amends, or even to induce the public to overlook other perhaps more undesirable features of the company or its products.

Whether, however, in conclusion, we address the subject of sponsorship or of advertising there is no doubt that they raise for serious consideration many ethical questions which extend well beyond the economic arguments. They influence and affect our views of society, of human relationships, of our use of material possessions, and of human communication. Ultimately, all such considerations appear to come down to what Kant referred to in considering our attitude to others, that in all our dealings we should treat each other as ends and never merely as means. Of course, in many ways we are always treating others partly as means – that is to some extent what business is significantly about. But to consider others simply and solely as potential sales and to regard their rational freedom as negotiable in the enterprise of making sales is to depersonalize them and to deprive them of their basic humanity and dignity as persons.

Additional reading

An indispensable reference is *Readings in Marketing Ethics* by Jan Willem Bol, Charles T. Crespy, James M. Stearn and John R. Walton, (Needham Heights, MA: Ginn Press, 1991). This book has more than two dozen articles covering a broad range of topics such as market research, strategy and product management. A balanced view is provided by the mixture of theoretical and empirical studies.

For a particularly European flavour, see the April 1992 issue of *Business Ethics – European Review* with its focus on marketing new products. In it, journalist Andrew Brown discusses 'The ethics of selling personalities' – a 'trade' in personalities is presented as being essential but the rules of the traffic must be established. Another article in the same issue is 'Marketing, reciprocity and ethics' by Bart Nooteboom. The case is made that manipulative behaviour (treating people only as a means of making money and not as sources of views, actions and opinions) is not only unethical but is also bad marketing.

Questions for discussion

● Consider an advertising campaign where essentially no information about the product is given. (The ads for the clothing company Benetton showing a photo of a dying AIDS patient or a black woman nursing a white baby are prime examples.) What do you believe the aims and strategies are of such campaigns? What information is given to the public? Are these ads persuasive? Are these ads ethical?

Chapter 9

Multinational decision-making: reconciling international norms

How should highly placed multinational managers, typically schooled in home-country moral traditions, reconcile conflicts between these traditions and those of their host country?

When host-country standards for bribery, pollution, discrimination and salary structures appear substandard from the perspective of the home country, should the manager take the high road and implement home-country, standards? Or does the high road imply a failure to respect cultural diversity and national integrity? In this contribution, Thomas Donaldson constructs and defends a practical ethical algorithm for multinational managers to use in reconciling such international normative conflicts.

By all accounts, this is a particularly apposite time to take stock of the international ethical issues described in this chapter. Recent geopolitical changes, such as the demise of communism, have created a sharper focus on the activities of the free market.

It is not at all uncommon for transnational companies to have real concerns about the way they conduct business in overseas markets. In some parts of the world business operations may well be impossible, for example, without recourse to 'commissions' of various kinds. As a result transnational companies have developed ways of handling these issues, including disengagement from countries where it has become impossible to reconcile such differences in moral standards. However, the growing pressures to establish ethical processes across such companies may place such problems into sharper focus.

In the financial services market, for example, simple terms such as 'insider-dealing' have different meanings in Australia and the UK. Indeed, such activities may be regarded as desirable in some parts of the world.

However, such dilemmas do not by any means stem solely from negative considerations, as is pointed out in this chapter. A company may fall foul of a host country simply by attempting to treat its employees similarly throughout the world, only to discover this move causes enormous disruption to host-country norms. This is where the algorithm proposed in this chapter is of particular value.

Multinational decision-making: reconciling international norms
Thomas Donaldson

Jurisprudence theorists are often puzzled when, having thoroughly analysed an issue within the boundaries of a legal system, they must confront it again outside those boundaries. For international issues, trusted axioms often fail as the secure grounds of legal tradition and national consensus erode. Much the same happens when one moves from viewing a problem of corporate ethics against a backdrop of national moral consensus to the morally inconsistent backdrop of international opinion. Is the worker who appeals to extranational opinion while complaining about a corporate practice accepted within his or her country the same as an ordinary whistleblower? Is a factory worker in Mexico justified in complaining about being paid three dollars an hour for the same work for which a US factory worker, employed by the same company, is paid eight dollars [1]? Is he justified when in Mexico the practice of paying workers three dollars an hour – and even much less – is widely accepted? Is an asbestos worker in India justified in drawing world attention to the lower standards of in-plant asbestos pollution maintained by an English multi-national relative to standards in England, when the standards in question fall within Indian government guidelines and, indeed, are stricter than the standards maintained by other Indian asbestos manufacturers?

What distinguishes these issues from standard ones about corporate practices is that they involve reference to a conflict of norms, either moral or legal, between home and host country. This article examines the subclass of conflicts in which host-country norms appear substandard from the perspective of home country, and evaluates the claim often made by multinational executives that the prevalence of seemingly lower standards in a host country warrants the adoption by multinationals of the lower standards. It is concerned with cases of the following form: a multinational company (C) adopts a corporate practice (P) which is morally and/or legally permitted in C's host country (B), but not in C's home country (A). The paper argues that the presence of lower standards in B justifies C's adopting the lower standards only in certain, well-defined contexts. It proposes a conceptual test, or ethical algorithm, for multinationals to use in distinguishing justified from unjustified applications of standards. This algorithm ensures that multinational practice will remain faithful at least to the enlightened standards of home-country morality.

If C is a non-national, that is to say a multinational, corporation, then one may wonder why home-country opinion should be a factor in C's decision-making. One reason is that, although global companies are multinational in doing business in more than one country, they are uninational in composition and character. They are chartered in a single country, typically have over 95% of their stock owned by citizens of their home country, and have managements dominated by citizens of their home country. Thus, in an important sense the term 'multinational' is a misnomer. For our purposes it is crucial to acknowledge that the moral foundation of a multinational, i.e. the underlying assumptions of its managers infusing corporate policies with a basic sense of right and wrong, is inextricably linked to the laws and mores of the home country.

Modern textbooks dealing with international business consider cultural relativity to be a powerful factor in executive decision-making. Indeed, they often use it to justify practices abroad which, although enhancing corporate profits, would be questionable in the multinational's home country. One prominent text, for example, remarks that: 'In situations where patterns of dominance–subordination are socially determined, and not a function of demonstrated ability, management should be cautioned about promoting those of inferior social status to positions in which they are expected to supervise those of higher social status' [2]. Later, referring to multiracial societies such as South Africa, the same text offers managers some practical advice: 'the problem of the multiracial society manifests itself particularly in reference to promotion and pay. And an equal pay for equal work policy may not be acceptable to the politically dominant but racial minority group' [3].

Consider two actual instances of the problem at issue:

Charles Pettis

In 1966 Charles Pettis, employee of Brown and Root Overseas, Inc., an American multinational, became resident engineer for one of his company's projects in Peru: a 146-miles, $46 million project to build a highway across the Andes. Pettis soon discovered that Peruvian safety standards were far below those in the USA. The highway design called for cutting channels through mountains in areas where rock formations were unstable. Unless special precautions were taken, slides could occur. Pettis blew the whistle, complaining first to Peruvian government officials and later to US officials. No special precautions were taken, with the result that thirty-one men were killed by slides during the construction of the road. Pettis was fired for his trouble by Brown and Root and had difficulty finding a job with another company [4].

American bank in Italy

A new American bank in Italy was advised by its Italian attorneys to file a tax return that misstated income and expenses and consequently grossly underestimated actual taxes due. The bank learned, however, that most other

Italian companies regarded the practice as standard operating procedure and merely the first move in a complex negotiating process with the Italian Internal Revenue Service. The bank initially refused to file a fallacious return on moral grounds and submitted an 'American-style' return instead. But because the resulting tax bill was many times higher than what comparable Italian companies were asked to pay, the bank changed policy in later years to agree with 'Italian style' [5].

The moral point of view

One may well decide that home-country standards were mandatory in one of the above cases, but not in the other. One may decide that, despite conforming to Peruvian standards, Peruvian safety precautions were unacceptable, while at the same time acknowledging that however inequitable and inefficient Italian tax mores may be, a decision to file 'Italian-style' is permissible.

Despite claims to the contrary, one must reject the simple dictum that whenever P violates a moral standard of country A, it is impermissible for C. Arnold Berleant has argued that the principle of equal treatment endorsed by most US citizens requires that US corporations pay workers in less developed countries exactly the same wages paid to US workers in comparable jobs (after appropriate adjustments are made for cost-of-living levels in the relevant areas) [6]. But most observers, including those from the less developed countries, believe this stretches the doctrine of equality too far in a way detrimental to host countries. By arbitrarily establishing US wage levels as the benchmark for fairness, one eliminates the role of the international market in establishing salary levels, and this in turn eliminates the incentive US corporations have to hire foreign workers. If US companies felt morally bound to pay Korean workers exactly the wages US workers receive for comparable work, they would not locate in Korea. Perhaps US firms should exceed market rate for foreign labour as a matter of moral principle, but to pay strictly equal rates would freeze less developed countries out of the international labour market [7]. Lacking, then, a simple formula of the sort 'P is wrong when P violates A's norms,' one seems driven to undertake a more complex analysis of the types and degrees of responsibilities multinationals possess.

The first task is to distinguish between responsibilities that hold as minimum conditions, and ones that exceed the minimum. We are reminded of the distinction, eloquently articulated by Kant, between perfect and imperfect duties. Perfect duties are owed to a specific class of persons under specified conditions, such as the duty to honour promises. They differ from imperfect duties, such as the duty of charity which, although mandatory, allow considerable discretion as to when, how, and to whom they are fulfilled. The perfect/imperfect distinction, however, is not appropriate for corporations since it is doubtful whether economic entities such as corporations must assume the same imperfect burdens, e.g. of charity, as individual persons.

For purposes of discussing multinationals, then, it is best to recast the distinction into one between minimal and enlightened duties, where a minimal duty constitutes a duty such that the persistent failure to observe it deprives the corporation of its moral right to exist, i.e. a strictly mandatory duty, and an enlightened duty is one whose fulfilment would be praiseworthy but not mandatory in any sense. In the present context, it is the determination of minimal duties that has priority since, in attempting to answer whether P is permissible for C in B, the notion of permissibility must eventually be cashed in terms of minimal standards. Thus, P is not impermissible for C simply because C fails to achieve an ideal vision of corporate conduct; and C's failure to contribute generously to the United Nations is a permissible, if regrettable, act.

Because minimal duties are our target, it is appropriate next to invoke the language of rights, for rights are entitlements that impose minimum demands on the behaviour of others.

The appeal to rights

Theorists commonly analyse the obligations of developed to less developed countries in terms of rights. James Sterba argues that 'distant peoples' (e.g. persons in Third World countries) enjoy welfare rights that members of the developed countries are obliged to respect [8]. Welfare rights are defined as rights to whatever is necessary to satisfy 'basic needs', and 'basic needs', in turn, as needs 'which must be satisfied in order not to seriously endanger a person's health and sanity' [9]. It follows that multinationals are obliged to avoid workplace hazards that seriously endanger workers' health.

A similar notion is advanced by Henry Shue in his book, *Basic Rights*. The substance of a basic right for Shue is 'something the deprivation of which is one standard threat to rights generally' [10]. He considers it a 'minimal demand' that 'no individuals or institutions, including corporations, may ignore the universal duty to avoid depriving persons of their basic rights' [11]. Since one's physical security, including safety from exposure to harmful chemicals or pollution, is a condition for one's enjoyment of rights generally, it follows that the right to physical security is a basic right that imposes specific obligations on corporations.

Equally important for our purposes is Shue's application elsewhere of the 'no-harm' principle to the actions of US multinationals abroad [12]. Associated with Mill and traditional liberalism, the 'no-harm' principle reflects a rights-based approach emphasizing the individual's right to liberty, allowing maximal liberty to each so long as each inflicts no avoidable harm on others. Shue criticizes as a violation of the no-harm principle a plan by a Colorado-based company to export millions of tons of hazardous chemical waste from the USA for processing and disposal in the West African nation of Sierra Leone [13]. Using the same principle, he is able to criticize any US asbestos manufacturing corporation which, in order to escape expensive regulations at home, moves its plant to a foreign country with lower standards [14].

Thus the Shue–Sterba rights-based approach recommends itself as a candidate for evaluating multinational conduct. It is irrelevant whether the standards of *B* comply or fail to comply with home-country standards; what is relevant is whether they meet a universal, objective minimum. In the present context, the principal advantage of a rights-based approach is to establish a firm limit to appeals made in the name of host-country laws and morals – at least when the issue is a clear threat to workers' safety. Clear threats, such as in-plant asbestos pollution exceeding levels recommended by independent scientific bodies, are incompatible with employees' rights, especially their right not to be harmed. It is no excuse to cite lenient host-country regulations or ill-informed host-country public opinion.

But even as a rights-oriented approach clarifies a moral bottom line for extreme threats to workers' safety, it leaves obscure not only the issue of less extreme threats, but of harms other than physical injury. The language of rights and harm is sufficiently vague so as to leave shrouded in uncertainty a formidable list of issues crucial to multinationals.

When refined by the traditions of a national legal system, the language of rights achieves great precision. But left to wander among the concepts of general moral theory, the language proves less exact. Granted, the celebrated dangers of asbestos call for recognizing the right to workers' safety, no matter how broadly the language of rights is framed. But what are we to say of a less toxic pollutant? Is the level of sulphur dioxide air pollution we should demand in a struggling nation, say, one with only a few fertilizer plants working overtime to help feed its malnourished population, the same we should demand in Portland, Oregon? Or, taking a more obvious case, should the maximal level of thermal pollution generated by a poor nation's electric power plants be the same as West Germany's? Since thermal pollution raises the temperature of a given body of water, it lowers the capacity of the water to hold oxygen and in turn the number of higher fish species, e.g. salmon and trout. But whereas the trade-off between more trout and higher output is rationally made by the West German in favour of the trout, the situation is reversed for the citizen of Chad, Africa. This should not surprise us. It has long been recognized that many rights, e.g. the right to medical care, are dependent for their specification on the level of economic development of the country in question [15].

Nor is it clear how a general appeal to rights will resolve issues that turn on the interpretation of broad social practices. For example, in the Italian tax case mentioned earlier, the propriety of submitting an 'Italian' versus 'American'-style tax return hinges more on the appraisal of the value of honesty in a complex economic and social system than on an appeal to inalienable rights.

An ethical algorithm

What is needed, then, is a test for evaluating P more comprehensively than a simple appeal to rights. In the end, nothing short of a general moral theory working in tandem with an analysis of the foundations of corporate existence is needed. That is, ultimately there is no escape for the multinational executive from merging the ordinary canons of economic decision-making, of profit maximization and market share, with the principles of basic moral theory [16]. But this formidable task, essential as it is, does not preclude the possibility of discovering lower-order moral concepts to clarify the moral intuitions already in use by multinational decision-makers. Apart from the need for general theories of multinational conduct there is need for pragmatic aids to multinational decision-making that bring into relief the ethical implications of views already held. This suggests, then, the possibility of generating an interpretive mechanism, or algorithm, that managers of multinationals could use in determining the implications of their own moral views about cases of the form: Is P permissible for C when P is acceptable in B but not in A?

The first step in generating such an ethical algorithm is to isolate distinct senses in which B's norms may conflict with the norms of A. Now, if P is morally and/or legally permitted in B, but not in A, then either:

1 The moral reasons underlying B's view that P is permissible refer to B's relative level of economic development; or
2 The moral reasons underlying B's view that P is permissible are independent of B's relative level of economic development.

Let us call the conflict of norms described in (1) a type 1 conflict. In such a conflict, an African country that permits slightly higher levels of thermal pollution from electric power-generating plants, or a lower minimum wage, than those prescribed in European countries would do so not because higher standards would be undesirable *per se*, but because its level of economic development requires an ordering of priorities. In the future, when it succeeds in matching European economic achievements, it may well implement the higher standards.

Let us call the conflict of norms described in (2) a type 2 conflict. In such cases levels of economic development play no role. For example, low-level institutional nepotism, common in many underdeveloped countries, is justified not on economic grounds, but on the basis of clan and family loyalty. Presumably the same loyalties should be operative even after the country has risen to economic success – as the nepotism prevalent in Saudia Arabia would indicate. The Italian tax case also reflects an Italian cultural style with a penchant for personal negotiation and an unwillingness to formalize transactions, more than a strategy based on level of economical development.

When the conflicts of norms occurs for reasons other than relative economic development (type 2), then the possibility is increased that there exists what Richard Brandt has called an 'ultimate ethical disagreement' [17]. An ultimate disagreement occurs when two cultures are able to consider the same set of facts surrounding a moral issue while disagreeing on the moral issue itself. An ultimate disagreement is less likely in a type 1 case since, after suitable reflection about priorities imposed by differing economic circumstance, the members of A may come to agree that *given* that facts of B's level of economic development, P is permissible. On the other hand, a type 2 dispute about what westerners call nepotism will continue even after economic variables are discounted [17].

The status of the conflict of norms between A and B, i.e. whether it is of type 1 or 2, does not fix the truth value of B's claim that P is permissible. P may or may not be permissible whether the conflict is of type 1 or 2. This, however, is not to say that the truth value of B's claim is independent of the conflict's type status, for a different test will be required to determine whether P is permissible when the conflict is of type 1 rather than type 2. In a type 1 dispute, the following formula is appropriate:

P is permissible if and only if the members of A would, under conditions of economic development relevantly similar to those of B, regard P as permissible.

Under this test, excessive levels of asbestos pollution would almost certainly not be tolerated by the members of A under relevantly similar economic conditions, whereas higher levels of thermal pollution would be. The test, happily, explains and confirms our initial moral intuitions.

Yet when, as in type 2 conflicts, the dispute between A and B depends upon a fundamental difference of perspective, the step to equalize hypothetically the levels of economic development is useless. A different test is needed. In type 2 conflicts the opposing evils of ethnocentrism and ethical relativism must be avoided. A multinational must forego the temptation to remake all societies in the image of its home society, while at the same time rejecting a relativism that conveniently forgets ethics when the payoff is sufficient. Thus, the task is to tolerate cultural diversity while drawing the line at moral recklessness.

Since in type 2 cases P is in conflict with an embedded norm of A, one should first ask whether P is necessary to do business in B, for if not, the solution clearly is to adopt some other practice that is permissible from the standpoint of A. If petty bribery of public officials is unnecessary for the business of the Cummins Engine Company in India, then the company is obliged to abandon such bribery. If, on the other hand, P proves necessary for business, one must next ask whether P constitutes a direct violation of a basic human right. Here the notion of a right, specifying a minimum below which corporate conduct should not fall, has special application. If Polaroid, an American company, confronts South African laws that mandate systematic discrimination against non-whites, then Polaroid must refuse to comply with the laws. Thus, in type 2 cases, P would be permissible if and only if the answer to both of the following questions is 'no'.

1 Is it possible to conduct business successfully in B without undertaking P?
2 Is P a clear violation of a basic human right?

What sorts of practice might pass both conditions 1 and 2? Consider the practice of low-level bribery of public officials in some underdeveloped nations. In some South American countries, for example, it is impossible for any company, foreign or national, to move goods through customs without paying low-level officials a few dollars. Indeed, the salaries of such officials are sufficiently low that one suspects they are set with the prevalence of the practice in mind. The payments are relatively small, uniformly assessed, and accepted as standard practice by the surrounding culture. Here, the practice of petty bribery would pass the type 2 test and, barring other moral factors, would be permissible.

A further condition, however, should be placed on multinationals undertaking P in type 2 contexts. The companies should be willing to speak out against, and be willing to work for change of P. Even if petty bribery or low-level nepotism passes the preceding tests, it may conflict with an embedded norm of country A, and as a representative of A's culture, the company is obliged to take a stand. This would be true even for issues related exclusively to financial practice, such as the Italian tax case. If the practice of underestimating taxes due: (1) is accepted in B; (2) is necessary for successful business; and (3) does not violate any basic human rights, then it satisfies the necessary conditions of permissibility. Yet in so far as it violates a norm accepted by A, C should make its disapproval of the practice known.

To sum up, then, two complementary tests have been proposed for determining the ultimate permissibility of P. If P occurs in a type 1 context, then P is not permissible if:

The members of A would not, under conditions of economic development relevantly similar to those of B, regard P as permissible.

If P occurs in a type 2 context, then P is not permissible if either:

1 It is possible to conduct business successfully in B without undertaking P; or
2 P is a direct violation of a basic human right.

Notice that the type 1 criterion is not reducible to the type 2 criterion. In order for the two criteria to have equivalent outcomes, four propositions would need to be true:

1 If P passes 1, it passes 2.
2 If P fails 1, it fails 2.
3 If P passes 2, it passes 1.
4 If P fails 2, it fails 1.

But none of these propositions is true. The possibility matrix given in Figure 9.1 lists in rows A and B the only combinations of outcomes that are possible on the assumption that the two criteria are equivalent. But they are not equivalent because the combinations of outcomes in C and D are also possible. To illustrate, P may pass 2 and fail 1; for example, the practice of petty bribery may be necessary for business, may not violate basic human rights, but may none the less be unacceptable in A under hypothetically lowered levels of economic development; similarly, the practice of allowing a significant amount of water pollution may be necessary for business, may not violate basic rights, yet may be hypothetically unacceptable in A. Or, P may fail 2 and pass 1; for example, the practice of serving alcohol at executive dinners in a strongly Muslim country may not be necessary for business in B (and thus impermissible by criterion 2) while being thoroughly acceptable to the members of A under hypothetically lowered economic conditions. It follows, then, that the two tests are not mutually reducible. This underscores the importance of the preliminary step of classifying a given case under either type 1 or type 2. The prior act of classification explains, moreover, why not all cases in row C or in row D will have the same moral outcome. Consider, for example, the two fail–pass cases from row C mentioned above, i.e. the cases of water pollution and petty bribery. If classified as a type 1 case, the water

	Criterion 1		Criterion 2	
A	Fail		Fail	equivalent outcomes
B	Pass		Pass	

	Criterion 1		Criterion 2	
C	Fail		Pass	non-equivalent outcomes
D	Pass		Fail	

Fig. 9.1   *Possibility matrix*

pollution would *not* be permissible, while petty bribery, if classified as a type 2 case, *would* be.

Some practical considerations and objections

The algorithm does not obviate the need for multinational managers to appeal to moral concepts both more general and specific than the algorithm itself. It is not intended as a substitute for a general theory of morality or even an interpretation of the basic responsibilities of multinationals. Its power lies in its ability to tease out implications of the moral presuppositions of a manager's acceptance of 'home' morality and in this sense to serve as a clarificatory device for multinational decision-making. But in so far as the context of a given conflict of norms categorizes it as a type 1 rather than type 2 conflict, the algorithm makes no appeal to a universal concept of morality (as the appeal to basic human rights does in type 2 cases) save for the purported universality of the ethics endorsed by culture *A*. This means that the force of the algorithm is relativized slightly in the direction of a single society. When *A*'s morality is wrong or confused, the algorithm can reflect this ethnocentricity, leading either to a mild paternalism or to the imposition of parochial standards. For example, *A*'s oversensitivity to aesthetic features of the environment may lead it to reject a given level of thermal pollution even under hypothetically lowered economic circumstances, thus yielding a paternalistic refusal to allow such levels in *B*, despite *B*'s acceptance of the higher levels and *B*'s belief that tolerating such levels is necessary for stimulating economic development. Or, *A*'s mistaken belief that the practice of hiring twelve-year-olds for full-time, permanent work, although happily unnecessary at its relatively high level of economic development, would be acceptable and economically necessary at a level of economic development relevantly similar to *B*'s, might lead it both to tolerate and undertake the practice in *B*.

Nor is the algorithm a substitute for more specific guides to conduct, such as the numerous codes of ethics now appearing on the international scene. A need exists for topic-specific and industry-specific codes that embody detailed safeguards against self-serving interpretations. Consider the Sullivan Standards, designed by the black American minister, Leon Sullivan, drafted for the purpose of ensuring non-racist practices by US multinationals operating in South Africa. As a result of a lengthy lobbying campaign by US activists, the Sullivan principles are now endorsed and followed by almost one-third of all American multinationals with South African subsidiaries. Among other things, companies complying with the Sullivan principles must:

1 Remove all race designation signs.
2 Support the elimination of discrimination against the rights of blacks to form or belong to government-registered unions.

3 Determine whether upgrading of personnel and/or jobs in the lower echelons is needed (and take appropriate steps) [18].

A variety of similar codes are either operative or in the process of development, e.g . . . . the United Nation's Code of Conduct for Transnational Corporations and its International Standards of Accounting and Reporting; the World Health Organization's Code on Pharmaceutical and Tobacco; the World Intellectual Property Organization's Revision of the Paris Convention for the Protection of Industrial Patents and Trademarks; the International Chamber of Commerce's Rules of Conduct to Combat Extortion and Bribery; and the World Health Organization's Infant Formula code against advertising of breast-milk substitutes [19].

Despite these limitations, the algorithm has an important application in countering the well-documented tendency of multinationals to mask immoral practices in the rhetoric of 'tolerance' and 'cultural relativity'. Utilizing it, no multinational manager can naively suggest that asbestos standards in Chile are permissible because they are accepted there. Nor can he or she infer that the standards are acceptable on the grounds that the Chilean economy is, relative to his or her home country, underdeveloped. A surprising amount of moral blindness occurs not because people's fundamental moral views are confused, but because their cognitive application of those views to novel situations is misguided.

What guarantees that either multinationals or prospective whistleblowers possess the knowledge or objectivity to apply the algorithm fairly? As Richard Barnet quips, 'On the 56th floor of a Manhattan skyscraper, the level of self-protective ignorance about what the company may be doing in Colombia or Mexico is high' [20]. Can Exxon or Johns Manville be trusted to have a sufficiently sophisticated sense of human rights, or to weigh dispassionately the hypothetical attitudes of their compatriates under conditions of relevantly similar economic development? My answer to this is 'probably not', at least given the present character of the decision-making procedures in most global corporations. I would add, however, that this problem is a contingent and practical one. It is no more a theoretical flaw of the proposed algorithm that it may be conveniently misunderstood by a given multinational than it is of Rawl's theory that it may be conveniently misunderstood by a trickle-down capitalist.

What would need to change in order for multinationals to make use of the algorithm? At a minimum they would need to enhance the sophistication of their decision-making mechanisms. They would need to alter established patterns of information flow and collection in order to accommodate moral information. The already complex parameters of corporate decision-making would become more so. They would need to introduce alongside analyses of the bottom-line, analyses of historical tendencies, nutrition, rights and demography. And they would need to introduce a new class of employee to provide expertise in these areas. However unlikely such changes are, I believe they are within the realm of possibility. Multinationals, the organizations capable of colonizing our international future, are also capable of looking beyond their national borders and applying – at a minimum – the same moral principles they accept at home.

References and notes

1 An example of disparity in wages between Mexican and US workers is documented in the case study, 'Twin-Plants and Corporate Responsibilities', by Haddox, John H. in: Werhane Patricia and D'Andrade, Kendall (eds) *Profits and Responsibility*, New York: Random House, 1985.
2 Robinson, Richard D. *International Business Management: A Guide to Decision Making*, 2nd edn, Hinsdale, IL: The Dryden Press, 1978, p. 241.
3 Robinson, Richard D. *Op. Cit.* p. 241.
4 Peters, Charles and Branch, Taylor *Blowing the Whistle: Dissent in the Public Interest*, New York: Praeger Publishers, 1972, pp. 182–185
5 Kelly, Arthur Italian bank mores. In: Donaldson, T. (ed) *Case-Studies in Business Ethics*, Englewood Cliffs, NJ: Prentice-Hall, 1984.
6 Berleant, A. 'Multinationals and the Problem of Ethical Consistency'. *Journal of Business Ethics* August 1982; **3**, 185–195.
7 One can construct an argument attempting to show that insulating the economies of the less developed countries would be advantageous to the less developed countries in the long run. But whether correct or not, such an argument is independent of the present issue, for it is independent of the claim that if P violates the norms of A, then P is impermissible.
8 Sterba, James 'The Welfare Rights of Distant Peoples and Future Generations: Moral Side Constraints on Social Policy'. *Social Theory and Practice* Spring 1981; **7**, 110.
9 Sterba, James Hazards *Social Theory and Practice* 1981; **7**, 111.
10 Shue, Henry *Basic Rights, Subsistence, Affluence, and US Foreign Policy*, Princeton, NJ: Princeton University Press, 1981 p. 34.
11 Shue, Henry *op. cit.* p. 170.
12 Shue, Henry Exporting hazards. *Ethics* July 1981; **91**, 579–606.
13 Shue, Henry *op. cit.*, pp. 579–580.
14 Considering a possible escape from the principle, Shue considers whether inflicting harm is acceptable in the event that overall benefits outweigh the costs. Hence, increased safety risks under reduced asbestos standards might be acceptable in so far as the economic benefits to the country outweighed the costs. The problem, as Shue correctly notes, is that this approach fails to distinguish between the no-harm principle and a naive greatest-happiness principle. Even classical defenders of the no-harm principle were unwilling to accept a simple-minded utilitarianism that sacrificed individual justice on the altar of maximal happiness. Even classical utilitarians did not construe their greatest-happiness principle to be a 'hunting license' (Shue, Henry *op. cit.* pp. 592–593.)
   Still another escape might be by way of appealing to the rigours of international economic competition. That is, is it not unreasonable to expect firms to place themselves at a competitive disadvantage by installing expensive safety equipment in a market where other firms are brutally cost-conscious? Such policies, argue

critics, could trigger economic suicide. The obligation not to harm, in turn, properly belongs to the government of the host country. Here, too, Shue's rejoinder is on target. He notes first that the existence of an obligation by one party does not cancel its burden on another party; hence, even if the host-country's government does have an obligation to protect its citizens from dangerous workplace conditions, its duty does not cancel that of the corporation (Shue, Henry *op. cit.*, p. 600). Second, governments of poor countries are themselves forced to compete for scarce foreign capital by weakening their laws and regulations, with the result that any 'competitive disadvantage' excuse offered on behalf of the corporation would also apply to the government (Shue, Henry *op. cit.*, p. 601).

15 Sterba himself reflects this consensus when he remarks that for rights 'an acceptable minimum should vary over time and between societies at least to some degree' (Sterba, J. 'Distant peoples', p. 112).

16 For the purpose of analysing the moral foundations of corporate behaviour, I prefer a social contract theory, one that interprets a hypothetical contract between society and productive organizations, and which I have argued for in my book, *Corporations and Morality* Englewood Cliffs, NJ: Prentice-Hall, 1982; see especially Chapter 3. There I argue that corporations are artefacts; that they are in part the products of our moral and legal imagination. As such, they are to be moulded in the image of our collective rights and societal ambitions. Corporations, as all productive organizations, require from society both recognition as single agents, and the authority to own or use land and natural resources and to hire employees. In return for this, society may expect that productive organizations will, all other things being equal, enhance the general interests of consumers and employees. Society may reasonably expect that in doing so corporations honour existing rights and limit their activities to accord with the bounds of justice. This is as true for multinationals as it is for national corporations.

17 Brandt, Richard 'Cultural Relativism'. In: Donaldson, T. and Werhane, P. (eds) *Ethical Issues in Business*, 2nd edn, Englewood Cliffs, NJ: Prentice-Hall, 1983.

18 See 'Dresser Industries and South Africa' by Mintz, Patricia and Hanson, Kirk O. In: Donaldson, Thomas (ed) *Case Studies in Business Ethics*, Englewood Cliffs, NJ: Prentice-Hall, 1984.

19 For a concise and comprehensive account of the various codes of conduct for international business now under consideration, see 'Codes of Conduct: Worry Over New Restraints on Multinationals'. *Chemical Week*, **129**, 15 July 1981, pp. 48–52.

20 Barnet, Richard J. and Muller, Ronald *Global Reach: The Power of Multinational Corporations*, New York: Simon and Schuster, 1974, p. 185.

Additional reading on international business ethics

An extended explanation of Donaldson's thoughts on this topic is given in his book *The Ethics of International Business* (Oxford: Oxford University Press, 1989). In addition to covering the ethical algorithm, the book addresses issues such as the concept of a fundamental human right and the theory and practice of the multinational. An in-depth case study, Union Carbide subjecting

ecting Bhopal citizens to higher technological risks, serves as an excellent vehicle to tie together many of the ethics concepts discussed.

Another valuable reference is *Ethics and the Multinational Enterprise: Proceedings of the Sixth National Conference on Business Ethics*, edited by Hoffman, W. Michael Lange, Anne E. and Fedo, David A. (Langam, MD, University Press of America, 1986). There are more than fifty contributions covering specific areas, such as: 'Corporate models for ethical decision making'; 'The impact of multinational business activity on women in the Third World' and 'International accords as tools for problem solving'.

Follow-up reading on bribery

The issue of bribery is a difficult one for many business people to come to grips with. The task is that much more demanding when dealing with people from other cultures. Donaldson's algorithm can provide much-needed practical advice for those doing business abroad.

Additional information on the topic can be found in *Bribery and Extortion in World Business* by Jacoby, Neil, Nehemkis, Peter and Eells, Richard. (New York: Macmillan, 1977). This book covers many critical issues including the crucial difference between bribery, extortion and tipping. The authors provide a useful way to look at bribery and extortion by treating these payments as commodities sold in the market. Insight into such transactions is gained by looking at the determinants of supply (such as political stability and pay of government officials) and determinants of demand (such as business opportunities and extent of government regulations).

Harold L. Johnson, in his article 'Bribery in international markets: diagnosis, clarification and remedy' (*Journal of Business Ethics* 1985; **4,** 447–455), provides a wide coverage of the topic. Included is a discussion on moral relativism (the 'when in Rome' argument) and an explanation of bribery dynamics drawing on game theory's prisoner's dilemma.

Questions for discussion

● Assume that you are in the final throes of negotiating a contract with a foreign government. The government negotiator agrees with all the terms but at the last minute insists that your company create a temporary job for the son of a government minister. According to Donaldson's algorithm, is it morally acceptable for you to agree to the demand? Do you agree with this conclusion? Would your employer agree with this? If you and your employer disagree, how would you present your argument?

Chapter 10

Business and environmental ethics

This contribution explores some interconnections between the business and environmental ethics movements. The first section argues that business has obligations to protect the environment over and above what is required by environmental law and that it should cooperate and interact with government in establishing environmental legislation. Business must develop and demonstrate environmental moral leadership.

The second section exposes the danger of using the rationale of 'good ethics is good business' as a basis for such business moral leadership in both the business and environmental ethics movements.

The third section cautions against the moral shallowness inherent in the position or in the promotion of ecological homocentrism which claims that society, including business, ought to protect the environment solely because of harm done to human beings and human interests.

Although the descriptions in this chapter are American, none the less one can see the development of many of these issues in Europe. The chapter also illustrates the depth and detail of the ethical debate in the USA, where it is not uncommon for those with an interest in the ethics of business to meet regularly to debate current issues; and the wealth of journals and publications dealing with the subject of business ethics.

Europe is less well-served, except perhaps through the European Business Ethics Network; the journal, *Business Ethics – A European Review*, and several business ethics conferences. One result of the relatively recent emergence of business ethics as a major subject in Europe is the scarcity of material on the connections between business and environmental ethics.

It is somewhat rare to find in the British media detailed discussion of ethics in reports on environmental topics. There is a rapidly growing industry devoted to environmental assessments and audits of various kinds.

Many of these audits have an arguably narrow definition of the environment and focus on conventional issues such as pollution, while paying little attention, for example, to corporate equal opportunity programmes and other internal processes.

In one sense this may be very appropriate, but it does suggest that for such issues to be covered there may be a need for corporate ethics audits, which might complement or include environmental audits.

An interesting point developed in this chapter is that you might find yourself a member of one or more stakeholder groups at the same time, in this case as a consumer and a citizen. This situation is often mirrored inside companies where an executive may be a consumer or customer, employee and shareholder simultaneously.

Business and environmental ethics
W. Michael Hoffman

The business ethics movement, from my perspective, is still on the march. And the environmental movement, after being somewhat silent for the past twenty years, has once again captured our attention – promising to be a major social force in the 1990s. Much will be written in the next few years trying to tie together these two movements. This is one such effort.

Concern over the environment is not new. Warnings came out of the 1960s in the form of burning rivers, dying lakes, and oil-fouled oceans. Radioactivity was found in our food, DDT in mother's milk, lead and mercury in our water. Every breath of air in the North American hemisphere was reported as contaminated. Some said these were truly warnings from Planet Earth of ecocatastrophe, unless we could find limits to our growth and changes in our lifestyle.

Over the past few years Planet Earth began to speak to us even more loudly than before, and we began to listen more than before. The message was ominous, somewhat akin to God warning Noah. It spoke through droughts, heat waves and forest fires, raising fears of global warming due to the build-up of carbon dioxide and other gases in the atmosphere. It warned us by raw sewage and medical wastes washing up on our beaches, and by devastating oil spills – one despoiling Prince William Sound and its wildlife to such an extent that it made us weep. It spoke to us through increased skin cancers and discoveries of holes in the ozone layer caused by our use of chloro-fluorocarbons. It drove its message home through the rapid and dangerous cutting and burning of our primitive forests at the rate of one football field a second, leaving us even more vulnerable to greenhouse gases like carbon dioxide and eliminating scores of irreplaceable species daily. It rained down on us in the form of acid, defoliating our forests and poisoning our lakes and streams. Its warnings were found on barges roaming the seas for places to dump tons of toxic incinerator ash. And its message exploded in our faces at Chernobyl and Bhopal, reminding us of past warnings at Three Mile Island and Love Canal.

Senator Albert Gore said in 1988: 'The fact that we face an ecological crisis without any precedent in historic times is no longer a matter of any dispute worthy of recognition' [1]. The question, he continued, is not whether there is a problem, but how we will address it. This will be the focal point for a public policy debate which requires the full participation of two of its major players – business and government. The debate must clarify such fundamental questions as:

1 What obligation does business have to help with our environmental crisis?
2 What is the proper relationship between business and government, especially when faced with a social problem of the magnitude of the environment crisis?
3 What rationale should be used for making and justifying decisions to protect the environment?

Corporations, and society in general for that matter, have yet to answer these questions satisfactorily. In the first section of this paper I will briefly address the first two questions. In the final two sections I will say a few things about the third question.

I

In a 1989 keynote address before the 'Business, ethics and the environment' conference at the Center for Business Ethics, Norman Bowie offered some answers to the first two questions [2]:

> Business does not have an obligation to protect the environment over and above what is required by law; however, it does have a moral obligation to avoid intervening in the political arena in order to defeat or weaken environmental legislation.

I disagree with Bowie on both counts.

Bowie's first point is very Friedmanesque [3]. The social responsibility of business is to produce goods and services and to make profit for its shareholders, while playing within the rules of the market game. These rules, including those to protect the environment, are set by the government and the courts. To do more than is required by these rules is, according to this position, unfair to business. In order to perform its proper function, every business must respond to the market and operate in the same arena as its competitors. As Bowie puts this [4]:

> An injunction to assist in solving societal problems [including depletion of natural resources and pollution] makes impossible demands on a corporation because, at the practical level, it ignores the impact that such activities have on profit.

If, as Bowie claims, consumers are not willing to respond to the cost and use of environmentally friendly products and actions, then it is not the responsibility of business to respond or correct such market failure.

Bowie's second point is a radical departure from this classical position in contending that business should not lobby against the government's process to set environmental regulations. To quote Bowie [5]:

> Far too many corporations try to have their cake and eat it too. They argue that it is the job of government to correct for market failure and then they use their influence and money to defeat or water down regulations designed to conserve and protect the environment.

Bowie only recommends this abstinence of corporate lobbying in the case of environmental regulations. He is particularly concerned that politicians, ever mindful of their re-election status, are already reluctant to pass environmental legislation which has huge immediate costs and in most cases very long-term benefits. This makes the obligations of business to refrain from opposing such legislation a justified special case.

I can understand why Bowie argues these points. He seems to be responding to two extreme approaches, both of which are inappropriate. Let me illustrate these extremes by the following two stories.

At the Center's First National Conference on Business Ethics, Harvard Business School Professor George Cabot Lodge told of a friend who owned a paper company on the banks of a New England stream. On the first Earth Day in 1970, his friend was converted to the cause of environmental protection. He became determined to stop his company's pollution of the stream, and marched off to put his new-found religion into action. Later, Lodge learned his friend went broke, so he went to investigate. Radiating a kind of ethical purity, the friend told Lodge that he spent millions to stop the pollution and thus could no longer compete with other firms that did not follow his example. So the company went under, 500 people lost their jobs, and the stream remained polluted.

When Lodge asked why his friend hadn't sought help from the state or federal government for stricter standards for everyone, the man replied that that was not the American way, that government should not interfere with business activity, and that private enterprise could do the job alone. In fact, he felt it was the social responsibility of business to solve environmental problems, so he was proud that he had set an example for others to follow.

The second story portrays another extreme. A few years ago [a TV programme] interviewed a manager of a chemical company that was discharging effluent into a river in upstate New York. At the time, the dumping was legal, though a bill to prevent it was pending in Congress. The manager remarked that he hoped the bill would pass, and that he certainly would support it as a responsible citizen. However, he also said he approved of his company's efforts to defeat the bill and of the firm's policy of dumping wastes in the meantime. After all, isn't the proper role of business to make as much profit as possible within the bounds of law? Making the laws – setting the rules of the game – is the role of government, not business. While wearing his business hat the manager had a job to do, even if it meant doing something that he strongly opposed as a private citizen.

Both stories reveal incorrect answers to the questions posed earlier, the proof of which is found in the fact that neither the New England stream nor the New York river was made any cleaner. Bowie's points are intended to block these two extremes. But to avoid these two extremes, as Bowie does, misses the real managerial and ethical failure of the stories. Although the paper company owner and the chemical company manager had radically different views of the ethical responsibilities of business, both saw business and government performing separate roles, and neither felt that business ought to cooperate with government to solve environmental problems [6].

If the business ethics movement has led us anywhere in the past fifteen years, it is to the position that business has an ethical responsibility to become a more active partner in dealing with social concerns. Business must creatively find ways to become a part of solutions, rather than being a part of problems. Corporations can and must develop a conscience, as Ken Goodpaster and others have argued – and this includes an environmental conscience [7]. Corporations should not isolate themselves from participation in solving our environmental problems, leaving it up to others to find the answers and to tell them what not to do.

Corporations have special knowledge, expertise and resources which are invaluable in dealing with the environmental crisis. Society needs the ethical vision and cooperation of all its players to solve its most urgent problems, especially one that involves the very survival of the planet itself. Business must work with government to find appropriate solutions. It should lobby for good environmental legislation and lobby against bad legislation, rather than isolating itself from the legislative process, as Bowie suggests. It should not be ethically quixotic and try to go it alone, as our paper company owner tried to do, nor should it be ethically inauthentic and fight against what it believes to be environmentally sound policy, as our chemical company manager tried to do. Instead business must develop and demonstrate moral leadership.

There are examples of corporations demonstrating such leadership even when this has been a risk to their self-interest. In the area of environmental moral leadership one might cite DuPont's discontinuing its Freon products, a $750-million-a-year business, because of their possible negative effects on the ozone layer, and Proctor and Gamble's manufacture of concentrated fabric softener and detergents which require less packaging. But some might argue, as Bowie does, that the real burden for environmental change lies with consumers, not with corporations. If we as consumers are willing to accept the harm done to the environment by favouring environmentally unfriendly products, corporations have no moral obligation to change so long as they obey environmental law. This is even more the case, so the argument goes, if corporations must take risks or sacrifice profits to do so.

This argument fails to recognize that we quite often act differently when we think of ourselves as *consumers* than when we think of ourselves as *citizens*. Mark Sagoff, concerned about our over reliance on economic solutions, clearly characterizes this dual nature of our decision-making [8]. As consumers, we act more often than not for ourselves; as citizens, we take on a broader vision and do what is in the best interests of the community. I often shop for things I don't vote for. I might support recycling referendums, but buy products in non-returnable bottles. I am not proud of this, but I suspect this is more true of most of us than not. To stake our environmental future on our consumer willingness to pay is surely short-sighted, perhaps even disastrous.

I am not saying that we should not work to be ethically committed citizen consumers, and investors for that matter. I agree with Bowie that 'consumers bear a far greater responsibility for preserving and protecting the environment than they have actually exercised' [9], but activities which affect the environment should not be left up to what we, acting as consumers, are willing to tolerate or accept. To do this would be to use a market-based method of reasoning to decide on an issue which should be determined instead on the basis of our ethical responsibilities as a member of a social community.

Furthermore, consumers don't make the products, provide the services, or enact the legislation which can be either environmentally friendly or unfriendly. Grass-roots boycotts and lobbying efforts are important, but we also need leadership and mutual cooperation from business and government in setting forth ethical environmental policy. Even Bowie admits that perhaps business has a responsibility to educate the public and promote environmentally responsible behaviour. But I am suggesting that corporate moral leadership goes far beyond public educational campaigns. It requires moral vision, commitment and courage, and involves risk and sacrifice. I think business is capable of such a challenge. Some are even engaging in such a challenge. Certainly the business ethics movement should do nothing short of encouraging such leadership. I feel morality demands such leadership.

II

If business has an ethical responsibility to the environment which goes beyond obeying environmental law, what criterion should be used to guide and justify such action? Many corporations are making environmentally friendly decisions where they see there are profits to be made by doing so. They are wrapping themselves in green where they see a green bottom line as a consequence. This rationale is also being used as a strategy by environmentalists to encourage more businesses to become environmentally conscientious. In December 1989 the highly respected Worldwatch Institute published an article by one of its senior researchers entitled 'Doing well by doing good' which gives numerous examples of corporations improving their [wallets] by improving the environment. It concludes by stating that 'fortunately, businesses that work to preserve the environment can also make a buck' [10].

In a recent Public Broadcast Corporation documentary entitled 'Profit the Earth', several efforts are depicted of what is called the 'new environmentalism' which induces corporations to do things for the environment by appealing to their self-interest. The Environmental Defense Fund (EDF) is shown encouraging agribusiness in Southern California to irrigate more efficiently and profit by selling the water saved to the city of Los Angeles. This in turn will help save Mono Lake. EDF is also shown lobbying for emissions trading that would allow utility companies which are under their emission allotments to sell their 'pollution rights' to those companies which are over their allotments. This is for the purpose of reducing acid rain. Thus the frequent strategy of the new environmentalists is to get business to help solve environmental problems by finding profitable or virtually costless ways for them to participate. They feel that compromise, not confrontation, is the only way to save the earth. By using the tools of the free enterprise system, they are in search of win–win solutions, believing that such solutions are necessary to take us beyond what we have so far been able to achieve.

I am not opposed to these efforts; in most cases I think they should be encouraged. There is certainly nothing wrong with making money while protecting the environment, just as there is nothing wrong with feeling good about doing one's duty. But if business is adopting or being encouraged to adopt the view that good environmentalism is good business, then I think this poses a danger for the environmental ethics movement – a danger which has an analogy in the business ethics movement.

As we all know, the position that good ethics is good business is being used more and more by corporate executives to justify the building of ethics into their companies and by business ethics consultants to gain new clients. For example, the Business Roundtable's *Corporate Ethics* report states [11]:

> The corporate community should continue to refine and renew efforts to improve performance and manage change effectively through programmes in corporate ethics . . . corporate ethics is a strategic key to survival and profitability in this era of fierce competitiveness in a global economy.

And, for instance, the book *The Power of Ethical Management* by Kenneth Blanchard and Norman Vincent Peale states in big red letters on the cover jacket that 'Integrity pays! You don't have to cheat to win'. The blurb on the inside cover promises that the book 'gives hard-hitting, practical, *ethical* strategies that build profits, productivity, and long-term success' [12]. Whoever would have guessed that business ethics could deliver all that! In such ways business ethics gets marketed as the newest cure for what ails corporate America.

Is the rationale that good ethics is good business a proper one for business ethics? I think not. One thing that the study of ethics has taught us over the past 2500 years is that being ethical may on occasion require that we place the interests of others ahead of or at least on par with our own interests. And this implies that the ethical thing to do, the morally right thing to do, may not be in our own self-interest. What happens when the right thing is not the best thing for the business?

Although in most cases good ethics may be good business, it should not be advanced as the only or even the main reason for doing business ethically. When the crunch comes, when ethics conflicts with the firm's interests, any ethics programme that has not already faced up to this possibility is doomed to fail because it will undercut the rationale of the programme itself. We should promote business ethics, not because good ethics is good business, but because we are morally required to adopt the moral point of view in all our dealings – and business is no exception. In business, as in all other human endeavours, we must be prepared to pay the costs of ethical behaviour.

There is a similar danger in the environmental movement with corporations choosing or being wooed to be environmentally friendly on the grounds that it will be in their self-interest. There is the risk of participating in the movement for the wrong reasons. But what does it matter if business cooperates for reasons other than the right reasons, as long as it cooperates? It matters if business believes or is led to believe that it only has a duty to be environmentally conscientious in those cases where such actions either require no sacrifice or actually make a profit. And I am afraid this is exactly what is happening. I suppose it wouldn't matter if the environmental cooperation of business was only needed in those cases where it was also in business's self-interest. But this is surely not the case, unless one begins really to reach and talk about that amorphous concept 'long-term' self-interest. Moreover, long-term interests, I suspect, are not what corporations or the new environmentalists have in mind in using self-interest as a reason for environmental action.

I am not saying we should abandon attempts to entice corporations into being ethical, both environmentally and in other ways, by pointing out and providing opportunities where good ethics is good business. And there are many places where such attempts fit well in both the business and environmental ethics movements. But we must be careful not to cast this as the proper guideline for business's ethical responsibility. Because when it is discovered that many ethical actions are not necessarily good for business, at least in the short run, then the rationale based on self-interest will come up morally short, and both ethical movements will be seen as deceptive and shallow.

III

What is the proper rationale for responsible business action towards the environment? A minimalist principle is to refrain from causing or prevent the causing of unwarranted harm, because failure to do so would violate certain moral rights not to be harmed. There is, of course, much debate over what harms are indeed unwarranted due to conflict of rights and questions about whether some harms are offset by certain benefits. Norm Bowie, for example, uses the harm principle, but contends that business does not violate it as long as it obeys environmental law. Robert Frederick, on the other hand, convincingly argues that the harm principle morally requires business to find ways to prevent certain harm it causes even if such harm violates no environmental law [13].

However, Frederick's analysis of the harm principle is largely cast in terms of harm caused to human beings and the violation of rights of human beings. Even when he hints at the possible moral obligation to protect the environment when no one is caused unwarranted harm, he does so by suggesting that we look to what we, as human beings, value [14]. This is very much in keeping with a humanistic position of environmental ethics which claims that only human beings have rights or moral standing because only human beings have intrinsic value. We may have duties with regard to non-human things (penguins, trees, islands, etc.) but only if such duties are derivative from duties we have towards human beings. Non-human things are valuable only if valued by human beings.

Such a position is in contrast to a naturalistic view of environmental ethics which holds that natural things other than human beings are intrinsically valuable and have, therefore, moral standing. Some naturalistic environmentalists only include other sentient animals in the framework of being deserving of moral consideration; others include all things which are alive or which are an integral part of an ecosystem. This latter view is sometimes called a biocentric environmental ethic as opposed to the homocentric view which sees all moral claims in terms of human beings and their interests. Some characterize these two views as deep versus shallow ecology.

The literature on these two positions is vast and the debate is ongoing. The conflict between them goes to the heart of environmental ethics and is crucial to our making of environmental policy and to our perception of moral duties to the environment, including business's. I strongly favour the biocentric view. And although this is not the place to try to argue adequately for it, let me unfurl its banner for just a moment.

A version of Richard Routley's 'last man' example [15] might go something like this: suppose you were the last surviving human being and were soon to die from nuclear poisoning, as all other human and sentient animals have died before you. Suppose also that it is within your power to destroy all remaining life or, to make it simpler, the last tree which could continue to flourish and propagate if left alone. Furthermore you will not suffer if you do not destroy it. Would you do anything wrong by cutting it down? The deeper ecological view would say yes because you would be destroying something that has value in and of itself, thus making the world a poorer place.

It might be argued that the only reason we may find the tree valuable is because human beings generally find trees of value either practically or aesthetically, rather than the atoms or molecules they might turn into if changed from their present form. The issue is whether the tree has value only in its relation to human beings or whether it has a value deserving of moral consideration inherent in itself in its present form. The biocentric position holds that when we find something wrong with destroying the tree, as we should, we do so because we are responding to an intrinsic value in the natural object, not to a value we give to it. This is a view which argues against a humanistic environmental ethic and which urges us to channel our moral obligations accordingly.

Why should one believe that non-human living things or natural objects forming integral parts of ecosystems have intrinsic value? One can respond to this question by pointing out the serious weaknesses and problems of human chauvinism [16]. More complete responses lay out a framework of concepts and beliefs which provides a coherent picture of the biocentric view with human beings as a part of a more holistic value system. But the final answer to the question hinges on what criterion one decides to use for determining moral worth – rationality, sentience or a deeper biocentric one. Why should we adopt the principle of attributing intrinsic value to all living beings, or even to all natural objects, rather than just to human beings? I suspect Arne Naess gives as good an answer as can be given [17]:

> Faced with the ever returning question of 'Why?,' we have to stop somewhere. Here is a place where we well might stop. We shall admit that the value in itself is something shown in intuition. We attribute intrinsic value to ourselves and our nearest, and the validity of further identification can be contested, and *is* contested by many. The negation may, however, also be attacked through a series of 'whys?' Ultimately, we are in the same human predicament of having to start somewhere, at least for the moment. We must stop somewhere and treat where we then stand as a foundation.

In the final analysis, environmental biocentrism is adopted or not depending on whether it is seen to provide a deeper, richer and more ethically compelling view of the nature of things.

If this deeper ecological position is correct, then it ought to be reflected in the environmental movement. Unfortunately, for the most part, I do not think this is being done, and there is a price to be paid for not doing so. Moreover, I fear that even those who are of the biocentric persuasion are using homocentric language and strategies to bring business and other major players into the movement because they do not think they will be successful otherwise. They are afraid, and undoubtedly for good reason, that the large part of society, including business, will not be moved by arguments regarding the intrinsic value and rights of natural things. It is difficult enough to get businesses to recognize and act on their responsibilities to human beings and things of human interest. Hence many environmentalists follow the counsel of Spinoza [18]:

> it is necessary that while we are endeavouring to attain our purpose . . . we are compelled . . . to speak in a manner intelligible to the multitude . . . For we can gain from the multitude no small advantages.

I understand the temptation of environmentalists employing a homocentric strategy, just as I understand business ethicists using the rationale that good ethics is good business. Both want their important work to succeed. But, just as with the good-ethics-is-good-business tack, there are dangers in being a closet ecocentrist. The ethicists in both cases fail to reveal the deeper moral base of their positions because it's a harder sell. Business ethics gets marketed in terms of self-interest, environmental ethics in terms of human interest.

A major concern in using the homocentric view to formulate policy and law is that non-human nature will not receive the moral consideration it deserves. It might be argued, however, that by appealing to the interests and rights of human beings, in most cases nature as a whole will be protected. That is, if we are concerned about a wilderness area, we can argue that its survival is important to future generations who will otherwise be deprived of contact with its unique wildlife. We can also argue that it is important to the aesthetic pleasure of certain individuals or that, if it is destroyed, other recreational areas will become overcrowded. In this way we stand a chance to save the wilderness area without having to refer to our moral obligations to respect the intrinsic value of the spotted owl or of the old-growth forest. This is simply being strategically savvy. To trot out our deeper ecological moral convictions runs the risk of our efforts being ignored, even ridiculed, by business leaders and policy-makers. It also runs head-on against a barrage of counter-arguments that human interests take precedence over non-human interests. In any event it will not be in the best interest of the wilderness area we are trying to protect. Furthermore, all of the above homocentric arguments happen to be true – people will suffer if the wilderness area is destroyed.

In most cases, what is in the best interests of human beings may also be in the best interests of the rest of nature. After all, we are in our present environmental crisis in large part because we have not been ecologically intelligent about what is in our own interest – just as business has encountered much trouble because it has failed to see its interest in being ethically sensitive. But if the environmental movement relies only on arguments based on human interests, then it perpetuates the danger of making environmental policy and law on the basis of our strong inclination to fulfil our immediate self-interests, on the basis of our consumer viewpoints, on the basis of our willingness to pay. There will always be a tendency to allow our short-term interests to eclipse our long-term interests and the long-term interest of humanity itself. Without some grounding in a deeper environmental ethic with obligations to non-human natural things, then the temptation to view our own interests in disastrously short-term ways is that much more encouraged. The biocentric view helps to block this temptation.

Furthermore, there are many cases where what is in human interest is not in the interest of other natural things. Examples range from killing leopards for stylish coats to destroying a forest to build a golf course. I am not convinced that homocentric arguments, even those based on long-term human interests, have much force in protecting the interests of such natural things. Attempts to make these interests coincide might be made, but the point is that from a homocentric point of view the leopard and the forest have no morally relevant interests to consider. It is simply fortuitous if non-human natural interests coincide with human interests, and are thereby valued and protected. Let us take an example from the work of Christopher Stone. Suppose a stream has been polluted by a business. From a homocentric point of view, which serves as the basis for our legal system, we can only correct the problem through finding some harm done to human beings who use the stream. Reparation for such harm might involve cessation of the pollution and restoration of the stream, but it is also possible that the business might settle with the people by paying them for their damages and continue to pollute the stream. Homocentrism provides no way for the stream to be made whole again unless it is in the interests of human beings to do so. In short, it is possible for human beings to sell out the stream [19].

I am not saying that human interests cannot take precedence over non-human interests when there are conflicts. For this we need to come up with criteria for deciding on interspecific conflicts of interests, just as we do for intraspecific conflicts of interest among human beings [20]. But this is a different problem from holding that non-human natural things have no interests or value deserving of moral consideration. There are times when causing harm to natural things is morally unjustifiable when there are no significant human interests involved and even when there are human interests involved. But only a deeper ecological ethic than homocentrism will allow us to defend this.

Finally, perhaps the greatest danger that biocentric environmentalists run in using homocentric strategies to further the movement is the loss of the very insight that grounded their ethical concern in the first place. This is nicely put by Lawrence Tribe [21]:

> What the environmentalist may not perceive is that, by couching his claim in terms of human self-interest – by articulating environmental goals wholly in terms of human needs and preferences – he may be helping to legitimate a system of discourse which so structures human thought and feeling as to erode, over the long run, the very sense of obligation which provided the initial impetus for his own protective efforts.

Business ethicists run a similar risk in couching their claims in terms of business self-interest.

The environmental movement must find ways to incorporate and protect the intrinsic value of animal and plant life and even other natural objects that are integral parts of ecosystems. This must be done without constantly reducing such values to human interests. This will, of course, be difficult, because our conceptual ideology and ethical persuasion are so dominantly homocentric; however, if we are committed to a deeper biocentric ethic, then it is vital that we try to find appropriate ways to promote it. Environmental impact statements should make explicit reference to non-human natural values. Legal rights for non-human natural things, along the lines of

Christopher Stone's proposal, should be sought [22]. And naturalistic ethical guidelines, such as those suggested by Holmes Rolston, should be set forth for business to follow when its activities impact upon ecosystems [23].

At the heart of the business ethics movement is its reaction to the mistaken belief that business only has responsibilities to a narrow set of its stakeholders, namely its stockholders. Crucial to the environmental ethics movement is its reaction to the mistaken belief that only human beings and human interests are deserving of our moral consideration. I suspect that the beginnings of both movements can be traced to these respective moral insights. Certainly the significance of both movements lies in their search for a broader and deeper moral perspective. If business and environmental ethicists begin to rely solely on promotional strategies of self-interest, such as good ethics is good business, and of human interest, such as homocentrism, then they face the danger of cutting off the very roots of their ethical efforts.

References and notes

This paper was originally presented as the Presidential Address to the Society for Business Ethics, 10 August 1990, at San Francisco, CA.

1 Gore, Albert 'What is Wrong With Us?' *Time* 2 January 1989, p. 66.
2 Bowie, N. 'Morality, Money, and Motor Cars'. In: Hoffman, W. Michael, Frederick, Robert and Petry, Edward S. Jr (eds) *Business, Ethics and the Environment: The Public Policy Debate*, New York: Quorum Books, 1990, p. 89.
3 See Friedman, Milton 'The Social Responsibility of Business is to Increase its Profits'. *The New York Times Magazine* 13 September 1970.
4 Bowie, Norman *op. cit.*, p. 91.
5 Bowie, Norman *op. cit.*, p. 94.
6 Robert Frederick, Assistant Director of the Center for Business Ethics, and I have developed and written these points together. Frederick has also provided me with invaluable assistance on other points in this paper.
7 Goodpaster, Kenneth E. 'Can a Corporation Have an Environmental Conscience?' In: Hoffman, W. Michael, Frederick, Robert and Petry, Edward S. Jr (eds) *The Corporation, Ethics and the Environment* New York: Quorum Books, 1990.
8 Sagoff, Mark 'At the Shrine of Our Lady of Fatima, or Why Political Questions Are Not All Economic'. In: Hoffman, W. Michael and Moore, Jennifer Mills (eds) *Business Ethics: Readings and Cases in Corporate Morality*, 2nd edn, New York: McGraw-Hill, 1990, pp. 494–503.
9 Bowie, N. *op. cit.*, p. 94.
10 Shea, Cynthia Pollock 'Doing Well By Doing Good'. *World-Watch* 1989: November/December, 30.
11 *Corporate Ethics: A Prime Business Asset*, a report by The Business Roundtable, New York, February, 1988, p. 4.
12 Blanchard, Kenneth and Peale, Norman Vincent *The Power of Ethical Management*, New York: William Morrow, 1988.
13 Frederick, Robert 'Individual Rights and Environmental Protection', presented at the Annual Society for Business Ethics Conference in San Francisco, 10 and 11 August 1990.

14 Frederick, Robert *op. cit.*
15 Routley, Richard and Routley, Val 'Human Chauvinism and Environmental Ethics'. In: Mannison, Dan, McRobbie, Michael and Routley, Richard (eds) *Environmental Philosophy*, Monograph series no. 2, Australian National University, 1980, pp. 121ff.
16 See Taylor, Paul W. 'The Ethics of Respect for Nature'. In: VanDeVeer, Donald and Pierce, Christine (eds) *People, Penguins and Plastic Trees*, Belmont, CA: Wadsworth, 1986, pp. 178–183. Also see Routley, R. and Routley, V. 'Against the Inevitability of Human Chauvinism'. In: Goodpaster, K.E. and Sayre, K.M. (eds) *Ethics and the Problems of the 21st Century*, Notre Dame, IN: University of Notre Dame Press, 1979, pp. 36–59.
17 Naess, Arne 'Identification as a Source of Deep Ecological Attitudes'. In: Tobias, Michael (ed) *Deep Ecology*, San Marcos, CA: Avant Books, 1988, p. 266.
18 de Spinoza, Benedict 'On the Improvement of the Understanding'. In: *Philosophy of Benedict de Spinoza*, translated by Elwes, R.H.M. New York: Tudor, 1936, p. 5.
19 Stone, Christopher D. 'Should Trees Have Standing? Toward Legal Rights for Natural Objects'. In: VanDeVeer, Donald and Pierce, Christine (eds) *People, Penguins, and Plastic Trees*, Belmont, CA: 1986, pp. 86–87.
20 See VanDeVeer, Donald Interspecific Justice. In: VanDeVeer, Donald and Pierce, Christine (eds) *People, Penguins, and Plastic Trees*, Belmont, CA: 1986, pp. 51–66.
21 Tribe, Lawrence H. 'Ways Not to Think About Plastic Trees: New Foundations for Environmental Law'. In: VanDeVeer, Donald and Pierce, Christine (eds) *People, Penguins, and Plastic Trees*, Belmont, CA: 1986, p. 257.
22 Stone, C.D. *op. cit.*, pp. 83–96.
23 Rolston, Holmes III *Environmental Ethics*, Philadelphia, PA: Temple University Press, 1988, pp. 301–313.

Additional reading

Two books which Hoffman refers to in notes 2 and 7 are particularly valuable: *Business, Ethics and the Environment* and *The Corporation, Ethics and the Environment*. These collections of articles are the proceedings from the 1989 National Conference on Business Ethics at Bentley College, USA.

There is, of course, a growing body of material on the environment which is not part of the ethics literature *per se*. These include:

1 Winter, George *Business and the Environment*, McGraw-Hill, Hamburg, 1988. This 248-page book has sections on the practical aspects of and arguments for environmentalist business management.
2 Elkington, John, Burke, Tom and Hailes, Julia *Green Pages*, London: Routledge, 1988. This is a collection of over forty contributions discussing actions by environmentalists and opportunities for business.

Examples of European business ethics/environmental work can be found in the proceedings from the 1991 European Business Ethics Network conference: *Business Ethics in a New Europe*, edited by Mahoney, Jack and Vallance,

Elizabeth (Dordrecht, Netherlands: Kluwer Academic Publishing, 1992). In it, Erik Schokkaert writes on 'Business Ethics and the Greenhouse Problem'. He argues that an imposition of a carbon tax is the most equitable and efficient way of reducing carbon dioxide emissions. Also included is Clive Wright's contribution 'Environmental conservation and the chemical industry'. Wright describes the Responsible Care Programme – an initiative by the chemical industry established in part to respond to criticisms by the public. This self-regulation addresses issues such as air emissions and community involvement.

Questions for discussion

- Do you agree with Hoffman's assertion that business should do more to protect the environment than is in its self-interest?
- If you do, how would you present this case to, say, a group of managers? What counterarguments would you expect?
- If you disagree with Hoffman, why?

Chapter 11

The future shape of ethical banking

In the light of recent scandals in the European financial services sector which have had a widespread impact, there are growing calls for increased regulation. Indeed, some critics would argue that the term 'financial services ethics' is an oxymoron. Yet most people would like to believe that integrity lies at the very heart of every financial transaction.

This is why its – perhaps occasional – absence creates such profound challenges for those inside and outside the financial services industry. Banks, in particular, will find the years ahead replete with ethical problems, not least because banks are under considerable pressure to protect margins in difficult trading conditions, while enhancing levels of customer service.

Moreover, banking is perhaps the only business which can require a customer to pay before submitting a bill. Furthermore, until recently British banks did not consider it necessary to indicate what their likely charges might be. Although the recent introduction of various banking charters has improved this position, none the less many observers feel it may take some time for banks in the UK to regain the reputation they once had with customers.

It might be expected therefore that all banks would have clearly set-out ethical standards describing their obligations to all stakeholder groups, and how they would resolve situations where the interests of stakeholder groups might conflict.

In practice the response of the banks to ethical challenges has been somewhat mixed and confusing. One British bank has chosen to describe its ethics code as a 'marketing initiative', thereby suggesting to some that its code may be replaced by another 'initiative' should it prove unsuccessful in marketing terms, or as other circumstances might require.

Some would argue that this attitude trivializes ethics to the degree that it may encourage those outside the banking industry to question whether integrity really is central to all banking operations. Yet our research has shown that the two principal areas where it is required that the highest ethical standards should prevail are health provision and financial services.

This chapter is of importance not just to those in financial services but to all business people, because of the crucial nature of the banking relationship in commercial activities. It is equally important to gain an insight into how this relationship may alter and change in the years ahead.

It is arguable that, while all businesses are subject to rapid change, perhaps these changes present a greater challenge to the banking industry than any other. However, it should also be of general interest to look at the future shape of ethical banking as the challenges there may herald difficulties that might be reflected in other business sectors.

The future shape of ethical banking
James J. Lynch

Introduction

The 1990s will witness changes in the four major geopolitical banking areas of the world – Europe, the USA, Japan and the Middle East. Some of these changes will be interactive, cutting across national and international boundaries to form a lattice-like network of cultural and financial relationships. These relationships will influence ethical codes and behaviour by bringing into play new mixtures of ethical traditions which hitherto have operated separately in their local markets.

European and US banks have followed the Hellenic and Judeo-Christian philosophies with emphasis on the golden rule, 'Do unto others as you would have them do unto you'. In the USA, banks in this century have been more circumscribed by law than has been the situation, until recently, in Europe. This reliance on the rule of law will become more marked but with a significant change of emphasis. Whereas since the 1930s US banking law has been primarily concerned with preventing fraud and safeguarding the savings of investors, the future trend will be to enforce banks to contribute to solving community problems. In ethical terms, the move is away from 'You can't do this' to 'You must do that'.

For example, under US federal law, those regulators responsible for approving bank mergers have a duty to ensure that banks lend in all areas, including poor ones, where their depositors live. The existence of this law was used by pressure groups in California, the 'Greenliners', to influence the policies of Japanese banks which now have a dominant role in that state. One of the problems facing Japanese banks in the USA has been a lack of experience in dealing with ethnic groups in a sensitive manner. This can result in perceptions of 'unethical' behaviour on the part of the Japanese, and sometimes oversensitivity to pressure groups. When California First (Japanese-owned) bought Union Bank, the latter invested $84 million in poor neighbourhoods due, it is claimed, to the 'Greenliners'. (The name 'Greenliners' was coined to counteract the practice of some US banks which 'redline' certain neighbourhoods which they consider too risky for loans.)

This one example reflects some of the forces at work in shaping ethical banking – legislation, social pressures, changes in ownership. There are others, as we shall see below.

Trends in European banking

The major factors shaping the European banking scene in the 1990s are:

1 The unification of Germany.
2 The single European market.
3 The rebirth of East European banking.

The unification of Germany will be the single greatest force on ethical banking in Europe because it will lead to the expansion of the concept of the 'universal bank', not only in the new Germany but in both the European Community and the countries of Eastern Europe.

The universal bank combines traditional banking with investment banking (corporate finance, stockbroking, dealing, etc.). A distinctive characteristic, in contrast to British and US banks, is that the universal banks own large stakes in their industrial clients; they are involved in the direction and operation of the companies in which they have a stake. Deutsche Bank is the largest universal bank.

A study published by the Centre for European Policy Studies in Brussels, in 1989, sought to cast doubts on the spread of the universal bank concept [1]. It argued that it is a phenomenon specific in time and place to the rebuilding of post-war Germany. At the time the report was prepared, Germany was still totally divided and its Eastern neighbours were under Communist rule. Now all that has changed.

The arguments against universal banks are:

1 They have not benefited from economies of scale.
2 They are slow to react and can be outmatched in performance by small 'boutique banks'.
3 They are at risk if one of their major industrial investments goes wrong.
4 There can be conflicts of interest between the roles of lender and investor to the same company.
5 There is a danger of concentration of power since universal banks dominate the credit system and investment market.

Against these economic arguments the significance of universal banks for ethical banking is that they perform a social role in their home market. By being willing to forgo part of their profit in the long-term interests of their clients or to further a particular project, they can help safeguard the interests of the economy as a whole. Furthermore, they can influence the ethical behaviour of clients in whom they have a stake. This means that they must be clear about their own ethical values and standards.

Universal banking was born in a post-war era of reconstruction in Germany. With all its faults, it has contributed to the development of Europe's strongest economy. There can be little doubt that universal banking will prosper in the post-peaceful-revolution era of the 1990s in the united Germany and its Eastern neighbours.

Turning to western Europe, there can be little doubt that 1992 marks a watershed in European banking. The ability of any bank to operate in every European Community member country on the basis of a single licence will increase competition as the 'newcomers' seek out the most lucrative segments of the financial markets, leaving the 'locals' to deal with the dross.

A survey by the Bank of England in 1989 on the views of British banks and financial institutions of the effects of the single European market revealed:

1 Change will be evolutionary rather than sudden.
2 There will be more opportunities than threats.
3 Major corporate products and services will be the first to create a single market, due in part to their wholesaling being already international.
4 Retail markets will remain fragmented for some time due to national characteristics.
5 Competition from the USA and Japan is likely to have more impact on the British market than will competition from within the European Community.

We shall now consider how these two major competitors are shaping up for the 1990s and their likely effects on ethical banking.

Trends in American banking

Just as the universal bank will provide a model in Europe, the 1990 banking model in the USA will be the 'superregional bank'. At the start of the 1980s such a bank did not exist; by 1990 there were over twenty, with combined assets of more than £600 billion. Superregional banks operate in more than one state. They are a consequence of a Supreme Court ruling to change the situation which had existed in the USA since the Pepper–McFadden Act.

Seeking to prevent a concentration of financial power, that Act prevented banks in one state from operating full branches in another. An unforeseen consequence of the Act, however, was the growth of the so-called money banks such as Citicorp, Bankers Trust, Chase in New York.

The new superregionals now want a larger slice of the national banking market which the 'New York giants' formerly shared among themselves.

In recent years, some superregionals have suffered large losses from bad property loans, but their woes were less than those of the money banks with their enormous exposure to Third World loans.

The superregionals are now sorting themselves into the three categories of:

1 Highly successful.
2 Successful.
3 Unsuccessful.

The highly successful are those like North Carolina's NCNB Corporation which have a clear vision and which concentrate on what they do best. (In this respect they are no different from any other highly successful company.) What most seem to do best is lend to medium-size companies. Cost control is a critical factor in these far-flung banks located in a number of states. Wells Fargo is the outstanding cost-controller. The successful superregionals are those which have merged with or acquired compatible partners and have maintained steady rather than speedy growth, such as Fleet/Norster, which runs two regional banks and several other businesses.

The unsuccessful are those which have become embroiled in post-merger drift or have concentrated their lending in a falling property market, such as the Bank of New England.

As legislation changes, the superregionals will grow by acquisition and will become real competitors of the money banks. Citicorp is the only one of these which seems ready to battle with the superregional. Its main weapon is technology. It has used its electronic networks and databanks to build itself into a national bank.

One outcome of these trends in the USA is that superregionals will become owned by 'non-banks', major manufacturing companies which have no banking traditions and different ethical codes – for better or worse – than the banking industry. Another outcome will be ownership by foreign banks and other institutions. We have already seen in this chapter that some leading superregionals in California are owned by the Japanese; this is a trend which will grow and will influence ethical banking in the USA.

Trends in Japanese banking

Adapting the British description of US Forces during World War II – 'Overpaid, oversexed and over here' – the Japanese banking industry can be described as 'overregulated, overcrowded and over everywhere'. Nine of the ten top banks worldwide are Japanese; the world's largest securities house, Nomura, is Japanese.

In recent years, the Japanese have paid heavily for their aggressive overseas expansion, resulting in painful write-offs of Mexican debt. The Japanese banks are highly regulated at home; this makes the freer conditions of other financial markets highly attractive. Although there is no immediate prospect of dismantling the legal barriers which separate different types of Japanese banks and securities companies, the very prospect of change is unsettling the industry.

Medium and small companies have become the key sectors for lending as the Japanese multimarket has grown financially self-sufficient. Sources of cheap money which fuelled the growth of Japanese banks have dried up as government restrictions on interest rates are removed. The competition for funds from rich industrialists has grown rapidly, causing the banks to respond to greater competition from life assurance and securities companies.

For many years Japanese banks have held huge portfolios of securities of client companies. These have been 'loss leaders', the cost of the low-yielding stock from the client and the growth in market value of the shares. Now that large companies are no longer borrowing and the stock-market is becoming more turbulent there will be a temptation to sell off the shares.

The financial markets in Japan are likely to become more volatile in the 1990s as the regulatory frameworks are taken down and replaced by new rules. The USA and the European Community are unlikely to tolerate the growth of Japanese influence in their markets without enjoying reciprocal rights.

As the Japanese respond to these pressures, their influence on new ethical banking will grow. The Judeo-Christian and Hellenic philosophies, with their emphasis on free will and truth and individual accountability, will have to adjust to that of Shintoism with its emphasis on collective duty and loyalty to superiors. While it would be wrong to suggest that one tradition is ethically superior to the other, it is important to recognize that they lead to different types of ethical behaviour. So too does another philosophy which is now a major force and will influence the new ethical banking – Islam.

Trends in Islamic banking

Islamic banking is a relatively new phenomenon. It was only in 1950 that Saudi Arabia established its own currency; Islamic banking (as distinct from European banks in the Middle East) began to develop in the 1960s. The oil boom of the 1970s spurred the growth of Islamic banks, but the main impetus in the spread of Islamic values in banking came with the revolution in Iran. Today, only that country and Pakistan have adopted the system completely but its influence spreads across the globe. In Britain, estimates of the volume of business conducted by banks conforming to Islamic principles range from \$1 to \$5 billion; worldwide estimates are from \$20 to \$40 billion and growing.

There are three categories of Islamic banks in operation:

1 Islamic development banks which concentrate on economic development in the Third World.

2 Islamic commercial banks, which are similar in the scope of their operations to British and American commercial banks.
3 Commercial banks which offer a limited range of Islamic products.

What links these categories together is the Koran; they all operate in varying degrees in accordance with the principles of *Sharia* or Islamic law.

The objectives of Islamic banking are:

1 To attract funds and employ these resources in Islamic countries;
2 To develop the saving habit among Muslim individuals;
3 To offer interest-free bank services according to Islamic *Sharia*.

The seven financial instruments of Islamic banking are:

1 *Mudaraba* – unit trust agreement.
2 *Murabaha* – resale contract.
3 *Musharaka* – a venture partnership.
4 *Ijara* – leasing.
5 *Wadia* – pawnbroking-type agreement.
6 *Takafol* – mutual insurance.
7 *Qard Hasan* – loan without interest.

These practices are described more fully in Figure 11.1. Most Islamic banking practices are cumbersome and can be in conflict with western banking legislation. They depend on very high levels of trust.

The Islamic prohibition on charging any interest on loans can have unusual consequences. An example is quoted by Hashi Syedain in a survey of Islamic banking in *Management Today* [2]. Many Muslims in the UK have used the services of an Islamic bank to finance house purchase. Interest-free house purchase is arranged by a combination of *musharaka* (venture principle) and *ijara* (leasing). Benefit is taken of British trust laws which make a distinction between legal and beneficial ownership.

> The bank and its customer buy a property together and the customer then buys back the bank's share by instalments at cost price. The bank makes its profit by leasing its interest in the house to the customer at a rate fixed on a yearly basis . . . There is one significant catch – because there is no interest involved, customers do not qualify for mortgage tax relief.

As far as ethical banking is concerned, Islamic banking is important because it raises a number of alternative approaches to the banker–customer relationship. It helps to stimulate new thinking about alternative banking and possible ethical solutions to emerging problems, such as coping with the underclass and financing small businesses based on networks or communes . . . what we are witnessing is the growth of a type of banking which states its ethical values explicitly.

Mudaraba	A unit-trust-type agreement between a bank (the lender) and a businessman whereby the bank agrees to finance a project on a profit-or-loss-sharing basis. The businessman undertakes to pay back the capital invested and a share of the profits. He acts as project manager while the bank acts as capital provider
Murabaha	A resale contract whereby the client requests the bank to buy specific goods. The bank resells these at a price which covers the purchase price plus the profit margin agreed upon by both parties. This changes traditional lending into a sale-and-purchase agreement, under which the bank buys the goods wanted by the client for resale to the client at a higher price, agreed upon by both parties
Musharaka	A partnership for a specific business activity, in which the bank and the partner create joint venture projects with the aim of making a profit, whereby, like the German universal bank concept, there is a participation in the management
Ijara	Straightforward leasing, renting or hiring
Wadia	An agreement to deposit an asset (excluding land) into the custody of the bank
Takafol	Mutual support whereby the various participants agree to pay instalments into a fund managed by the bank. The bank acts as a management company – admitting participants, collecting instalments, investing funds and paying benefits – under the conditions of the contract
Qard Hasan	Literally a 'good loan'. This is a loan whereby a borrower is obliged to repay the lender the principal sum borrowed on the loan. It is left to the discretion of the borrower to reward the lender for the loan by paying any sum over and above the amount of the principal. Usually this is used in a transaction between the state and a less wealthy member of society.

Fig. 11.1 *Islamic banking practices*

Ethics and culture

The significance for ethical banking of this growth in internationalism of banks is plain to see. It has long been recognized that there are wide differences in what is ethically acceptable, both across national cultures and over time within a single culture. Lying is, in most western cultures, considered more wrong than in Eastern cultures where the 'wrongness' depends on the context in which the lie occurs. The Japanese place a higher value on social harmony as an ethical goal than they do on truthfulness. In Japan, a person has a moral duty to lie in certain social situations.

The core elements of ethical behaviour are determined by time and circumstances shaping society. A country under constant military threat will emphasize physical courage and have no moral qualms about treating its perceived enemies in ways which others consider to be unethical . . .

An affluent society will emphasize charity towards needy persons. The UK in the 1980s was an example of such a society where charities emerged in great numbers to stir the conscience of rich individuals. The drive by some banks and building societies to provide charity-oriented credit cards, whereby a tiny proportion of a customer's credit turnover is allocated to a designated charity, can be seen either as a spur to social conscience or a cynical exploitation of a trend.

In contrast to rich society, poor societies, such as India, develop a moral code which encourages detachment from the poor and the sick. Hence the work of Mother Teresa which we hold up as an example of virtue in the west is perceived, in a sense, as 'unethical' in the Indian subcontinent. The growing number of poor across the world is another force shaping ethical banking.

Trends in alternative banking

There are four types of alternative banks (and alternatives to banks) which are influencing ethical banking since they are based on more explicit ethical values than are the traditional banks:

1 Social collateral banking.
2 Viewpoint banking.
3 Mutual societies.
4 'Ethical' investments.

Social collateral banking

This began in Bangladesh in 1977. The problem of poor people without ownership of homes or land is acute in that country. Such people find it impossible to raise loans and invest in improving their standard of living. The Grameen Bank has addressed this problem by developing a system of social collateral. People wanting to use the bank are asked to organize themselves into groups of fifty and subgroups of five. Members of each subgroup are asked to act as guarantor for each other's loans. Each group and subgroup also act as the evaluator and approver of each loan. Thus credit scoring moves from the bank to the community.

The success of this non-traditional approach can be gauged by the traditional measures of banking: a 97.3% on-time repayment of loans totalling over £54 million to more than 290 000 borrowers, three-quarters of whom are women. And the bank makes a profit.

Social collateral banking is moving into India and South America. It is also catching on in the affluent west – South Shore Bank of Chicago and Mercury Provident in the UK are experimenting with ways of using social collateral to lend to the so-called underclass.

Viewpoint banking

This is my term for alternative banks based on a shared philosophy or viewpoint (Islamic banking is the prime example). Mercury Provident, mentioned in the previous paragraph, is a British 'licensed deposit taker' whose clients tend to share the ideas of Rudolph Steiner. An 'ecologist' ahead of his time, Steiner viewed money as a representation of social and spiritual energy. It should be used in a fully conscious way – knowing where it is going and the purposes for which it is being used.

Members of Mercury Provident can have an account similar to a building society savings account – but with some differences. They can specify their own terms of withdrawal and their own rates of interest (up to a specified ceiling). Each member can specify either a particular project or area of work to which they want their money to be lent. By this means both lenders and borrowers become much more aware of each other's interests. Projects financed by Mercury Provident range from publishing to retirement homes, as well as investments in organic research, Steiner schools and Marged Shoes (a women's cooperative making shoes in Wales). Mercury Provident uses National Westminster as its clearing bank.

Another example of viewpoint banking is doing without conventional currency. Pioneered in Canada under the title Local Employment and Trade System (LETS system), it has spread to the USA, Australia, New Zealand and the UK.

The system is designed not to replace conventional currency completely, but as a complementary system that helps local communities to thrive independently of national and international economics. LETS uses a 'green pound' to replace barter trading; green pounds are intangible, existing only in the books and computers of the system and are created simply by trading. It works as follows. Whenever someone trades with another member, for example buying food or renting a room, they simply inform the office which debits one account and credits the other. The buyer need not have any green pounds to start buying, and there is no interest charged anywhere in the system. The creation of 'money' is linked solely to the creation of real value, so no one can hoard money and profit from other people's shortage.

LETS is still in the experimental stage but it has lessons for the new ethical banking. It requires active participation rather than passive consumption. More importantly, it focuses on the need for trust, commitment from members and skilful management.

Mutual societies

Mutual societies are not new; they are the concept behind the building society movement. However, as building societies move to become banks there is another long-established form of mutuality which is gaining strength – credit unions.

In the USA, there are now 14 000 credit unions, in Nigeria 7000; total assets are over $200 billion. Thus the credit union movement is significantly larger than Islamic banking. In the UK, there are around 150 credit unions and some local authorities are supporting their growth. There are credit unions among London taxi drivers, the Pentecostal Church and many local communities.

A credit union is a mutual financial cooperative which offers savings and low-interest loans to its members. Members save a regular amount each week and borrow from the common pool as and when they need to. By law a credit union must be formed by people sharing a 'common bond'. This can mean working for the same employer or resident in the same area, or members of the same association.

In the UK, the Credit Union Act of 1979 provides the legal framework within which credit unions must operate. Currently, the maximum interest rate is 1% a month for borrowers and a maximum of 8% for savers. Loans and savings are limited to a maximum of £2000.

'Ethical' investments

These are not a new phenomenon but are the fastest-growing new idea in banking.

Since the mid 1980s an increasing number of conventional banks has offered 'ethical investment funds'. By this they mean companies which are engaged in producing environmentally friendly products as distinct from companies involved in armaments, animal testing for products, harmful chemicals, or South Africa.

Lines can become blurred in these categories. To assist UK investors in making the 'right' choice, the Ethical Investment Research and Information Service (EIRIS) was started in 1983. It provides lists of acceptable companies given particular criteria.

It emphasizes that it does not 'make judgements about the moral acceptability of the activities of individual firms', but it can tell potential investors a company's policy on arms, nuclear power or South Africa [3].

We have already seen that Mercury Provident predated the new enlightenment of so-called ethical investment funds. Another pioneer is the Ecology Building Society.

Founded in 1981 with only ten members and £5000, it now has assets of over £4 million. The Ecology Building Society operates similarly to its long-established counterparts, lending its money as mortgages on property. Where it differs from other societies is in its criteria for lending, which shall be 'most likely to lead to the saving of non-renewable resources, the promotion of self-sufficiency in individuals or communities, or the most ecologically efficient use of land'. This must surely be one of the most value-laden criteria of any financial institution. For ethical banking it holds a lesson – beware of being overzealous in imposing your values on customers. For example, the Ecology Building Society will lend to an organically farmed smallholding, but not to barn conversions for holiday homes, no matter how much they improve the local environment.

All the examples of alternative banking described in this section are a reality. Each signals a trend which conventional banks need to take into account:

1 Extending the criteria for lending.
2 Giving more decision-making to customers on where their money is invested.
3 Devising new ways of meeting the financial needs of the poor.

At the other end of the spectrum from helping the poor is helping the rich to safeguard and increase their wealth. This is no new challenge for banks but it is one which is receiving increased attention in the new ethical banking.

Banks for the rich

For bankers, the rich, like the poor, are always with us. But they like to be treated differently.

Mass-market banks are a relatively recent phenomenon. For legal reasons, they have not existed in the USA. In the UK, they are less than a hundred years old, being a response to the growth of industry at the turn of the century, but only coming into active life as purveyors of a range of saving and lending products on a vast scale since the 1960s.

The 1980s in both the UK and the USA have seen an unprecedented growth in affluence. The common millionaire has given way to the billionaire. Senior executives receive six-figure salaries; entrepreneurs have become 'seriously rich' in their thirties, dealers in the money markets have become seriously rich and seriously poor in their twenties.

In 1987, the most wealthy 10% of the adult population of the UK owned half the total marketable wealth. This minority has been passionately courted by the banks; the day of the personal banker has arrived. Personal knowledge of clients' individual circumstances and the ability to respond to them swiftly and flexibly is the main selling point of small banks.

One characteristic is to appear to eschew modern technology by providing detailed account statements. Drummonds (a subsidiary of the Royal Bank of Scotland), located at Charing Cross in London, panders to this nostalgia by providing customers with quill pens and even snuff on request.

The management of assets tends to be dealt with in an impersonal manner by the large clearing banks. Not so in the old and new private banks. Duncan Lawrie, founded in London in 1971, manages funds of its clients of at least £45 000 at a 1% charge plus VAT. Unlike Duncan Lawrie, most private banks on both sides of the Atlantic are subsidiaries of large banks. In the UK, the largest and best known 'private bank', Coutts, with fourteen branches, is owned by the National Westminster Bank. The Royal Bank of Scotland has three private banks under its wing: (1) Child and Co., which caters particularly for the law and bloodstock industries; (2) Holts, which focuses on the armed services; and (3) Drummonds, which caters particularly for affluent Scots who have exiled themselves to London.

In the USA, the parentage of private banks is more clearly identified. One of the largest – American Express Bank – advertises the traits which'it seeks in its 'élite corps' of bankers:

1 *Character* Cast-iron integrity, energy, stamina and grace under pressure.
2 *Verve* We admire activists who are willing to break some china within the bank in order to be effective for their clients.
3 *Entrepreneurship* We reward those whose solutions to one client's needs create fertile opportunities for other clients.
4 *Unselfishness* Every account officer must be a 'switchboard' connecting clients with *whoever* will best serve their needs.
5 *Resilience* People who thrive on weeks of sustained effort, and who display a genius for keeping up with change.

Putting to one side copy-writers' hyperbole, this mixture of ethical values and physical characteristics does at least attempt to reveal an ethical code, particularly the definition of 'unselfishness'. This is one of the contributions which both private banks and the more specialized 'banking boutiques' can make to ethical values – a spelling out of what they stand for.

In the USA, private banking concentrates on lending to affluent individuals; in Switzerland, the primary focus is on investment management with particular emphasis on the preservation of capital and assurance of secrecy, though this is now under threat.

The private banker provides a highly personalized service and charges for it accordingly. They are masters of the relationship approach to banking rather than the more common transactional approach. This is difficult for the larger banks to provide, hence there will be an increasing trend by the major banks in the UK and elsewhere to set up private bank subsidiaries, probably under a different name. The Coutts–National Westminster relationship and the three offshoots of the Royal Bank of Scotland provide a model.

One other contribution which the private bank phenomenon will make to ethical banking is a greater openness by all banks on their charges and on criteria for opening an account. The rich are generally more demanding than the poor; they like to know what they will be charged for their banking services. Therefore, as more 'private banks' are established by the large banks (and building societies which have transformed into banks), there will be pressure from consumers' groups, and probably legislation, to force banks to be more open about charges to all their customers. The key issue will be not so much the amount charged but the ability of a bank, or rather a branch manager, to *justify* the level of charge to the satisfaction of customers.

Another contribution to ethical banking will be to force larger banks to devise a type of customer interaction which blends the relationship approach with the transactional approach. This I call the 'situational approach'.

The situational approach

As major banks have grown it has proved increasingly difficult to provide the relationship approach of serving the needs of each customer through an indepth knowledge of the individual and his/her personal circumstances built up over many years. This has not solely been the fault of banks. Customers have become more geographically mobile; also, the spread of services through automated teller machines (ATMs) has kept the customer out of contact. Indeed, the manager has become increasingly like the priest in the confessional, meeting only those who have sinned.

The transactional approach, with its focus on relating to customers on a series of one-off contacts based on a specific transaction, be it a home loan or insurance purchase, has become more common. This is probably due to the numbers of customers who have to be serviced and also to the proliferation of products, each accompanied by a sales drive.

A further factor is the use of credit scoring which leads to each loan application being treated separately. This can also apply in loan applications being evaluated by a lending officer.

The situational approach would require that all customers with a certain amount of assets deposited with the bank should be contacted annually and offered the opportunity to discuss their financial situation and ways in which the bank might help them. This would include determining if they are getting the best deal on their investments, taking account of their needs and priorities. For example, by being proactive in offering to transfer funds to a higher-interest account, a branch manager might find that the customer has preference for accessibility which makes the existing arrangements more satisfactory. Equally, every customer with credit facilities over a certain sum should have an annual meeting with an appropriate bank official to review the situation and determine whether there are alternative arrangements to his/her benefit.

Situational banking is not altruism. The risk of losing a few interest points has to be set against the risk of the customer closing the account and transferring the business to a competitor.

Trends in technology

Few industries have undergone the technology revolution of banking. Billions of pounds have been invested in the establishment of networks, the development of ATMs/cash machines, the provision of on-line data to branches and even to clients. Looking ahead, the two major technological innovations in banking will be the use of the telephone and the television.

Telephone banking enables customers to phone and interrogate their banks' computer system and be answered by a recorded voice. Midland Bank has gone further and provides the customers of their First Direct telephone banking service with a response from a human operator. Their prelaunch research showed that the vast majority of people prefer to talk to people rather than computers. At the time of writing, it is too early to assess the success or otherwise of First Direct.

However, the longer-established computer response systems have got off to a slow start in the UK. Only twenty of over 600 banks and building societies provide this type of service. Just over one million customers use the system, the TSB group accounting for a quarter of the total.

There are three types of telephone banking systems in operation:

1 Modern telephone.
2 Tone pads.
3 Voice recognition.

The modern telephone, with its push buttons for dialling, enables the customer to give the account and personal identification number. The customer then dials different numbers for different services – updated account statement, new cheque book, etc. Customers can also pay bills and use other bank services by telephone, provided they have completed the necessary documentation at their branch to set up the system.

Tone pads – small electronic units which imitate the bleeps made by a telephone – are provided by some banks to customers who do not have the modern phones. The procedure for using the telephone banking service using the tone pad is the same as with the modern telephone.

Voice recognition is still in its infancy, being pioneered by the Royal Bank of Scotland. There are three types of voice response systems:

1 *Voice print*: This is the most sophisticated system. The words of the customer are compared to a voice print which is stored in the customer's branch. Only when the two match can any transaction take place. The number of words which can be recognized is limited.
2 *Isolated words*: This system recognizes a spoken digit at a time and simple words like 'yes' and 'no', between a 'bleep'.
3 *Continuing digits*: This allows a complete string of numbers to be uttered for recognition to take place.

Telephone technology, like the use of ATMs, raises problems of confidentiality. Furthermore, a voice recognition system which mistakes one digit for another can cause problems for both bank and customer.

Ethical banking will require a drawing-up of codes of conduct for banking technology.

Television banking has been pioneered by the Bank of Scotland under the acronym HOBS (Home and Office Banking Service). This allows customers to check details of their accounts and order services over the telephone line by pressing a key pad in front of their television set. A simple, cheap keyboard (£100) plugs into the television and the telephone. When used, the television will show on its screen the information sought by the customer. Providing prior arrangements have been made, HOBS will pay bills 'just in time' to gain maximum credit. It also makes easier the transfer of funds from one account to another to gain maximum interest. The technological effectiveness of HOBS is restricted by the inadequacies of customers' televisions. The provision of data on screens is sometimes blurred and it can take, in computer terms, a long time to respond to instructions.

More sophisticated types of television banking, using personal computers, are on the horizon. The spread of this type of banking will increase. It is feasible for a Japanese bank to service the needs of British customers from Tokyo without having to open a single branch. Though that time may be far off, it is necessary now to establish codes of conduct which will be in accord with . . . ethical banking . . . .

Conclusion

The future shape of banking will result from the monumental changes taking place in the industry across the world. Increasing customer sophistication will force banks to design and deliver products in new ways to take advantage of the growing internationalism of banking.

In Europe, the Second Banking Directive, which allows banks to establish themselves in other countries, will lead to new alliances and increased competition for lucrative niches. The concept of the universal bank, pioneered in Germany, will spread its wings in the new Germany and in Eastern Europe.

Superregional banks, increasingly owned by 'non-banks', will capture much of the US domestic market, forcing the giant money banks to be more aggressive overseas. Changes in the legal framework of Japanese banking will have consequences which will reverberate across the globe as the Japanese giants flex their muscles. New forms of banking drawing on different value systems will appear and be treated as either a threat or a source of inspiration by traditional banks. The need to provide a personal touch for more demanding and increasingly affluent customers will spur the development of 'private banking'. Large banks will need to offer different levels of service, and for their core of customers will adopt a 'situational approach'. In addition, the march of technology will continue, with greater use of telephones and television to enable customers to be served at home.

All these trends will raise new ethical issues and revive some old ones. There will be a need to think through the principles on which banks will respond to new needs from their customers and new pressures from their competitors. Banking will be a more demanding and exciting industry to work in; the question is, faced with all these changes, will it be more or less ethical?

References

1 Steinherr, Alfred and Huveneers, Christian, 'Universal Banks: The Prototype of Successful Banks in the Integrated European Market?' Centre for European Policy Studies.
2 Syedain, Hashi 'Counting on the Quran'. *Management Today*, March 1989; p. 104–108.
3 Choosing an Ethical Fund, EIRIS, 1990.

Additional reading

In an illuminating ten-page interview led by Jack Mahoney, Edward George, the Governor of the Bank of England, reflects on the place of ethics in banking. Topics covered range from the interest charge on credit cards to the failure of the Bank of Credit and Commerce International (*Business Ethics – European Review*, 1992; **1**, 162–172.

In a forthcoming paper titled 'Ethical banking: the case of the Co-operative Bank', Brian Harvey describes the philosophy and actions of this innovative UK bank. With the core value 'the responsible sourcing and distribution of funds', the bank is 'committed to an alternative, socially responsible approach to the provision of banking services'. This case can be analysed from various perspectives, such as a bank being ethical or a bank utilizing niche marketing.

Questions for discussion

- To what do you attribute the recent growing feeling that banks no longer act with the level of integrity that has underpinned the banking industry for decades?
- What action is needed to re-establish trust in the banking industry?

Chapter 12

Accountancy and ethics

Anyone taking a serious interest in ethics of business quickly comes to the conclusion that accountants have a key, if not a central, role to play. However, it is a role that is becoming increasingly controversial.

Written by one of the UK's most prestigious journalists, this chapter can be approached on at least two levels.

On a general level, Andrew Jack's contribution examines the challenges confronting the ethos of self-regulation in an industry passing through a period of rapid change.

In particular, he has taken a long, hard look at the place, attitudes and techniques of UK accountants. He deals with the real, practical challenges facing the accountancy profession and its reaction to these challenges.

Corporate executives are clearly in a position to place considerable pressure on their accountants and, as this chapter demonstrates, this has tended to increase the charms of creative accounting.

There is also an important section on accountancy as a business, which will provoke a number of questions for both managers and accountants.

The audit conflict raises interesting points about relationships within the accountancy profession, and with company boards. Independence is clearly what counts. But what happens when auditors press forward with their view in the teeth of opposition from the board? One outcome is that they may be replaced. What price independence then?

The section dealing with other conflicts of interest spells out the dangers and difficulties that arise as accountancy companies diversify. This point crops up again later in the chapter with the interesting comment from a member of an ethics committee: 'Lawyers withdraw from conflicts of interest. Accountants manage them'.

The segment on changing times challenges the view that there may have been a recent halcyon period when integrity was not an issue.

There is an important section on the profession's response, which covers the work of the Accounting Standards Board and its efforts to deal with ethical problems.

Accountancy and ethics
Andrew Jack

Introduction

Ask a group of consumers whether business has ethics and they are likely to laugh in derision. Ask a group of business executives the same about accountants, and the answer is not likely to be so different.

That is an extreme view, perhaps even an unfair one, but it is certainly one that can be expressed with far more conviction than would have been possible even a decade ago. Lawyers may be a more common butt of jokes, but accountants have suffered at least as much denigration as any of the other professions.

It reflects a number of factors: not least the growth in creative accounting; the large number of companies which failed as a result of fraud which the auditors were apparently unable to detect; and the structural issues in the current organization of the accounting industry.

The literature on ethics in accountancy – and on the professions in general – is sparse. There seems to be an assumption that the professions – proud bearers of codes of ethics – are less relevant or interesting – and perhaps less questionable in their practices – than businesses. It is a field that demands more serious consideration.

The image of accountants – reflected by the Monty Python sketches of the 1970s – was of people who were grey, unimaginative and boring. But above all, they were cautious, backward-looking, a brake on excess. By the late 1980s, that conservatism had been replaced by something altogether more aggressive.

Creative accounting

An important influence was the changing nature of the equity markets. There was growing pressure, as never before, from company investors to improve profits and strengthen the balance sheet. That helped ensure that there was healthy demand for the shares, creating scope for rights issues, reducing the need for bank borrowing, and helping justify the case of acquisitions or to defend against other corporate predators looking for takeover targets.

One essential response was the development of an enormous array of creative accounting techniques, which broke with the caution of the past and seemed to spurn a predominant emphasis on the true underlying financial position of the company. In its place came a range of devices rather more flattering to corporate performance in the short term – at the expense of shareholders more interested in the future, as defined in any way beyond a few months.

Manipulation was helped by a weak framework of legislation: companies law has scant reference to financial reporting other than the vaguely defined requirement for the profit and loss account and the balance sheet to show 'a true and fair view'. This was particularly the case before the introduction of the accounts directives promulgated by the European Community as the 1980s progressed.

There were standards produced by the profession, through the Accounting Standards Committee. But their legal status was uncertain, and the committee finally had to be radically restructured towards the end of the decade as companies simply refused to comply with its more controversial guidelines.

In general, with the connivance of lawyers and other professional advisers, there was an emphasis on the letter rather than the spirit of standards; and of legal form over the substance of financial transactions.

There is an almost endless catalogue of examples, many designed specifically to evade new rules which were introduced to stamp out previous abuses. Efforts to reduce the scale of debt – and hence reduce the risk of breaching banking covenants – generated off-balance sheet finance, sale and leaseback arrangements, and 'quasi-equity' capital instruments such as convertible capital bonds which were debt in all but name. Balance sheet assets were boosted with intangible assets such as brands, calculated using dubious valuation methods.

There were 'non-subsidiary subsidiaries' which permitted the exclusion of loss-making companies from the consolidated accounts; 'extraordinary items' to exclude costs from the profit figure; 'circular transactions' which inflated profits by selling assets held for years at historic cost, booking the difference to the sale price, and purchasing them back almost immediately; and preacquisition provisions which could be fed back discreetly to boost profits at a later date.

These devices were a poor reflection both on accountants and on accountancy. It is all too often forgotten that by law it is a company's directors – and not its accountants – who are responsible for ensuring that the accounts show a true and fair view. None the less, the accounts must be approved by the auditors; and many of the directors, internal accounts staff, financial engineers in banks and other external advisers to companies were trained with the larger accountancy firms.

There is no single correct way to present financial information. But many accountants would agree that the pendulum swung too far in the 1980s away from fair financial reporting. At the very least, the growth of the creative accounting industry reflects inadequacies in accounting standards.

More seriously, it highlights auditors' willingness to bow under commercial pressures to the treatment of information favoured by company management. At its worst, there are instances of direct complicity between external accountants and executives, at the expense of shareholders. This reflects the changing shape of the profession as it has been transformed into an aggressive, expanding business sector.

Accountancy as a business

While the last few years brought new and important pressures to bear on companies, there were also fundamental changes affecting the accounting firms. One of the most significant came in the late 1960s, when the professional bodies relaxed the restrictions on the number of partners any firm could have. Some had already begun circumventing the rules by creating semiautonomous regional partnerships, each below the maximum limits. Now this was legitimized, and partnerships sprawled. Coopers & Lybrand in the UK had more than 700 partners in 1993. The largest thirty firms all had more than twenty partners. The idea of all the owners in the firms gathering around a table regularly to determine policy became a thing of the past. Management committees and elaborate information systems took over.

The second important change has been the relaxation on marketing in the early 1980s. After a wave of initial ambitious advertising campaigns – including on television – of questionable worth, the public statements have become less frequent. But marketing has become more sophisticated and aggressive. This reflects a much harsher climate of competition between the firms. One accountant commented recently that in the past, if he had heard two executives on a train complaining about their auditor, he would have called the firm in question to warn them. Now, he says, the attitude would be to approach the company to win it as a client.

A third and related factor is the growing diversity of the firms. Many no longer describe themselves as accountants at all, but as consultants or business advisers. Tax advice, non-audit accounting work, insolvency and management consultancy have long existed. But the practices have grown ever more diverse – and profitable – than the core of traditional accounting. Executive recruitment, treasury management, environmental consulting, pensions advice and economic forecasting are among the activities now on offer.

Cross-selling other services to audit clients has become ever more important. The scope for conflicts of interests has grown correspondingly. This has been reflected in a relaxation in 1991 of professional rules, so that up to 25% of partners in a firm do not have to be chartered accountants.

There is a final concern in the early 1990s. The profession – often after heady expansion and substantial expenditure on offices and other overheads –

was suddenly faced with a recession just as severe in its consequences for accountancy firms as for clients. That has led to wide-ranging cost-cutting, including a reduction in staff and partner numbers. It has also resulted in a substantial growth in 'low-balling' or very low competitive tenders for contracts, with rival firms undercutting each other, arguably below rates which are viable.

The audit conflict

The result of this growing commercialism is epitomized in a joke told by David Tweedie, chairman of the Accounting Standards Board, against his own colleagues: 'What's the difference between an auditor and an airport luggage trolley? The trolley has a mind of its own'.

This view partly reflects the difficulties of accountants in coping with their own standards once they fall into the hands of others. Tweedie himself tells the story of how, as technical partner at KPMG Peat Marwick, he would refuse to accept a particular accounting treatment, but would then be pressured by the client company and its lawyers, demanding to know where the standards showed the presentation offered was illegal.

Auditors always have the final decision, because they can 'qualify' a client company's accounts in their report to alert shareholders to treatments with which they disagree. One senior audit partner argued recently that qualified accounts are a sign of failure, an admission that persuading the board to change its mind has been unsuccessful. But since any such discussion takes place behind closed doors, it is difficult for others to know how controversial are any policies used in the accounts which fall just short of qualification or some other public statement.

The fundamental problem lies in the nature of the relationship between auditor and company board. Executive management usually hires and fires auditors, determines their remuneration and receives their detailed reports. The shareholders merely receive the published accounts. In exceptional cases they may be able to question audit matters at the annual general meeting, but their power is unlikely to be significant without substantial support from institutional investors.

The consequence is a fear by the auditors that too much opposition may result in the company removing them in favour of another firm. That may jeopardize a prestigious client with substantial marketing and other benefits. It will certainly result in the loss of the audit fee. There is even more financial pressure when the accounting firm providing the audit is also offering a range of other non-audit services, with a value which may easily exceed the audit fee itself. The consequence may even be that the audit partners end up under pressure to lose their jobs.

This commercial pressure can be wielded by the company threatening to conduct a 'beauty parade' of rival accounting firms to tender for future audits. At a more mild level, other firms will often be asked for a second opinion on a controversial matter, as the company searches for a more sympathetic view. This leads to the process of 'opinion shopping' – again to the detriment of shareholders – when a view the company favours emerges. A rival firm may be more liberal in the interpretation of standards in the hope of gaining the audit; the auditor is persuaded to accepted this alternative view on pain of possibly losing the audit.

Other conflicts of interest

Given that accountancy firms are increasingly pushing their activities into more diverse areas, an ever-wide range of potential conflicts is emerging. In general, there is the concern that the provision of other services could conflict with the audit: not simply that many fees will be sacrificed if the audit comes under threat, but also that the auditors may be less severe in examining and questioning work – such as computer systems consultancy – carried out by their own colleagues from the same firm.

Of equal concern to the client may be a range of issues concerning the quality of other services provided by the auditing firm. If the audit department is tough, perhaps consultants will be more reluctant to provide the most imaginative options which stretch the limits of acceptability, for fear of incurring their colleagues' wrath.

Then there is the tension between client confidentiality and the 'industry knowledge' which the firms so aggressively market to win work with rival companies in the same sector. How far does any skills transfer constitute a leakage of commercial information from competitors as much as a benefit to the new client? A good example is executive recruitment. If an accountancy firm recommends one client company's finance director for an equivalent post with another client, it is doing a disservice to the first; if it refuses to consider this finance director, has it served the latter client well?

There are also conflicts within the functional units. In corporate finance, for example, there are few restrictions on an accountancy firm acting on different sides of the same transaction – such as advising both buyer and seller on a potential corporate sale, or both the management team on a buy-out and also the bankers deciding whether to support them.

Backing the right side could also mean audit and other work in the future.

In insolvency, one key question so far untouched by ethical guidelines is whether the investigating accountants – who may be appointed by a bank to assess whether a company should survive – can also become its receivers.

There may be the temptation to recommend insolvency proceedings in the hope of picking up the work that follows.

Changing times?

Accountants are prone to wallow in the nostalgia of a previous golden era. If they concede that there are troubles with the profession now, it is often so they can refer misty-eyed to an ex-senior partner, long since retired or dead, who would have taken a firmer view; someone whose word was respected and feared by clients and with whom argument was pointless, a guardian of integrity with no doubt about what constituted a true and fair view.

That is not borne out entirely by the facts. Elements of marketing, aggressive competition and diversity of services provided have been evident over many decades. The Accounting Standards Committee was created in the early 1970s in response to public criticism at the time to a previous era of creative accounting, not least the activities of the late Robert Maxwell and Pergamon, which were subject to a government inquiry.

One Big 6 partner says that after he qualified in the early 1960s, his partner advised him with a wink to invest in shares in a client company, as he himself was doing. That was just before an announcement which pushed the share price up substantially. Nowadays, the mood on insider-trading has changed entirely, while accountants are specifically forbidden from holding shares in client companies.

Perhaps the most promising changes have come since 1990, with the creation of the Accounting Standards Board, which has the power to set tougher standards with the backing of the law, and its sister body, the Financial Reporting Review Panel, which has the power to take companies to court and if necessary force their presentation in the required format at the directors' own expense.

Ironically, while the panel's power is focused most on directors, it has had at least as much effect on auditors. It allows essentially upstanding accountants to have a new threat for directors who are proving resistant to their recommendations. It may also force them to take a tougher line, on fear of disciplinary action by their professional bodies, humiliation in the press and the threat of losing the client anyway as a result.

The profession's response

Aside from work in developing and supporting the review panel and the Accounting Standards Board, the professional bodies have been most involved in ethical issues through the chartered accountants' joint ethics committee, representing the institutes covering the UK and Ireland.

There has certainly been substantial recent progress, with a new version of the overall guide to professional ethics published in 1992, and specific guidelines underway on topics such as opinion shopping, low-balling ('predatory pricing'), the rotation of audit partners, and on the introduction of a 'quarantine' period after a partner leaves a firm before being allowed to join a client as an executive.

Ian Plaistowe, past president of the Institute, suggests that the focus has also changed in the last decade, away from self-interest – when ethics meant how to protect the firms from each other through restrictions on marketing – towards a concentration on the public interest.

But that begs the question of how the public interest is defined and how it is best served. Jock Worsley, the joint ethics committee's chairman, says many of the items now on the agenda have been driven by criticisms of events highlighted in government reports or through negative press comments. What gets approved depends on the consensus built within the committee.

Some sceptics suggest that the accountancy profession has proved reluctant to tackle the most important issues head-on. Practitioners within the firms tend to argue that they can create 'Chinese walls' or other safeguards to prevent compromise of quality. As one official from the ethics committee of the Institute of Chartered Accountants in England and Wales puts it: 'Lawyers withdraw from conflicts of interest. Accountants manage them.' [1]

While some of the committee's decisions have made the firms take its operations seriously for the first time, little of its guidance has attacked the most lucrative existing practice areas. One exception is the ban on a firm providing specialist valuations on items such as brands for the same client. But even on this topic, a significant valuation was excluded – that of pensions valuations – on the grounds that it was to be tackled by the Goode committee, a government inquiry on pensions regulation.

Elsewhere, ethics rules often appear to have been diluted or withdraw over time as newer, less 'professional' practices have gained currency, such as 'cold-calling' potential clients, or the creeping use of contingency fees.

A final question is that of discipline. Ethics codes are of little use unless there is an effective mechanism for enforcement. Only recently have the professional bodies begun to tackle a number of outstanding issues, such as examining the conduct of a firm rather than simply its individual members.

Conclusion

The last few years have seen rapid changes in accountancy, with the firms transformed from small professional bodies into large international industrial conglomerates, though without the same level of disclosure or external accountability as companies.

Over that time, the firms and their professional bodies have largely succeeded in maintaining a self-regulated system, with accounting, auditing and ethical standards drawn up internally with little interference from legislators or other outside entities.

But growing public awareness and criticism of accountants, linked to their failure to detect fraud and their weakness in giving in to – or even conniving with – executives in presenting financial figures in the best light suggest that this position has remained unchallenged for too long. Accountancy is too important to be left to accountants.

Notes and references

1 Zünd, André *Ethics in Auditing* p. 235–237.

Additional reading

For specific additional material see the 'Focus on Accountancy' in Volume 1 Number 4 of *Business Ethics – A European Review,* 1992. This focus deals with ethics in auditing; whistleblowing auditors – the ultimate oxymoron; and a note on teaching ethics in accounting. In the same issue there is also a select bibliography on auditor independence.

For a discussion on the new guide to professional ethics that has been approved by the three UK and Irish Institutes of Chartered Accountants, see F.E. Worsley's article 'A Guide to Good Practice' in *Accountancy,* March 1992; **109**, 116–131.

Questions for discussion

- What advice would you give the Accounting Standards Board in choosing to deal with the ethical problems in this chapter?
- What measures would you take as an auditor to preserve your independence?

Chapter 13

Business ethics: practical proposals

This final chapter concentrates on the practical aspects of applied business ethics, and pulls together many of the recommendations made in earlier chapters. It also includes several international perspectives as these apply to companies and employees in the Far East.

The interesting point about the seeming lack of enthusiasm amongst human resource professionals is borne out by our practical experience. Business ethics is a subject which deals very much with the individual and his or her place and behaviour within an organization, yet it is relatively rare for human resource departments to play an active part in ventilating ethics as a corporate concern. More commonly corporate affairs and, of course, chief executives and chairpersons play an important role in corporate ethics developments. In many cases human resource departments will respond to these initiatives, but rarely make the first move.

Very helpful in this regard, the chapter covers the individual dimension, group and peer influence and organizational strategies. All of this is of the utmost importance for the executive who wishes ethics to progress in his or her organization but needs to be clear about the different dimensions to the question, before pressing ahead.

It is also interesting to see how many companies are active in the application of ethics in their firms and the degree to which they have considered the various elements of what we call the ethics process. Typically, an ethics process would include some form of ethical awareness training for example, together with arrangements to monitor and enforce any code of ethics.

The need for training in ethics has never been greater, as perhaps is illustrated from an August 1992 review of the 1992 A level results by the Examining Board in England, which showed that an examination question dealing with the *Merchant's Tale* by Chaucer was rarely attempted because most students did not know what the word 'ethical' meant.

There is a fine description in this chapter of why good managers make bad ethical choices, which should be of interest to every aspiring chief executive officer, illustrating as it does that a manager may well make a poor ethical judgement but that is not to say that he or she is 'unethical'.

The arguments for and against codes of ethics are also covered in this chapter. And we would echo the plea for 'meaningful' codes. Too often, codes of ethics consist of a set of prohibitions, and bear all the hallmarks of being hastily put together to satisfy external requirements without much thought for their internal reception within the company.

As such, these are a waste of time and indeed may be counterproductive, since it could be argued that any management which allocates so little importance to its own ethos does not deserve the support of its staff.

In closing these comments on this chapter, and the book itself, we should like to make a few final remarks.

First, it is likely that ethics will command a greater level of management attention in the years to come. We believe this to be so, not just because of the rapid economic changes that are taking place, but also because of perceived changes in society's values. And in order to survive and prosper, companies will need to pay very close attention to the nature of these changes. This will mean studying in detail the significance of even small shifts in public values.

Then, organizations will need to be able to adapt quickly to meet these altered demands. New markets will appear suddenly, and, most likely, some established markets may disappear as quickly.

So companies will need to encourage and empower employees at all levels to identify these shifts and to adapt accordingly. For this to happen, staff will need to have a very clear understanding of corporate values and their company's ethical standards. Then, top management can give staff maximum freedom to make adaptations, safe in the knowledge that the corporate ethos remains intact.

Business ethics: practical proposals
Gael M. McDonald and Raymond A. Zepp

Given the volume of writing on the topic of business ethics, it is perhaps surprising that the issue is often swept aside or greeted with a 'ho-hum' reaction: 'Bring up ethics and most people mumble something about knowing right from wrong. It's a subject that tends to elicit cynicism, self-righteousness, paranoia, and laughter' [1].

The popular understanding of ethical concern is a narrow view of personal behaviour related to sex, alcohol, gambling, lying, stealing and cheating at the most obvious and blatant level. This view ignores the subtlety of decision-making in a variety of business settings. Bryson [2] suggests that the concept of ethics in business has multiple layers rather than a single meaning. These layers are common sense, philosophical appreciation, etymological appreciation and the notion of religious ethics.

It has been suggested appropriately that studies into business ethics should take a contextual approach as the search for general answers is unrealistic. Each situation is in a sense unique, and what is perceived to be the case is a function of the facets and circumstances of the specific situation. This situational emphasis should not be confused with the theory of ethical relativity, for the relativist asserts that what morality ordains in one place, age or culture, may be quite different in another age, place or culture.

It appears that there has been an evolution in the study of business ethics. Initially, the discussion was related to the theoretical framework of moral philosophy. By the 1970s, the study of business ethics had fragmented into a proliferation of field observations in such areas as purchasing (e.g. Mayer [3]), field sales personnel (e.g. Dubinsky [4]) and international marketing (e.g. Kaikati and Label [5]). As the business community has become more international, research into business ethics has developed into survey-based, cross-cultural investigations [6, 7].

While much has been written of a theoretical and observational nature, only a few articles have presented action-related suggestions for practising managers (e.g. Noah [8] and Bivens [9]). The absence of pragmatism could be a contributing factor to the lukewarm reception that a discussion of business ethics evokes from those responsible for the human resources function. Without adequate direction and well-thought-out plans based on existing research findings, it is difficult for those responsible to manage and enhance the ethical behaviour of employees.

Based on earlier findings, this article intends to provide guidelines for establishing ethical priorities from the individual, group and organizational perspectives.

Before addressing practical suggestions in the area of business ethics, one must first address the fundamental question surrounding the difference between social responsibility and ethics. In order to clarify this point, collectivity *vis-à-vis* individuality appears to be the key distinction between the two related concepts. Simplistically, social or corporate responsibility relates to the broadening of organizational accountability, particularly in relation to the immediate operating environment; ethics pertains to individual value-guided behaviour. While social responsibility provides the overall framework from which the ethical action can be evaluated, ethics fundamentally relates to individual behaviour. Drucker [10] describes this individual aspect of ethics in an Asian environment: 'For the Confucian, but also for the philosopher of Western tradition, only law can handle the rights and objectives of collectives. Ethics is always a matter of the person'.

If ethics is a personal matter, why then should the organization be involved? One might rightly argue that such an involvement blurs the distinction between ethics and social responsibility. It appears that organizational involvement, whether directed by the personnel function or not, is undertaken with the interests of the organization in mind. Ultimately the corporate image is influenced by the ethical behaviour of individuals. It is becoming apparent that sound ethics is good business in the long run. Becker and Fritzsche [11] found that French, German and American managers overwhelmingly agreed with this view.

Once it is accepted that organizations should intervene in the development of ethical standards, how can those in the planning and administrative role influence the ethical perceptions and behaviour of their employees? To address this question, it appears appropriate to approach the problem from three perspectives:

1 The individual dimension.
2 Group/peer influence.
3 Organizational strategies.

The individual dimension

An increasing number of corporations are devoting time to business ethics training, for example, Alcoa, Atlantic Richfield, Chemical Bank, Cummins Engine and McDonnell-Douglas [12]. In any corporation it is axiomatic that not all employees will possess the same ethical values; each will be guided by his/her own personal value system and experiences. However, some could be developed.

Basic awareness programmes

As a preliminary step in creating sensitivity to the ethical dimensions of behaviour and corporate decision-making, basic awareness programmes could be initiated by exposure to current articles and published material on the topic of ethics, or the purchasing and circulation of books and audiovisual materials. Counsellor-assisted discussion with individuals can use as examples problems experienced in the past by employees. Employees may be asked to recount decisions with which they have felt uncomfortable, along with the reasons for their discomfort. In multinationals, the sharing of basic value systems could provide a basis for understanding cultural variations and their effect on decision-making. For example, different cultures view bribery with varying degrees of opprobrium, and employees should be made aware of these differences.

Specific ethical training programmes

One of the earliest examples of an internal programme devoted specifically to the topic of ethics was initiated in the mid 1980s by Allied-Signal [1], at its conglomerate headquarters in Morris Township, New Jersey. Allied-Signal conducts an annual three-day programme for high-level managers with three specific objectives:

1 To enable managers to recognize the ethical component of a business decision.
2 To decide what to do with it once they recognized it.
3 To learn how to anticipate emerging ethical issues.

The first day is devoted to defining business ethics to the firm; the second day focuses on the obligation the firm has to its employees and includes such issues as an employee relations decision model and corporate values at Allied, and the final day's topic is the firm's obligation to others [13]. The programme content emphasizes the use of case studies posing difficult ethical decisions, together with discussion.

Another dimension of Allied-Signal's programme is the encouragement of airing difficulties faced in day-to-day operations, i.e. the support shown to employees so that they feel free to discuss ethical problems that may confront them.

It is imperative that training in ethics should not be a set of rules to be dictated by management to employees. For this reason, Polaroid was reluctant to establish a formal ethics training programme, but rather opted for a conference in 1983, attended by 250 employees, which featured discussions with philosophers, ethicists and business professors, on the language and concepts of ethics. Polaroid was conscious that the establishment of a formal ethics programme might suggest that the employees were viewed as unethical.

As an outgrowth of the 1983 conference, Polaroid has developed a series of dilemma workshops which assist participants in applying ethical concepts to cases drawn from actual events in the corporation.

When designing programmes, trainers should be aware that ethical situations are not always black-and-white issues, but rather present a series of possible rationalizations that are used to justify unethical behaviour. Gellerman [14] has identified four types of rationalizations that can lead to misconduct:

1 A belief that the activity is within reasonable ethical and legal limits, that it is not 'really' illegal or immoral.
2 A belief that the activity is in the individual's or the corporation's best interests, that the individual would somehow be expected to undertake the activity.
3 A belief that the activity is 'safe' because it will never be found out or publicized – the classic crime-and-punishment issue of discovery.
4 A belief that because the activity helps the company, the company will condone it and even protect the person who engages in it.

Awareness of these rationalizations can prove helpful in the designing of programme material and case studies.

Support for separate ethics programmes is mounting: 'Some experts . . . feel that separate courses are the only effective way to teach ethics' [8]. Noah also states that 89% of all accredited business schools claim to teach ethics 'in some manner'. To conclude, Lickona [15] has provided specific strategies for enhancing the instructional influence of corporate-directed training programmes. These are:

1 The use of socratic questioning in order to isolate views and confront reasoning.
2 Creating open, integrative discussions.
3 Eliciting a full range of ethical views.
4 Utilizing an experiential approach drawing upon employees' own personal cases showing value conflict and ethical dilemmas.
5 Taking care not to present cases that continually show the most difficult choices and high levels of cognitive strain.

Developing an appreciation for individual differences

Any attempt by organizations to regulate the ethical behaviour of their employees must take into consideration individual differences, particularly in multicultural environments, such as Malaysia and Singapore. Differences in age have been found to lead to differences in ethical perceptions, with managers over thirty years old more readily agreeing to certain unethical practices. This has been found to be especially true in multinational organizations [6]. One explanation of this fact is that younger employees are more willing to tap into an organization's *esprit de corps*, and accept more readily the corporate culture, acting more considerately towards them. But as they grow older, they may become more cynical towards the organization's game rules and act in an independent manner.

A number of researchers have concluded that there is little consistency in ethical perceptions of different situations; a person cannot be labelled 'unethical' in an overall sense; each circumstance should be examined separately. Acceptance of unethical behaviour in one situation cannot be used as an indication of likely acceptance of unethical behaviour in another, nor can it be taken as a measure of overall agreement to unethical behaviour.

As potentially unethical situations are perceived independently, supervising management should not evaluate or prejudge the overall ethical standards of employees on the basis of isolated incidents.

The administration of questionnaires indicating the level of agreement or disagreement to potentially unethical situations could alert managers to focus attention and instigate controls in certain areas. For example, in the Asian environment, potentially unethical action which subjects agree to have been identified, such as practices of the gaining of competitor information, exposure of personal error and deceptive advertising [6, 16]. Not reporting a colleague's violation of company policy, distribution of gifts, using company facilities for personal purposes and padding an expense account (up to 10%) are practices found acceptable in a Singaporean study [17].

The higher the level of education, the less unethical respondents seem to perceive the situation. This conclusion suggests that more education may make executives either more alienated towards others, or else more tolerant of malpractice.

Selection procedures

If businesses are concerned with the ethical behaviour of their employees, it is easier to hire individuals possessing adequate ethical standards than to undertake the reshaping of ethical standards after hiring:

> First hire the right people. Employees who are inclined to be ethical are the best insurance you have. They may be the only insurance. Look for people with principles; let them know that those principles are an important part of their qualifications for the job [18].

Within the interviewing procedure, hypothetical situations containing an ethical dimension could be presented to the interviewee and the decision response evaluated. For example, questions such as the following could be used:

- You are interviewing a former product manager who has just left a competitor's company. He is not the best applicant, although if pressed he would tell you about the competitor's plans for the coming year. Would you hire him and to what extent would you go to obtain this information?
- The research and development department has modernized one of your products. It is not really 'new and improved' but you know that putting this statement on the package will significantly increase sales. How would you react to the suggestion of using 'new and improved'?

As a source of job-related information, reference-checking has always provided verification of information contained in application forms/résumés. Comments on the ethical standards of potential employees could be solicited from the candidate's referees or previous supervisor.

Group/peer influence

Self and peer perceptions

It is well-documented that peers can exert a strong influence on the ethical behaviour of colleagues. Numerous studies have found that employees frequently perceive peers as having lower ethical standards than themselves [19, 20]. This suggests that when considering possible actions in a decision-making situation, an unspoken evaluation of what a peer might do is an influential factor that is often overlooked. If employees are contemplating a possible unethical action, they may be influenced by their own evaluation of what others (peers) would do in the same situation. Greater understanding of the *true* ethical standards of peers, rather than perceived beliefs, could lead to an increased security in making decisions that are in harmony with one's own value system.

The effect of peer influence varies among cultures. Dolecheck and Dolecheck [7] found that the behaviour of one's peers had more of an effect in Hong Kong than in the USA.

Group dynamics

There is some evidence [21] that individuals interacting in a group sometimes produce group decisions of a higher level of moral reasoning than the average of the individual members acting alone. As Posner and Schmidt [22] noted: 'Levels of moral reasoning and judgement are likely to be higher when members get together and discuss ethical issues than when the choices have to be made in solitude' (p. 213). It appears that further research is needed to resolve the paradox of the apparent contradiction between Nichols and Day's finding [21] and that of Janis [23], who coined the term 'groupthink' in relation to highly cohesive groups. Janis defines groupthink as 'a deterioration of mental efficiency, reality testing, and moral judgement that results from in-group pressures' (p. 9).

The recent Irangate scandal is yet another classical example of the groupthink phenomenon.

In situations where highly cohesive groups have developed and can be identified, caution is therefore to be recommended, as well as the occasional monitoring of decisions.

Group seminars

Encouraging group discussion of ethical issues can be beneficial: 'Counselling with others about ethical situations in the workplace can provide perspective, understanding, and comfort' [7] (p. 37). The mutual support and transfer of information could be of particular value in multinational companies, as cultural differences in ethical values could be aired and appreciated.

Mentor schemes

When an employee is experiencing doubt regarding a difficult ethical decision but does not want to expose his or her uncertainty within the formal decision process, mentors could be useful in their advisory capacity as an avenue of private discussion and guidance. A description is given by Flippo [24]: 'A Mentor is an older and respected manager or professional who counsels protégés, exhibits genuine concern, listens for feelings as well as facts, and stimulates people through ideas and information' (p. 261). There is evidence that mentors are more useful with employees who are experiencing crisis periods in their lives [25].

Whistleblowing/finger-pointing

Ralph Nader [26] coined the term 'whistleblower', which has been defined by Hauserman [27] as 'a person who reports a real or perceived wrongdoing of her or his employer' (p. 5). One might extend this definition to include the reporting of peer wrong-doings, although management may be reluctant to have this information aired publicly.

One must ask to what extent companies should encourage the practice of finger-pointing within the organization as a means of identifying wrong-doing at an early stage before the problem escalates. This question is difficult to answer due to differences in cultural acceptance, but encouragement of the practice could be viewed as an additional communication channel between management and employees, while, on the other hand, the deleterious effect on *esprit de corps* and interpersonal relations cannot be ignored.

Internal staff associations

The fostering of internal staff associations could provide needed support and terms of reference for new employees. In particular, they encourage team spirit and the opportunity for additional checks and balances. Regrettably, such associations in Asia are often viewed by management as a threat and tend to be lumped together in the same category as antagonistic trade unions.

Organizational strategies

It has now become widely accepted that the ethical behaviour of employees can be influenced by specific organizational strategies. It should be noted, however, that the efficacy of different strategies tends to provoke lively discussion.

Codes of ethics

Distinction must be made between codes of ethics and rules of ethics, as expressed by Hosmer [28]:

> Ethical codes are statements of the norms and beliefs of an organization . . . they are the ways that the senior people in the organization want others to think. This is not censorship. Instead, the intent is to encourage ways of thinking and patterns of attitudes that will lead towards the wanted behaviour (p. 153).

Ethical rules, on the other hand, are:

> requirements to act in a given way, not just expectations or suggestions or petitions to act in that way. There is an aura of insistency about the law; it defines what you must do (p. 68).

In practice, the above distinction is sometimes blurred, as an employee knows that repeated violation of a code will undoubtedly lead to his/her dismissal.

A number of companies, such as Borg-Warner Corporation, Whirlpool and Johnson & Johnson, have in the past decade developed ethical codes that have been disseminated through company booklets, annual reports and/or during induction programmes. General Dynamics Corporation, the US government's largest defence contractor, was instructed by the Defense Department in 1985 to enforce a code of ethics, with mandatory sanctions for violations. The company now has a twenty-page ethical code book and forty ethics programme directors [29].

According to a 1979 study by the Ethics Resource Centre, over 70% of large corporations have codes of ethics [30]. It appears that companies who wish to influence ethical standards establish ethical codes as their first step. The Centre for Business Ethics [31] has estimated that, of those companies taking steps to institutionalize ethics, over 90% have written codes of ethics. This represents a strong trend over the past twenty years. From the same study, the communication of codes appears more common through printed material than through the advice from a superior, through entrance interviews, or through workshops and seminars.

The primary advantages of codes of ethics are:

1 To clarify management's thoughts of what constitutes unethical behaviour.
2 To help employees think about ethical issues before they are faced with the realities of the situation.
3 To provide employees with the opportunity for refusing compliance with an unethical action.
4 To define the limits of what constitutes acceptable or unacceptable behaviour.
5 To provide a mechanism for communicating the managerial philosophy in the realm of ethical behaviour.
6 To assist in the induction and training of employees.

Arguments against ethical codes express the following concerns:

1 Even a detailed list of guidelines cannot be expected to cover all the possible grey areas of potentially unethical practices.
2 Like fair employment practice statements, codes of ethics are often too generalized to be of specific value.
3 Rarely are codes of ethics prioritized; for example, loyalty to the company and to fellow employees does not resolve the potential conflict when a colleague is seen to be acting contrary to company interests.
4 As an individual phenomenon, ethical behaviour which has been guided by

ethical codes of conduct will only be effective if the codes have been internalized and are truly believed by employees.

Ethical policy statements

From writings in the field of ethics, it appears that many authors use the term 'ethical policy statement' as synonymous with 'ethical rule', in the sense that it is enforceable. The fundamental question is whether ethical policy statements promote ethical behaviour. There is evidence to suggest the answer is 'yes'.

Hegarty and Sims [32] simulated a situation in which a company president wrote a letter to employees reinforcing ethical behaviour and warning of dismissal for non-compliance. The result was an increase in ethical behaviour. In another study, Staff [33] found that a written company policy had a significant effect on the acceptance of gratuities by purchasing officers.

Policy statements naturally suffer from some of the same defects as ethical codes. Policies cannot cover all possible situations; they are not prioritized, and they may lead to conflicting and potentially incompatible instructions. Formal policies may also be inconsistent with day-to-day practices for getting a job done. It has been found that the more decentralized the decision-making function (and consequently the direct supervision of managers), the greater the likelihood of inadvertent non-compliance. It could also be suggested that if employees do not perceive senior managers to be complying with ethical policy, they may tend not to comply themselves.

Leadership

In Loucks's statement of four principles for ethical management [18], he states that the most important principle is effective leadership: 'Let your ethical example at all times be absolutely impeccable . . .indeed, without a good example from the top, ethical problems are probably inevitable within your organization' (p. 8). Dolecheck and Dolecheck [7] found that of six factors which contribute to unethical behaviour, the behaviour of superiors was ranked as the most influential by both Hong Kong and US managers. The same study highlighted cultural differences in ethical perceptions, as the Hong Kong managers gave behaviour of superiors a higher absolute ranking than did the Americans.

One way in which top management can be seen to be setting an example is in the practice of accepting speaking engagements. Sending executives out to speak on ethical topics serves to convince not only the public, but also employees and management of the company and, ultimately, themselves.

At its extreme, heavy-handed leadership can lead to difficulties when the policy-maker attempts to transfer his/her personal value system to organizational behaviour. This is particularly true in family owner-operated businesses that are prevalent in Asia.

It is clear that top management can influence ethical behaviour, although it is imperative that the ethical value system of the corporation be accepted by all employees and not merely confined to the senior management stratum.

Ethical ombudsperson

An increasing number of organizations are investigating the position of corporate ombudsperson. While a formal definition varies from company to company, it appears that some characteristics are common to most ombudsperson positions:

1 *An investigative, counselling and advisory role* – as a consequence of being approached or on his/her own initiative, an ombudsperson could investigate ethical circumstances and advise on potential problem areas. He/she may on occasion attempt to resolve ethical conflicts.
2 *Independent* – the ombudsperson must not be seen to be taking sides in any discussion and must have the trust of both management and employees. A prerequisite for independence is confidentiality if the position is to be effective.
3 *Experience within the company* – the position is suitable for an older respected employee who has, with experience, assimilated the corporate value system. Specifically, the position is appropriate for an individual nearing retirement or a 'plateau employee'.

An important question is: 'who chooses the ombudsperson?' If top management unilaterally nominates the title holder, there is a risk that the position may not have the confidence of lower-level employees.

Although doubts are sometimes expressed that the position of ethical ombudsperson does not really work [28], a small but increasing number of companies are experimenting with this position. A survey of Fortune 500 companies found that, of those which initiate ethics programmes, 8% have an ethical ombudsperson [31].

Ethics committees

An additional effort to focus attention on past and current decisions could take the form of an ethics committee. The committee membership should be rotated among all employees, thereby exposing them to ethical problems submitted by either employees or managers. A decision by the committee would provide firm, clear guidelines for action. Motorola has experimented successfully with the concept. The Centre for Business Ethics study cited earlier found that ethics committees are more than twice as popular as ethical ombudsperson positions and, where they exist, their functions seem more oriented to policy-making than dealing with specific violations or complaints. Only 40% of them handled infractions, and 25% responded to employee complaints [31].

Realistic, performance and reward plans

All expectations of employee performance are based on value systems, and yet the pressure to perform can often override personal ethical standards. Management may want to reconsider corporate pressures, such as management by objectives, surpassing last year's accomplishments, unrealistic goals, cost savings plans and pay-to-performance schemes which may unknowingly be rewarding unethical behaviour. Reassessment of what we reward and how we reward obviously requires careful thought and consideration of viable alternatives.

Establishment of ethical corporate cultures

Corporate culture is one of the most frequently mentioned but most often confused terms in modern management theory. Many companies consciously and actively promote the corporate culture that reflects the 'attitudes and values, management style and problem behaviour of its people' [34]. The corporate culture will naturally affect the ethical values of its personnel, and the more an employee feels him/herself a member of the company team, the stronger will be the tendency to conform to the ethical standards of the company.

Everett [30] discusses the parallel between corporate culture and organized religion, emphasizing the need for a common faith that binds its members together. This faith is a 'deep conviction about the overreaching commitments of the group. This faith not only needs clear articulation, it needs to be ritualized continuously and colourfully in the activities of the organisation' (p. 316).

However, as seen in the earlier discussion of group behaviour, highly cohesive groups run the risk of groupthink. It would seem, therefore, that each corporation should aim at an optimal degree of cohesiveness or group spirit, which will maximize the positive effects of an established corporate culture without becoming so cohesive that groupthink sets in.

Conclusion

This article has attempted to present many actions which are available to practising managers who wish to improve the ethical climate of their organizations. Having discussed the pros and cons of each proposal, we have refrained from stating that one option is better than another, or that, on implementation, success is guaranteed. While most people agree that the inculcation of ethical awareness is desirable, the means of stimulating this awareness will vary among companies, industries and cultures.

While much more research is needed to determine the efficacy of these methods, scientific experimentation under controlled conditions will be difficult indeed. In order to compare method A with method B, identical environments are necessary. While this methodological difficulty does preclude absolute proof, it does not undermine the partial evidence and practical assistance that can be provided by each of the recommendations.

Ethics is not subject to the 'flavour-of-the-month' syndrome; it is not about to go away; in fact, increasing concern for higher ethical standards is resulting in the consideration and development of creative programmes, many of which have been outlined in this article. No doubt improvements will be sought and achieved, given the professionalism and expansion of the human resource function.

References

1 Lee, C. 'Ethics Training: Facing the Tough Questions'. *Training*, 30, March, 1986; 30–40.
2 Bryson, W. 'The Meaning of Ethics in Business'. *Business Horizons*, 20, November 1977; 31.
3 Mayer, R.R. 'Management's Responsibility for Purchasing Ethics'. *Journal of Purchasing*, 4, 1970; 13–20.
4 Dubinsky, A.J., 'Ethical Problems of Field Sales Personnel'. *MSU Business Topics*, 28, Summer 1980; 11–16.
5 Kaikati, J. and Label, W. 'American Bribery Legislation: An Obstacle to International Marketing'. *Journal of Marketing*, 44, Fall 1980; 38–43.
6 McDonald, G. and Zepp, R. 'Ethical perceptions of Hong Kong business managers'. In: *Proceedings of the Conference on the Changing Role of Hong Kong Management*, Hong Kong Baptist College, 1987.
7 Dolecheck, M. and Dolecheck, C. 'Business Ethics: A Comparison of Attitudes of Managers in Hong Kong and the United States'. *Hong Kong Manager*, April-May 1987; 28–43.
8 Noah, T. 'The Business Ethics Debate: Do B-School Courses Alter Executive Behaviour?' *Newsweek*, 25 May 1987; 44.
9 Bivens, T. 'Applying Ethical Theory to Public Relations'. *Journal of Business Ethics*, 1987; 6, 195–200.

10 Drucker, P. 'What is Business Ethics?' *The Public Interest*, **64**, Spring 1981; 18.
11 Becker, H. and Fritzsche, D. 'Business Ethics: A Cross-Cultural Comparison of Managers' Attitudes'. *Journal of Business Ethics*, **6**, 1987; 289–295.
12 Cooke, R.A., and Ryan L. 'The Relevance of Ethics in Management Education'. *Journal of Management Development*, **7**, 1988; 29–30.
13 Genfan, H. 'Formalizing Business Ethics'. *Training and Development Journal*, November 1987; 35–37.
14 Gellerman, S.W. 'Why 'Good' Managers Make Bad Ethical Choices'. *Harvard Business Review*, July-August 1986; 85–90.
15 Lickona, T. 'What Does Moral Psychology Have to Say to the Teacher of Ethics?', In: Callahan, D. and Bok, S. (eds) *Ethics Teaching in Higher Education*, Plenum Press, New York, pp. 103–32.
16 Kam, H.L. 'Ethical Beliefs in Marketing Management: A Cross-Cultural Study'. *European Journal of Marketing*, **15**, 1981; 58.
17 Mehta, S. and Kau, S.A.K. 'Marketing Executives' Perceptions of Unethical Practices'. *Singapore Management Review*, **6**, 1984; 25–35.
18 Loucks, V. 'A CEO Looks at Ethics'. *Business Horizons*, **30**, March-April 1987; 2–6.
19 Pitt, L.F. and Abratt, R. 'Corruption in Business: Are Management Attitudes Right?' *Journal of Business Ethics*, **5**, February 1986; 39–44.
20 McDonald, G. 'Comparative Ethic Perceptions of Advertising Practitioners'. Unpublished MBA thesis, 1982.
21 Nichols, M.L. and Day, V.E. 'A Comparison of Moral Reasoning of Groups and Individuals on the "Defining issues test"'. *Academy of Management Journal*, **25**, 1982; 201–208.
22 Posner, B. and Schmidt, W. 'Values and the American Manager: An Update'. *California Management Review*, 1984; **26**, 1984; 210–212.
23 Janis, I.L. *Victims of Groupthink*, Boston, MA: Houghton Mifflin, 1972.
24 Flippo, E.B. *Personnel Management*, (6th edition) New York: McGraw-Hill, 1984.
25 Halcomb, R. 'Mentors and the Successful Woman'. *Across the Board*, **17**, February 1980; 13.
26 Nader, Ralph, Petkas, Peter and Blackwell, Kate *Whistle Blowing*, New York: Bantam Books, 1972.
27 Hauserman, Nancy R. 'Whistle Blowing: Individual Morality in a Corporate Society'. *Business Horizons*, **29**, March-April 1986. pp. 4–9.
28 Hosmer, L.T. *The Ethics of Management*, New York: Irwin, 1987.
29 Buchanan, S. 'Corporate Ethics Codes can Lack Punitive Punch'. *New Straits Times*, 27 November 1987.
30 Everett, W.J. 'OIKOS: Convergence in Business Ethics'. *Journal of Business Ethics*, **5**, 1986; 313–325.
31 Centre for Business Ethics. 'Are Corporations Institutionalising Ethics?' *Journal of Business Ethics*, **5**, 1986; 85–91.
32 Hegarty, W.H. and Sims, H. 'Organizational Philosophy, Policies, and Objectives Related to Unethical Behaviour: A Laboratory Experiment'. *Journal of Applied Psychology*, **64**, 1979; 331–338.
33 Staff. 'Gifts to buyers'. *Purchasing*, 11 April 1979; 19.
34 Schwart, H. and Davies, S. 'Matching Corporate Culture and Business Strategy'. *Organizational Dynamics*, **10**, 1981; 36.

Additional reading

In 'Making Integrity Pay' (*Scottish Banker*, November 1992; 16–17), John Drummond outlines an ethical framework for business decision-making. Included is a discussion on the public perception of business people.

For a unique perspective on why some business people behave unethically, see Dena C. Ludwig and Clinton O. Longenecker's article 'The Bathsheba Syndrome: The Ethical Failure of Successful Leaders' in *Journal of Business Ethics*, April 1993; 265–273. These authors argue that ethical failure is brought on by success and not by competitive pressures.

Questions for discussion

- Who in your organization should have day-to-day responsibility for ethical processes?
- What arrangements should be put in place to monitor and enforce ethical standards?
- How should ethical standards be measured in large corporations? How would you make these measurements credible?

Index